ISBN: 9781290767071

Published by:
HardPress Publishing
8345 NW 66TH ST #2561
MIAMI FL 33166-2626

Email: info@hardpress.net
Web: http://www.hardpress.net

Heath's English Classics

CYMBELINE

EDITED BY

ALFRED J. WYATT, M.A.

SOMETIME SCHOLAR OF CHRIST'S COLLEGE, CAMBRIDGE EXAMINER IN
ENGLISH AT VICTORIA UNIVERSITY

D. C. HEATH & CO., PUBLISHERS

BOSTON   NEW YORK   CHICAGO

THE ARDEN SHAKESPEARE

A MIDSUMMER NIGHT'S DREAM.
  Edited by Edmund K. Chambers, B.A., Oxford.
ANTONY AND CLEOPATRA.
  Edited by Harold N. Hillebrand, Ph.D., Harvard.
AS YOU LIKE IT.
  Edited by J. C. Smith, M.A., Edinburgh.
CORIOLANUS.
  Edited by Edmund K. Chambers, B.A., Oxford.
CYMBELINE.
  Edited by A. J. Wyatt, M.A., Cambridge.
HAMLET.
  Edited by Edmund K. Chambers, B.A., Oxford.
HENRY IV — PART I.
  Edited by F. W. Moorman, B.A., Yorkshire College.
HENRY IV — PART II.
  Edited by L. Winstanley.
HENRY V.
  Edited by G. C. Moore Smith, M.A., Cambridge.
HENRY VIII.
  Edited by D. Nichol Smith, M.A., Edinburgh.
JULIUS CÆSAR.
  Edited by Arthur D. Innes, M.A., Oxford.
KING JOHN.
  Edited by G. C. Moore Smith, M.A., Cambridge.
KING LEAR.
  Edited by D. Nichol Smith, M.A., Edinburgh.
LOVE'S LABOUR'S LOST.
  Edited by H. B. Charlton, M.A.
MACBETH.
  Edited by Edmund K. Chambers, B.A., Oxford.
MUCH ADO ABOUT NOTHING.
  Edited by J. C. Smith, M.A., Edinburgh.
OTHELLO.
  Edited by C. H. Herford, Revised by R. M. Alden, Ph.D.
RICHARD II.
  Edited by C. H. Herford, Litt.D., Cambridge.
RICHARD III.
  Edited by George Macdonald, M.A., Oxford.
ROMEO AND JULIET.
  Edited by Robert A. Law, Ph.D., Harvard.
THE MERCHANT OF VENICE.
  Edited by H. L. Withers, B.A., Oxford.
THE TEMPEST.
  Edited by F. S. Boas, M.A., Oxford.
TWELFTH NIGHT.
  Edited by Arthur D. Innes, M.A., Oxford.
WINTER'S TALE.
  Edited by H. B. Charlton, M.A.

The remaining volumes are in preparation.

3 B 7

GENERAL PREFACE.

In this edition of SHAKESPEARE an attempt is made to present the greater plays of the dramatist in their literary aspect, and not merely as material for the study of philology or grammar. Criticism purely verbal and textual has only been included to such an extent as may serve to help the student in the appreciation of the essential poetry. Questions of date and literary history have been fully dealt with in the Introductions, but the larger space has been devoted to the interpretative rather than the matter-of-fact order of scholarship. Aesthetic judgments are never final, but the Editors have attempted to suggest points of view from which the analysis of dramatic motive and dramatic character may be profitably undertaken. In the Notes likewise, while it is hoped that all unfamiliar expressions and allusions have been adequately explained, yet it has been thought even more important to consider the dramatic value of each scene, and the part which it plays in relation to the whole. These general principles are common to the whole series; in detail each Editor is alone responsible for the play or plays that have been intrusted to him.

Every volume of the series has been provided with a Glossary, an Essay upon Metre, and an Index; and Appendices have been added upon points of special interest, which could not conveniently be treated in the Introduction or the Notes. The text is based by the several Editors on that of the *Globe* edition: the only omissions made are those that are unavoidable in an edition likely to be used by young students.

By the systematic arrangement of the introductory matter, and by close attention to typographical details, every effort has been made to provide an edition that will prove convenient in use.

CONTENTS

INTRODUCTION

1. DATE, HISTORY, AND BIBLIOGRAPHY OF THE PLAY.

The First Folio of 1623, the first collected edition of Shakespeare's plays (now one of the most precious books in the world), contained thirty-six of the thirty-seven plays now usually associated with Shakespeare's name—*Pericles* was not included until the Third Folio of 1664—one half of which had previously appeared as single plays in "quarto" editions, the other eighteen being then published for the first time. Among the latter was *Cymbeline*, the last of the "tragedies", and the last play in the book.

Date of Composition.—It is not possible to fix the date of composition of this play with certainty. The items of external and external-internal evidence are four in number:

(*a*) Dr. Simon Forman, the astrologer, in his MS. "book of plays, and notes thereof", has under the year 1611, but undated, a brief sketch of the plot of "Cimbalin King of England", which was Shakespeare's play. Forman died in September of that year, and his diary, which also contains dated descriptions of *Macbeth* and *Winter's Tale*, belongs to the years 1610–1611. It is not improbable that, when Forman saw it, *Cymbeline* was a new play.

(*b*) The suggestion for the character of Euphrasia in Beaumont and Fletcher's *Philaster* was apparently taken from Imogen. Moreover, compare these two passages:

> "*Phi.* I hear the tread of people. I am hurt:
> The gods take part against me: could this boor
> Have held me thus else?"   —*Philaster*, iv. 3.[1]

[1] Mermaid Series, London, 1893, p. 164.

> "*Iach.*   I have belied a lady,
> The princess of this country, and the air on 't
> Revengingly enfeebles me; or could this carl,
> A very drudge of nature's, have subdued me
> In my profession?"   —*Cymbeline*, v. 2. 2–6.

Philaster is dated 1608–1611; 1611 would then be the downward limit for *Cymbeline*.

(*c*) The main plot of the play is derived from the ninth "novel" of the second day in Boccaccio's *Decamerone*. From the same source Shakespeare took part of a speech of Autolycus in *Winter's Tale*, as will be manifest to anyone who compares these two passages following:

> "*Aut.* He has a son, who shall be flayed alive; then 'nointed over with honey, set on the head of a wasp's nest; then stand till he be three quarters and a dram dead; then recovered again with aqua-vitæ or some other hot infusion; then, raw as he is, and in the hottest day prognostication proclaims, shall he be set against a brick-wall, the sun looking with a southward eye upon him, where he is to behold him with flies blown to death."
>   —*Winter's Tale*, iv. 4. 812–821.

> "But as for Ambrogiuolo, the very same day that he was impaled on a stake, anointed with honey, and fixed in the place appointed to his no mean torment, he not only died, but likewise was devoured to the bare bones by flies, wasps, and hornets, whereof the country notoriously aboundeth."   —*Decamerone*, ii. 9.[1]

The date of the *Winter's Tale* is 1610–1611, and it is inferred that *Cymbeline* preceded it by no long interval.

(*d*) From the allusion to the story of Antony and Cleopatra in ii. 4. 69–72:

>   "the story
> Proud Cleopatra, when she met her Roman,
> And Cydnus swell'd above the banks, or for
> The press of boats or pride ";

and to the Troy legend in iv. 2. 252, 253:

> "Thersites' body is as good as Ajax',
> When neither are alive ";

[1] Morley's Universal Library, No. 15, London, 1885.

it has been supposed that *Cymbeline* comes after *Antony and Cleopatra* and *Troilus and Cressida*, that is, after 1607.

If the foregoing evidence be valid, the limits of date are 1607 and 1611, and between these two years the composition of the play has been held to fall.

Malone conjectured that, inasmuch as Shakespeare drew material from the same parts of Holinshed's *Chronicles* for *Lear*, *Macbeth*, and *Cymbeline*, these three plays were written about the same time. Basing himself partly on this conjecture, Mr. Fleay[1] postulates a double date for the play — part written in 1606–1607, the remainder about 1610. Dr. Ingleby,[2] relying mainly on some similarities of phrase between this play and *Macbeth* which are pointed out in the notes on act ii. scene 2, came to the same general conclusion, but differs widely from Mr. Fleay as to the scenes to be assigned to the earlier date. Thus the hypothesis of a double date, which would require very strong evidence, is far from being proved at the present time.

It is more satisfactory to turn to the internal evidence, which will be found to point unmistakably towards the later date.

Cymbeline, *The Tempest*, and *The Winter's Tale* (with *Pericles*) form a small group with marked points of resemblance. They have been well christened "romances". "There is a romantic element about these plays. In all there is the same romantic incident of lost children recovered by those to whom they are dear—the daughters of Pericles and Leontes, the sons of Cymbeline and Alonso. In all there is a beautiful romantic background of sea or mountain." They all deal with divided and reunited families, with a background composed largely of country scenes, as if the dramatist's thoughts and steps were now often turned in the direction of Stratford, where he may even have written parts of these plays. Not less marked are the resemblances in style, language, — often outpaced by the thought—metre. There are laxities in the dramatic construction of *Cymbeline*

---

[1] *Shakespeare Manual*, London, 1876, p. 53; and *Life and Work of Shakespeare*.   [2] *Shakespeare's Cymbeline*, London, 1886, p. xi.

(see, *e.g.*, note on iii. 3. 99) which place it without doubt among the author's latest plays.

The metrical evidence of date is threefold: (*a*) The proportion of unstopped to end-stopped lines in his verse increases steadily throughout Shakespeare's dramatic life, although the former are never the majority. Compare the blank verse of *Love's Labour's Lost* with that of our play: the ratios of unstopped to end-stopped lines are 1 : 18·14 and 1 : 2·52 respectively; in *The Tempest* and *The Winter's Tale* they are 1 : 3·02 and 1 : 2·12. (*b*) The number of eleven-syllabled lines, lines with double or feminine endings, increases in like manner with the lateness of Shakespeare's work. In *Love's Labour's Lost* they form only 4 per cent of the total lines; in *Winter's Tale* they are 31·09 per cent, in *Cymbeline* 32 per cent, in *The Tempest* 33 per cent. (*c*) Weak endings, or decasyllabic lines ending in unemphatic words such as pronouns, prepositions, conjunctions, are not found in the earlier plays; in the later plays, beginning with *Macbeth*, they increase in number almost continuously. In *Cymbeline* they form 4·83 of the whole, *Tempest* 4·59, *Winter's Tale* 5·59. Five wonderful lines in *Cymbeline*—iv. 2. 220-224—illustrate all the above metrical characteristics in briefest space:

> "thou shalt not lack
> The flower that's like thy face, pale primrose, nor
> The azured harebell, like thy veins, no, nor
> The leaf of eglantine, whom not to slander,
> Out-sweeten'd not thy breath".

Thus it will be seen that the metrical unites with the other internal evidence in bringing the three plays of *Cymbeline*, *The Tempest*, and *The Winter's Tale* closely together in date of composition. If the last belongs to 1610–1611, and *The Tempest* to 1610, as is almost certain, we cannot be far wrong in dating *Cymbeline* 1609–1610.

Subsequent History.—There is little of importance in the subsequent history of the play. We know from the *Office-book* of Sir Henry Herbert, Master of the Revels, that it was acted at Court in January, 1633, and was "well liked by the king".

Thomas D'Urfey's *Injured Princess, or the Fatal Wager*, first played in 1682, is an adaptation of *Cymbeline*; perhaps its worth may be gauged by the line:

" Fly, sirrah, with this to the packet-boat ".

The most famous stage version of the play is Garrick's, produced at Drury Lane in 1761. The changes, with the exception of a few added words, were confined to omissions and transpositions. Henry Brooke, author of *The Fool of Quality*, wrote a tragedy of *Cymbeline*, based on Shakespeare's, and published in 1778, but it was never acted.

Commentators upon Shakespeare have been only too plentiful and only too foolish. At first there was room for careful revision and correction of the earlier editions; but, this done, Shakespeare was improved upon, and other men's language and thoughts, save for an occasional suggestion of genius, were put in the place of his. Of most of the emendations— save the mark!—that have been suggested we do well to be impatient. A wise conservatism is the best attitude of mind in textual criticism.

The following list of editions may be useful, and may explain some references in the notes:

Quartos of single plays from 1597;
First Folio, 1623;
Second Folio, 1632;
Third Folio, 1663 and 1664;
Fourth Folio, 1685;
Rowe's (first critical edition), 1709;
Pope's, 1725;
Theobald's, 1733;
Hanmer's, 1744–1746;
Warburton's, 1747;
Dr. Johnson's, 1765;
Capell's, 1768;
Johnson and Steevens', 1773;
Malone's, 1790;
Variorum editions, 1803, 1813;
Bowdler's ("family"), 1818;
Boswell's Malone, 1821;

and, among more recent ones, those of Singer, Knight, Collier, Halliwell-Phillipps, Hudson, Dyce, Grant White, Staunton, the " Globe ", the " Cambridge ", and the Furness Variorum (in progress).

2. SOURCES.

In seeking out the sources of a play of Shakespeare, it must be borne in mind that no attempt is made to take away from the glory and greatness of the dramatist's share of the work.   On the contrary, Shakespeare contributed to the making of his plays almost every element of their greatness. To use a familiar metaphor, he almost always borrowed the rough ore of a story or plot and transmuted it into the pure gold of one of his complete plays.   Mere stories lay ready to his hand in abundance: Shakespeare made them dramatic; gave to the principal actors in the stories distinctive characters, and revealed those characters to us, often by slight but masterly indications; showed us the play of motives, of feelings, of passions; made his *personæ* as real to us as our personal friends and foes.

The sources of *Cymbeline* are twofold—one simple, the other more complicated.   The main plot of the play is a medieval fiction; the setting is early British history.   This historical framework, such as it is, Shakespeare took from Holinshed's *Chronicles*.   It consists chiefly of a few names, especially those of Cymbeline and his sons (but see notes on dramatis personæ) ; of a few allusions, as, for instance, to Mulmutius and his laws; and of the incident of a handful of men staying the flight of an army and turning defeat into victory, which Shakespeare, as was his wont, took from quite another part of Holinshed.   Since the passages of Holinshed are quoted in full in Appendix B and references made to them in the notes, nothing more need be said here than that the Queen, Cloten (all but the name), the life of the Court, Belarius and his theft and its consequences, are not in Holinshed, and no other source has been found for them.

The story of the wager, out of which Shakespeare constructed his main plot, is known to us, intact in all its essentials, in at least six different forms.   They are: (1) A French miracle-play, entitled "Un Miracle de Nostre-Dame", probably of the 13th century, printed in the "Théâtre Français au -Moyen-Age" (1839): of this Collier[1] quotes a summary. (2) A French poetical "Roman de la Violette" of the 13th century, by Gibert de Montreuil, of which Collier[1] gives an analysis taken from "Le Journal des Savans". (3) Another poetical French romance of the same century, "Le Compte de Poitiers", of which also Collier[1] gives an analysis. It differs from "La Violette" in little more than the names. (4) The ninth "novel" of the second day in Boccaccio's *Decamerone*, which first appeared complete in English dress in 1620; but the dedicatory epistle of that edition states that many of Boccaccio's novels had been translated into English long before. (5) The tale of the fish-wife of Stand on the Green (see Appendix C) in *Westward for Smelts*, a collection of tales, which Malone[2] dated 1603, but of which no edition earlier than 1620 is known; and the entry in the registers of the Stationers' Company confirms the latter date. (6) "Frederick of Jennen", which Steevens[3] describes as "an ancient translation, or rather a deformed and interpolated imitation, of the ninth novel of the second day of the Decameron". He adds: "This novel exhibits the material features of its original; though the names of the characters are changed, their sentiments debased, and their conduct rendered still more improbable than in the scenes before us". The colophon states that it was printed in Antwerp in 1518![4]

In all these the plot is essentially the same: the wager, the repulse of the villain, the husband's attempted revenge, the wife's escape, the discovery of the fraud, the happy reconciliation of husband and wife, and the punishment of the criminal. The variety of form—miracle-play, romance, novel; the extent of time, from about 1200 to the 17th century; show how wide-spread the legend must have been, and how more than possible it is that Shakespeare knew the story in more than one form, which may or may not be those

---

[1] *Shakespeare's Library*, vol. ii.
[2] *Boswell's Malone*, xiii. 229.   [3] *Ib.* xiii. 2–3.
[4] It should be clearly understood that some of these six versions are almost identical with one another, but at least none of them professes to be a mere translation.

which we now possess. This much at least is clear, that it would be absurd to speak in a tone of certainty about the matter.

For the present purpose (1) the miracle-play, (4) the *Decamerone* tale, and (5) that in *Westward for Smelts*, stand out from the rest. It seems to me impossible to decide whether Shakespeare went direct to the Italian original, or borrowed from an English translation or close adaptation now lost; but that he drew material from the one or the other, I consider there is no room to doubt. The only other known source that can compete with the *Decamerone* is *Westward for Smelts*. That the student may judge for himself, I give Skottowe's[1] abridgment of the former here; in Appendix C he will find a rough sketch of the latter, designed chiefly to bring out the points of difference. This is the story in Boccaccio:

Several Italian merchants met accidentally in Paris at supper, and conversed freely of their absent wives. "I know not", one jestingly remarked, "how my wife conducts herself in my absence, but of this I am certain, that whenever I meet with an attractive beauty, I make the best advantage I can of the opportunity." "And so do I," quoth another, "for whether I believe my wife unfaithful or not, she will be so if she pleases." A third said the same, and all readily coincided in the licentious opinion, except Bernabo Tomekin of Genoa, who maintained that he had a wife perfectly beautiful, in the flower of youth, and of such indisputable chastity, that he was convinced if he were absent for ten years she would preserve her fidelity. A young merchant of Piacenza, Ambrogiuolo, was extremely facetious on the subject, and concluded some libertine remarks by offering to effect the seduction of this modern Lucretia, provided opportunity were afforded him. Bernabo answered his confident boast by the proposition of a wager, which was instantly accepted.

According to agreement, Bernabo remained at Paris, while Ambrogiuolo set out for Genoa, where his enquiries soon convinced him that Zinevra, the wife of Bernabo, had not been too highly praised, and that his wager would be lost, without he could effect by stratagem what he had certainly no probability of obtaining by direct

[1] *Life of Shakespeare*, London, 1824; ii. 261 foll. The tale will be found in full in No. 15 of Morley's *Universal Library*, 1s.

solicitation. Chance threw in his way a poor woman, often employed in the house of Zinevra, whom he secured in his interest by
a bribe. Pretending unavoidable absence for a few days, the woman
entreated Zinevra to take charge of a large chest till she returned.
The lady consented, and the chest, with Ambrogiuolo secreted in it,
was placed in Zinevra's bed-chamber. When the lady retired to
rest, the villain crept from his concealment, and by the light of a
taper took particular notice of the pictures and furniture, and the
form and situation of the apartment. Advancing to the bed, he
eagerly sought for some mark about the lady's person, and at last
espied a mole and tuft of golden hair upon her left breast. Then
taking a ring, a purse, and other trifles, he returned to his concealment, whence he was not released till the third day, when the woman
returned and had the chest conveyed home.

Ambrogiuolo hastily summoned the merchants in Paris, who were
present when the wager was laid. As a proof of his success he
produced the stolen trinkets, called them gifts from the lady, and
described the furniture of the bed-room. Bernabo acknowledged the
correctness of the account, and confessed that the purse and the ring
belonged to his wife; but added, that as Ambrogiuolo might have
obtained his account of the room, and procured the jewels also, from
some of Zinevra's servants, his claim to the money was not yet
established. "The proofs I have given", said Ambrogiuolo, "ought
to suffice; but as you call on me for more, I will silence your scepti-
cism at once;—Zinevra has a mole on her left breast." Bernabo's
countenance testified the truth of the assertion, and he shortly
acknowledged it by words: he then paid the sum he had wagered,
and instantly set out for Italy. Arriving near his residence, he
despatched a messenger for Zinevra, and gave secret orders that she
should be put to death upon the road. The servant stopped in a
lonely place, and declared his master's harsh instructions. The lady
vehemently protested her innocence of any crime against her husband;
besought the compassion of her conductor, and promised to conceal
herself in some distant and obscure abode. Her life was spared,
and the servant returned to his master with some of Zinevra's clothes, ·
reporting that he had killed her, and left her body to the ferocity of
beasts of prey.

Zinevra disguised herself in the garments of a man, and entered
the service of a Catalonian gentleman, who carried her to Alexandria.
Here she was fortunate enough to attract the attention of the Sultan,
who solicited her from her master. She soon became a favourite,

and under the name of Sicurano was appointed captain of the guard. For the security of both Christian and Turkish merchants, who resorted to the fair at Acre, the Sultan annually sent an officer with a band of soldiers. Sicurano was employed on this service, when, being in the shop of a Venetian merchant, she cast her eye upon a purse and girdle, which she recognized as her own. Without declaring her discovery, she enquired to whom they belonged, and whether they were for sale. Ambrogiuolo, who had arrived with a stock of merchandise, now stepped forward, and replied, that the trinkets were his, and begged Sicurano, since he admired them, to accept of them. Sicurano asked why he smiled; when Ambrogiuolo related, that the purse and girdle were presents to him from a married lady of Genoa, whose love he had enjoyed; and that he smiled at the folly of her husband, who had laid five thousand against one thousand florins, that the virtue of his wife was incorruptible.

The jealousy and revenge of Bernabo were now explained to Zinevra, and the base artificer of her ruin stood before her. She feigned pleasure at Ambrogiuolo's story, cultivated his acquaintance, and took him with her to Alexandria. Her next care was to have Bernabo, now reduced to great distress, brought privately to Alexandria. Then, watching a favourable opportunity, she prevailed with the Sultan to compel Ambrogiuolo to relate publicly every circumstance of his villainy. Bernabo confessed that he had caused his wife to be murdered on the supposition of her guilt with Ambrogiuolo. "You perceive", said Sicurano to the Sultan, "how little reason the unhappy lady had to be proud either of her gallant or her husband: if you, my lord, will punish the deceiver, and pardon the deceived, the traduced lady shall appear in your presence." The Sultan assented; Sicurano fell at his feet, and discarding her assumed demeanour, declared herself to be Zinevra: the display of the mole upon her breast banished every doubt. Ambrogiuolo was then put to a cruel death; and his immense wealth was given to Zinevra. The Sultan pardoned Bernabo, and, making Zinevra a princely donation of jewels and money, provided a ship, and suffered ·her and her husband to depart for Genoa.

The deviations of Shakespeare from his original make up the play itself. Even where he has followed most closely, he has changed and glorified his loan until it is barely recognizable. In all the circumstances of the wager, in the repentance of the husband and of the villain, and in the punishment of the latter, how great the changes are must be apparent to all. It is more to the purpose here, therefore, to indicate some particulars in which it is possible that Shakespeare followed versions of the story other than that in the *Decamerone*. That he knew the *Decamerone* version is proved by the quotation from *Winter's Tale* above (see p. viii), and by the fact that the device of the trunk for conveying the concealed villain into the lady's bed-room is peculiar to that version;[1] in *Westward for Smelts* he conceals himself under the bed. The mark on the lady's person is on the left breast[1] in Boccaccio as in Shakespeare; it is not mentioned in *Westward for Smelts*. But, on the other hand, there are a few remarkable resemblances between the Fishwife's tale and Shakespeare, which are also divergences from Boccaccio: (1) the villain proposes the wager, not the husband as in Boccaccio; (2) the villain converses with the lady and is entertained by her, whereas in the *Decamerone* he only sees her asleep, being convinced of the hopelessness of his errand by the report he hears of her virtue; (3) the lady requests the servant to fulfil his master's command and kill her, while in Boccaccio she begs for her life to be spared; (4) she is found in great distress in her disguise by King Edward IV. (in *Westward for Smelts*), becomes one of his pages (*Cymbeline*, v. 5. 86), and follows him to battle. Whether Shakespeare took these variations of the story from a lost edition of *Westward for Smelts* I am unable to decide; possibly he was as capable of making them for himself as "kinde Kitt of Kingstone". It is noteworthy that, while the principal actors are all Italian in Boccaccio, and all English in the English tale, in Shakespeare two are English and one Italian.

It only remains to give, from a tract quoted by Collier,[2] two points of resemblance between the French *Miracle* and

---

[1] Hudson states that the discovery of a private mark on the lady's person, and her disguise in male attire, are also "not found in any other version of the tale". This is an error. Both are in the miracle-play; the mark on the person is in *Violette* (but upon the *right* breast); the male attire in *Westward for Smelts*.

[2] *Shakespeare's Library*, vol. ii. The tract bears date 1839, and is entitled ": Farther Particulars of Shakespeare and his Works".

Shakespeare which may deserve remark. Count Berengier, the villain of the piece, boasts to the husband that he knows no woman living, but if he might *speak to her twice*, at the third time he might have all his desire. Compare this with Iachimo's (i. 4. 113–114): "with no more advantage than the opportunity of a second conference". Again, Berengier says to Denise, the lady of the play: "I come from Rome, where I left your lord, who does not value you the stalk of a cherry: he is connected with a girl for whom he has so strong a regard, that he knows not how to part from her". Compare this with *Cymbeline*, i. 6. These two coincidences, whatever they may be worth, are absent alike from Boccaccio and from *Westward for Smelts*; they go some way towards proving the truth of the suggestion, that the tale may have been known to Shakespeare in some form now lost.

3. CRITICAL COMMENTS.

Probably no play of Shakespeare's is generally appreciated so far below its real merits as *Cymbeline*. This is partly due to the supposed "essential indecency of the plot"; partly to the fact that it yields its gold only to the earnest miner, not to the mere scraper of the surface. That gold is, firstly, the charming sylvan picture of the royal rustics Guiderius and Arviragus; secondly, a *dénouement* of unsurpassed interest in the unravelling of a most intricate plot; lastly, the most fully drawn "portrait of a lady" in the whole gallery of Shakespeare's women, his ideal of womanhood, the peerless Imogen.

The earliest notable criticism of the play is Dr. Johnson's: "This play has many just sentiments, some natural dialogues, and some pleasing scenes, but they are obtained at the expense of much incongruity. To remark the folly of the fiction, the absurdity of the conduct, the confusion of the names and manners of different times, and the impossibility of the events in any system of life, were to waste criticism upon unresisting imbecility, upon faults too evident for detection and too gross for aggravation." Fortunately it

is unnecessary in our day to reply to this in detail. Shakespeare borrowed the fiction, as was his wont, and the use he
has made of it may be held even in this instance to have
justified his choice. "The confusion of the names and
manners of different times" is admitted: Caius Lucius and
Iachimo, the Roman general and the medieval Italian, hailing
from the same country in the same play. Shakespeare could
be as consistent in such matters as Ben Jonson when he
chose; witness *The Tempest.* But it is clear that he did
not often choose: here and in *Winter's Tale* he silently and
effectually claims the utmost freedom for himself and for the
English romantic drama. "The impossibility of the events
in any system of life" I deny. If we take the medieval plot
out of its setting of mythical early British history, there is
nothing impossible or even improbable about it; the alleged
incongruity between the nature of the plot and the character
of Posthumus will be dealt with later on.

Cymbeline is neither a "history", a comedy, nor a tragedy.
Hazlitt called it a "dramatic romance". Our greatest living
Shakespeare-critic says of *Cymbeline, The Winter's Tale,* and
The Tempest, which he classes together: "Characteristics of
versification and style, and the enlarged place given to scenic
spectacle, indicate that these plays were produced much about
the same time. But the ties of deepest kinship between them
are spiritual. There is a certain romantic element in each.
They receive contributions from every portion of Shakspere's
genius, but all are mellowed, refined, made exquisite; they
avoid the extremes of broad humour and of tragic intensity;
they were written with less of passionate concentration
than the plays which immediately precede them, but with
more of a spirit of deep or exquisite recreation." And the
same writer adds with reference to the same plays: "When
a man has attained some high and luminous tableland of
joy or of renouncement, when he has really transcended self,
or when some one of the everlasting, virtuous powers of the
world—duty or sacrifice or the strength of anything higher
than oneself—has assumed authority over him, forthwith a
strange, pathetic, ideal light is shed over all beautiful things

in the lower world which has been abandoned".[1] All Shakespeare's latest plays tell of reconciliation and reunion of husbands and wives, of parents and children, and it is impossible not to think of the great poet himself returning at the close of his career to his quiet country home with his heart full of the mellowed practical wisdom that abounds in these plays.

If it is hard to find a better term for this play, yet "romance" is not altogether a happy one because of its exceeding ambiguity, and because it does the play bare justice. *Cymbeline* is almost as comprehensive as life itself. In the struggle between the evil and the good, in the intervention of the powers above on the side of the righteous in affliction, in the threefold action and the varied and distracting interests, in the wonderful disentanglement of the last scene, though we miss the intensity of passion of *Lear* and the headlong precipitation of *Macbeth*, we are compensated by the many-sided, all-embracing fulness of the play. The divine intervention must be brought into connection with its happy termination. "For", as a well-known critic remarks, "the personages who here act and err are friends and favourites of the gods, because even that which in calm certainty or uncertain passion they do contrary to the maxims of morality, is done from moral motives or in moral indignation; so that the drama with a tragic ending would have been an impeachment of the world's government."

The same critic[2] expends much ingenuity in showing that there is an underlying "idea" in each of Shakespeare's plays, "would men observingly distil it out". That Shakespeare consciously and of set purpose wrote a play round an idea for a centre-piece, as it were, I do not believe. But that the actions and characters of this play can be made to group themselves around one all-pervading "idea", which they express and impress in many ways and situations, I am bound to admit. But let the writer speak for himself. [The

---

[1] *Shakspere: A Critical Study of his Mind and Art*, by Edward Dowden, LL.D., pp. 403, and 414, 415.

[2] Gervinus: *Shakespeare Commentaries*, translated by F. E. Bunnett; p. 644 ff.

play] "treats uniformly throughout two opposite ideas or moral qualities, namely, truth in word and in deed (fidelity), and untruth and faithlessness,—falseness in deed or perfidy, falseness in word or slander. All the actions and characters of the play combine to exemplify these ideas." This opening statement is then enforced by many examples and quotations. The court is the world of falsehood, the sylvan home of Belarius is the abode of truth. The Queen is false to every one but Cloten. The happiness of Posthumus and Imogen depends on their confidence in one another. When they swerve, as they both do, from perfect trust, the direst nemesis follows. The true Posthumus is contrasted with the false Iachimo. The good characters of the play can often be true to their better selves only by being false to the evil characters. Thus the Physician deceives the Queen, and Pisanio deceives Cloten. Such words as "truth", "true", "falsehood", "false", "lie", are of constant occurrence. Imogen says:

> "To lapse in fulness
> Is sorer than to lie for need, and falsehood
> Is worse in kings than beggars" (iii. 6. 12–14).

Cornelius:

> "She is fool'd
> With a most false effect; and I the truer,
> So to be false with her" (i. 5. 42–44).

Pisanio :

> "for true to thee
> Were to prove false, which I will never be,
> To him that is most true" (iii. 5. 151–153).

And again:

"Wherein I am false I am honest; not true, to be true" (iv. 3. 42).

Posthumus:

> "villain-like, I lie—
> That caused a lesser villain than myself,
> A sacrilegious thief, to do't" (v. 5. 218–220).

Fidelity is the cardinal virtue of an heroic age; nothing then is nobler or more valuable than a true and tried friend,

servant, or wife. Posthumus and Imogen, in spite of everything, preserve their fidelity unspotted. "And this it is, and
this alone, which at last overcomes misfortune and wickedness: that we do not shape our own course after that of the
world, that we do not let the vices of others tempt us to our
own nor believe them excusable. ' By constancy', says
Bacon, ' fate and fortune return like Proteus to their former
being.' Faithlessness, in revenge for faithlessness, as recommended by Iachimo to Imogen, would have for ever destroyed
the love and happiness of both; the true constancy of both,
in spite of the supposed falsehood of each, surmounted the
wicked report and even the incurable evil—the supposed
death."

Mention has been made of the threefold action of this play.
The imperial or political action of the relations between the
courts of Britain and Rome in the reign of Cymbeline is the
least interesting of the three. Cymbeline himself is a king
only in outward show; in act he is a mere tool of the queen,
in speech he is an echo of her or even of "that harsh, noble,
simple nothing" Cloten. Hence his title to give the name
to the play has been called in question. It may be defended
on the ground that in him alone are the threads of the different actions and interests united.[1]

The second action—the rustic life, of Belarius and his
foster-sons among the Welsh mountains—is Shakespeare's
own invention. It stands in no very vital relation to the rest
of the play; but its justification is its great and inherent
charm, that is far indeed from being dulled by greater famili-
arity. At first acquaintance it may appear that the two
brothers are but a doubling of the same character; a more
careful reading will reveal that the dramatist has limned
them as differently as the size and nature of his canvas would
allow.

But it is in the main action of the wager and its consequences that interest must always centre; it is upon the chief
actors therein that Shakespeare has showered all the wealth

[1] See Appendices B and E.

of his own intense interest, and consequently all the matured power of his inimitable portraiture. That there is something repugnant to modern notions in the very wager itself is no doubt true; that it will repay every reader a hundredfold to overcome and banish that repugnance is still more true.

It remains for us to glance at the persons chiefly concerned in this wager; to note, if we can, its effect upon them, and their influence upon one another; and to see in what way they were different from their former selves at the close of the play.

The devil has been declared to be "not so black as he is painted"; the utter revulsion and contempt we feel for Iachimo make it all the more necessary to point out some redeeming traits in his character. In the first place there are the facts, "writ large" upon the play, that he is deeply impressed by a moral purity which he had never before encountered, and that in the end he feels and expresses sincere contrition for his own wickedness. Before his meeting with Posthumus he had not known, or had not sought to know, virtuous men and women, and did not believe that such existed. His first glance at Imogen gives this disbelief a rude shock:

> "If she be furnish'd with a mind so rare,
> She is alone the Arabian bird, and I
> Have lost the wager".

After this first encounter with her and the following scene in her bed-chamber Iachimo is never the same man again. His life and reputation depend upon the result of the wager, and he carries his part through with effrontery; but—mark this well—there is no exaggerated bravado in his report of his successful errand, he keeps as near the exact truth as circumstances permit, he does not drag the "heavenly angel" any deeper into the hell of slander than he can avoid. Then, with Posthumus, he disappears for two acts, and when we meet him again, when he has been vanquished and his life nobly spared by him whom he had so woefully wronged, he ejaculates:

> "The heaviness and guilt within my bosom
> Takes off my manhood".

And in the last scene he prefaces his enforced confession with these significant conscience-stricken words:

"I am glad to be constrain'd to utter that
Which torments me to conceal".

Thus the last state of this man is better than the first.

Imogen's choice of a husband has been assailed on account of his conduct in the matter of the wager, and for the sake of both the hero and the heroine the charge must be examined and if possible rebutted. In the court of Britain there is but one opinion of Posthumus among the disinterested:

" to seek through the regions of the earth
For one his like, there would be something failing
In him that should compare ".

But abroad "this matter of marrying his king's daughter" is not allowed to "word him a great deal from the matter", and the cynical, sceptical Iachimo puts him through an awful ordeal from which he is ultimately saved, "yet so as by fire": The successive steps of Iachimo's demoniacally cunning provocation and challenge must be carefully traced in i. 4., before one can attempt to answer the question posed ·by the detractors of Posthumus: Ought he to have accepted the wager? Regarded not as a question of morality, but as properly a question of medieval chivalry, the answer can but be, Yes. Iachimo's challenge is against the whole sex: "I durst attempt it against any lady in the world". Posthumus was the more bound to accept it. By doing so he was acting in the spirit of the most exalted ideals of chivalry. Indeed alike himself and the cause he was championing would have been held for ever disgraced if he had acted otherwise. Posthumus had the uttermost confidence in his lady; she would put the slanderer of her sex to ignominious rout (as she actually did), and her champion would then take fitting revenge on the "Italian fiend" for his gross and blatant disbelief. That this is Iachimo's own view of the matter is evident from his admiring testimony in the final scene to the conduct of Imogen's "true knight".

There is a second count in the indictment—that Posthumus ought not to have accepted Iachimo's proofs that he had "convinced the honour of his mistress". The answer is the same as before—let the reader follow step by step the diabolical cleverness of Iachimo's report in ii. 4., and he will infallibly come to the same conclusion as Philario: "You have won". The behaviour of Posthumus when he believes the wager lost compares unfavourably enough with Imogen's when convinced of *his* unfaithfulness. But even in his murderous letter to Pisanio we read: "the testimonies whereof *tie bleeding in me*", and of "proof *as strong as my grief*". Later, while his wife's guilt is still not disproved, he makes not unworthy reparation. When he reappears in the fifth act it is as a heart-broken penitent, purified and ennobled, even to the point of silently and greatly sparing the life of him who was the cause of all his woe.

In the character of Imogen we have the dramatic study of an almost perfect woman, the crowning glory of that incomparable galaxy which contains Miranda, Desdemona, and Rosalind, Portia, Cordelia, and Hermione. This would seem to have been the opinion alike of Shakespeare himself and of his critics. Every intimate student of *Cymbeline* takes up the chorus of praise. Hazlitt is a partial exception; but his depreciatory remark, that Imogen "is only interesting herself from her tenderness and constancy to her husband", is too extraordinary for discussion, and is disproved by the unfailing interest with which each reader follows her every word and action. Against it may be set the opinions of the last great actress who has played the part, Helen Faucit, Lady Martin —"In drawing her he has made his masterpiece"—and that of a critic who is also one of the two[1] greatest of living English poets: "The play of plays, which is *Cymbeline*", says Swinburne.[2] "Here is depth enough with weight enough of tragic beauty and passion, terror and love and pity, to approve the presence of the most tragic master's hand; subtlety enough of sweet and bitter truth to attest the passage of the mightiest

[1] Alas! the other is gone from us since these words were penned: William Morris died October 3rd, 1896.   [2] *A Study of Shakespeare*, p. 226.

and wisest scholar or teacher in the school of the human spirit; beauty with delight enough and glory of life and grace of nature to proclaim the advent of the one omnipotent Maker among all who bear that name. Here above all is the most heavenly triad of human figures that ever even Shakespeare brought together. . . . The passion of Posthumus is noble, and potent the poison of Iachimo; . . . but we think first and last of her who was 'truest speaker' and those who 'called her brother, when she was but their sister; she them brothers, when they were so indeed'. The very crown and flower of all her father's daughters—I do not speak here of her human father, but her divine—the woman above all Shakespeare's women is Imogen. . . . In Imogen we find half glorified already the immortal godhead of womanhood. I would fain have some honey in my words at parting—with Shakespeare never, but for ever with these notes on Shakespeare; and I am therefore something more than fain to close my book upon the name of the woman best beloved in all the world of song and all the tide of time; upon the name of Shakespeare's Imogen."

That she is the incarnation of the poet's own ideal of womanly grace, beauty, and intellect, may be inferred from the almost universal admiration he showers upon her throughout the play. Even Cloten is fain to admit that

> "she's fair and royal,
> And that she hath all courtly parts more exquisite
> Than lady, ladies, woman; from every one
> The best she hath, and she of all compounded,
> Outsells them all".

The most striking testimony to her personal beauty is the admiration and awe which almost make a pure man of the defeated libertine in the famous bed-chamber scene. To Belarius, who had fled from court before her birth, she appears (in her male attire) "a fairy", "an angel", "an earthly paragon", "divineness no elder than a boy". Her brothers' welcome and treatment of her cannot be taken out of its context, but it is one prolonged tribute to her charms. Lucius never had

> "A page so kind, so duteous, diligent,
> So tender over his occasions, true,
> So feat, so nurse-like".

Pisanio, when instructing her in a page's part, bids her change

> "fear and niceness—
> The handmaids of all women, or, more truly,
> Woman it pretty self—into a waggish courage;
> Ready in gibes, quick-answer'd, saucy and
> As quarrelous as the weasel . . . and forget
> Your laboursome and dainty trims, wherein
> You made great Juno angry".

It is no doubt partly because Imogen cannot change her very nature after this fashion, and only succeeds in maintaining her incognita by keeping the part she has to play ever present to consciousness, that she wins all men's hearts as much in male attire as in her proper person. In whatever attire, in whatever company, in whatever situation, Imogen's unchangeable nature is "a shop of all the qualities that man loves woman for". Even her "neat cookery" was, at least in the opinion of her unsophisticated brothers, fit for Juno "sick"; to the same judges her singing was "angel-like", and Pisanio delicately implies that her natural voice was musical (iii. 4. 175). Her qualities of mind and heart are not inferior to the endowments of her person. She is blest with a native healthiness of feeling and of intellect that makes her equal to every emergency, and invariably leads her to do and to say the right thing. Her keen penetration makes her an excellent judge of character. Thus in the very first scene, in spite of all the Queen's protestations, she sees through her "dissembling courtesy".

It is inevitable that we should compare her conduct with that of Posthumus to his detriment. Both of them are led to believe that the other has proved false. It never occurs to either of them to take revenge by similar faithlessness. But while Posthumus determines on the murder of his wife without even giving her a chance of proving her innocence, she, in similar circumstances, commands Pisanio to fulfil his master's bidding and take her life, without a single thought of revenge. While Posthumus rails at the whole sex because he believes its most virtuous ornament to have fallen a prey to the wiles of Iachimo, Imogen, on her part, fears that

> "all good seeming,
> By thy revolt, O husband, shall be thought
> Put on for villany";
>   "so thou, Posthumus,
> Wilt lay the leaven on all proper men;
> Goodly and gallant should be false and perjur'd
> From thy great fail".

What a height of nobility and self-command to attain at this moment of supreme anguish!

Imogen had never been ambitious for the throne or even for a courtly life; she had chosen a poor husband; she once wished she had been "thief-stol'n", like her two brothers, and thought those blest,

> "How mean soe'er, that have their honest wills".

When she met her brothers in the cave, she could not refrain the wish that she had been their sister, "and so more equal ballasting to thee, Posthumus". The close of the play finds these wishes partly fulfilled. She has lost a kingdom, but gained two worlds by it. She has her honest will. "See", says Cymbeline,

> "Posthumus anchors upon Imogen,
> And she, like harmless lightning, throws her eye
> On him, her brothers, me, her master, hitting
> Each object with a joy".[1]

[1] It is a pleasure to acknowledge my indebtedness to Fletcher's *Studies of Shakespeare*.

CYMBELINE

DRAMATIS PERSONÆ

CYMBELINE, king of Britain.
CLOTEN, son to the Queen by a former husband.
POSTHUMUS LEONATUS, a gentleman, husband to Imogen.
BELARIUS, a banished lord, disguised under the name of Morgan.
GUIDERIUS, ⎰ sons to Cymbeline, disguised under the names of Polydore
ARVIRAGUS, ⎱ and Cadwal, supposed sons to Morgan.
PHILARIO, friend to Posthumus, ⎱ Italians.
IACHIMO, friend to Philario, ⎰
CAIUS LUCIUS, general of the Roman forces.
PISANIO, servant to Posthumus.
CORNELIUS, a physician.
A Roman Captain.
Two British Captains.
A Frenchman, friend to Philario.
Two Lords of Cymbeline's court.
Two Gentlemen of the same.
Two Gaolers

Queen, wife to Cymbeline.
IMOGEN, daughter to Cymbeline by a former queen.
HELEN, a lady attending on Imogen.

Lords, Ladies, Roman Senators, Tribunes, a Soothsayer, a Dutchman, a Spaniard,
Musicians, Officers, Captains, Soldiers, Messengers, and other attendants.

Apparitions.

SCENE: *Britain; Rome.*

CYMBELINE

ACT I.

SCENE I. *Britain. The garden of Cymbeline's palace.*

Enter two Gentlemen.

First Gent. You do not meet a man but frowns: our bloods
No more obey the heavens than our courtiers
Still seem as does the king.
   Sec. Gent.   But what's the matter?
   First Gent. His daughter, and the heir of 's kingdom, whom
He purposed to his wife's sole son—a widow
That late he married—hath referr'd herself
Unto a poor but worthy gentleman: she's wedded;
Her husband banish'd; she imprison'd: all
Is outward sorrow; though I think the king
Be touch'd at very heart.
   Sec. Gent.   None but the king?   10
   First Gent. He that hath lost her too; so is the queen,
That most desired the match; but not a courtier,
Although they wear their faces to the bent
Of the king's looks, hath a heart that is not
Glad at the thing they scowl at.
   Sec. Gent.   And why so?
   First Gent. He that hath miss'd the princess is a thing
Too bad for bad report: and he that hath her—
I mean, that married her, alack, good man!
And therefore banish'd—is a creature such
As, to seek through the regions of the earth   20
For one his like, there would be something failing
In him that should compare.   I do not think
So fair an outward and such stuff within
Endows a man but he.
   Sec. Gent.   You speak him far.
   First Gent. I do extend him, sir, within himself,

Crush him together rather than unfold
His measure duly.
  Sec. Gent.   What's his name and birth?
  First Gent. I cannot delve him to the root: his father
Was called Sicilius, who did join his honour
Against the Romans with Cassibelan,   30
But had his titles by Tenantius, whom
He served with glory and admired success,
So gain'd the sur-addition Leonatus;
And had, besides this gentleman in question,
Two other sons, who in the wars o' the time
Died with their swords in hand; for which their father,
Then old and fond of issue, took such sorrow
That he quit being, and his gentle lady,
Big of this gentleman our theme, deceased
As he was born. The king he takes the babe   40
To his protection, calls him Posthumus Leonatus,
Breeds him and makes him of his bed-chamber,
Puts to him all the learnings that his time
Could make him the receiver of; which he took,
As we do air, fast as 't was minister'd,
And in 's spring became a harvest, lived in court—
Which rare it is to do—most praised, most loved,
A sample to the youngest, to the more mature
A glass that feated them, and to the graver
A child that guided dotards; to his mistress,   50
For whom he now is banish'd, her own price
Proclaims how she esteem'd him and his virtue;
By her election may be truly read
What kind of man he is.
  Sec. Gent.   I honour him
Even out of your report. But, pray you, tell me,
Is she sole child to the king?
  First Gent.   His only child.
He had two sons: if this be worth your hearing,
Mark it: the eldest of them at three years old,
I' the swathing-clothes the other, from their nursery
Were stol'n, and to this hour no guess in knowledge 60
Which way they went.
  Sec. Gent.   How long is this ago?
  First Gent. Some twenty years.
  Sec. Gent. That a king's children should be so convey'd,
So slackly guarded, and the search so slow,
That could not trace them!
  First Gent.   Howsoe'er 't is strange,

Or that the negligence may well be laugh'd at,
Yet is it true, sir.
   Sec. Gent.   I do well believe you.
   First Gent. We must forbear: here comes the gentleman,
The queen, and princess.   *[Exeunt.*

     Enter the QUEEN, POSTHUMUS, *and* IMOGEN.

   Queen. No, be assured you shall not find me, daughter,
After the slander of most stepmothers,   71
Evil-eyed unto you: you 're my prisoner, but
Your gaoler shall deliver you the keys
That lock up your restraint.   For you, Posthumus,
So soon as I can win the offended king,
I will be known your advocate: marry, yet
The fire of rage is in him, and 't were good
You lean'd unto his sentence with what patience
Your wisdom may inform you.
   Post.   Please your highness,
I will from hence to-day.
   Queen.   You know the peril.   80
I 'll fetch a turn about the garden, pitying
The pangs of barr'd affections, though the king
Hath charged you should not speak together. *[Exit.*
   Imo.   O
Dissembling courtesy!   How fine this tyrant
Can tickle where she wounds!   My dearest husband,
I something fear my father's wrath; but nothing—
Always reserved my holy duty—what
His rage can do on me: you must be gone;
And I shall here abide the hourly shot
Of angry eyes, not comforted to live,   90
But that there is this jewel in the world
That I may see again.
   Post.   My queen! my mistress!
O lady, weep no more, lest I give cause
To be suspected of more tenderness
Than doth become a man.   I will remain
The loyal'st husband that did e'er plight troth:
My residence in Rome at one Philario's,
Who to my father was a friend, to me
Known but by letter: thither write, my queen,
And with my eyes I 'll drink the words you send, 100
Though ink be made of gall.

Re-enter QUEEN.

Queen.   Be brief, I pray you:
If the king come, I shall incur I know not
How much of his displeasure. [*Aside*] Yet I 'll move him
To walk this way: I never do him wrong,
But he does buy my injuries, to be friends;
Pays dear for my offences.   [*Exit.*
　Post.   Should we be taking leave
As long a term as yet we have to live,
The loathness to depart would grow.   Adieu!
　Imo. Nay, stay a little:
Were you but riding forth to air yourself,   110
Such parting were too petty.   Look here, love;
This diamond was my mother's: take it, heart;
But keep it till you woo another wife,
When Imogen is dead.
　Post.   How, how! another?
You gentle gods, give me but this I have,
And sear up my embracements from a next
With bonds of death! [*Putting on the ring.*]   Remain, re-
　　main thou here
While sense can keep it on.   And, sweetest, fairest,
As I my poor self did exchange for you,
To your so infinite loss, so in our trifles   120
I still win of you: for my sake wear this;
It is a manacle of love; I 'll place it
Upon this fairest prisoner. [*Putting a bracelet upon her arm.*
　Imo.   O the gods!
When shall we see again?

Enter CYMBELINE *and* Lords.

　Post.   Alack, the king!
　Cym. Thou basest thing, avoid! hence, from my sight!
If after this command thou fraught the court
With thy unworthiness, thou diest: away!
Thou 'rt poison to my blood.
　Post.   The gods protect you!
And bless the good remainders of the court!
I am gone.   [*Exit.*
　Imo.   There cannot be a pinch in death   130
More sharp than this is.
　Cym.   O disloyal thing,
That shouldst repair my youth, thou heap'st
A year's age on me.

Imo.   I beseech you, sir,
Harm not yourself with your vexation:
I am senseless of your wrath; a touch more rare
Subdues all pangs, all fears.
    Cym.   Past grace? obedience?
Imo. Past hope, and in despair; that way, past grace.
Cym. That mightst have had the sole son of my queen!
Imo. O blest, that I might not!   I chose an eagle,
And did avoid a puttock.   140
    Cym. Thou took'st a beggar; wouldst have made my throne
A seat for baseness.
    Imo.   No; I rather added
A lustre to it.
    Cym.   O thou vile one!
    Imo.   Sir,
It is your fault that I have loved Posthumus:
You bred him as my playfellow, and he is
A man worth any woman, overbuys me
Almost the sum he pays.
    Cym.   What, art thou mad?
Imo. Almost, sir: heaven restore me!   Would I were
A neat-herd's daughter, and my Leonatus
Our neighbour shepherd's son!
    Cym.   Thou foolish thing!   150

Re-enter QUEEN.

They were again together: you have done
Not after our command.   Away with her,
And pen her up.
    Queen.   Beseech your patience.   Peace,
Dear lady daughter, peace!   Sweet sovereign,
Leave us to ourselves; and make yourself some comfort
Out of your best advice.
    Cym.   Nay, let her languish
A drop of blood a day; and, being aged,
Die of this folly!   [*Exeunt Cymbeline and Lords.*
    Queen.   Fie! you must give way.

Enter PISANIO.

Here is your servant.   How now, sir!   What news?
 Pis. My lord your son drew on my master.
    Queen.   Ha!   160
No harm, I trust, is done?
 Pis. .   There might have been,
But that my master rather play'd than fought

And had no help of anger: they were parted
By gentlemen at hand.
    Queen.   I am very glad on't.
    Imo. Your son's my father's friend; he takes his part,
To draw upon an exile! O brave sir!
I would they were in Afric both together;
Myself by with a needle, that I might prick
The goer-back. Why came you from your master?
    Pis. On his command: he would not suffer me   170
To bring him to the haven; left these notes
Of what commands I should be subject to,
When't pleased you to employ me.
    Queen.   This hath been
Your faithful servant: I dare lay mine honour
He will remain so.
    Pis.   I humbly thank your highness.
    Queen. Pray, walk awhile.
    Imo.   About some half-hour hence,
I pray you, speak with me: you shall at least
Go see my lord aboard: for this time leave me.   [*Exeunt.*

SCENE II. *The same. A public place.*

Enter CLOTEN *and two* Lords.

    First Lord. Sir, I would advise to shift a shirt; the violence
of action hath made you reek as a sacrifice: where air comes
out, air comes in: there's none abroad so wholesome as that
you vent.
    Clo. If my shirt were bloody, then to shift it. Have I hurt
him?
    Sec. Lord. [*Aside*] No, 'faith; not so much as his patience.
    First Lord. Hurt him! his body's a passable carcass, if he
be not hurt: it is a throughfare for steel, if it be not hurt.
    Sec. Lord. [*Aside*] His steel was in debt; it went o' the
backside the town.   11
    Clo. The villain would not stand me.
    Sec. Lord. [*Aside*] No; but he fled forward still, toward
your face.
    First Lord. Stand you! You have land enough of your
own: but he added to your having; gave you some ground.
    Sec. Lord. [*Aside*] As many inches as you have oceans,
Puppies!
    Clo. I would they had not come between us.
    Sec. Lord. [*Aside*] So would I, till you had measured how
long a fool you were upon the ground.   21

Clo. And that she should love this fellow and refuse me!

Sec. Lord. [*Aside*] If it be a sin to make a true election, she is damned.

First Lord. Sir, as I told you always, her beauty and her brain go not together: she's a good sign, but I have seen small reflection of her wit.

Sec. Lord. [*Aside*] She shines not upon fools, lest the reflection should hurt her.

Clo. Come, I'll to my chamber. Would there had been some hurt done!   31

Sec. Lord. [*Aside*] I wish not so; unless it had been the fall of an ass, which is no great hurt.

Clo. You'll go with us?

First Lord. I'll attend your lordship.

Clo. Nay, come, let's go together.

Sec. Lord. Well, my lord.   [*Exeunt.*

SCENE III.   *A room in Cymbeline's palace.*

Enter IMOGEN *and* PISANIO.

Imo. I would thou grew'st unto the shores o' the haven,
And question'dst every sail: if he should write,
And I not have it, 't were a paper lost,
As offer'd mercy is.   What was the last
That he spake to thee?

Pis.   It was his queen, his queen!

Imo. Then waved his handkerchief?

Pis.   And kiss'd it, madam.

Imo. Senseless linen! happier therein than I!
And that was all?

Pis.   No, madam; for so long
As he could make me with this eye or ear
Distinguish him from others, he did keep
The deck, with glove, or hat, or handkerchief
Still waving, as the fits and stirs of's mind
Could best express how slow his soul sail'd on,
How swift his ship.

Imo.   Thou shouldst have made him
As little as a crow, or less, ere left
To after-eye him.

Pis.   Madam, so I did.

Imo. I would have broke mine eye-strings, crack'd them, but
To look upon him, till the diminution
Of space had pointed him sharp as my needle,

Nay, follow'd him, till he had melted from   20
The smallness of a gnat to air, and then
Have turn'd mine eye and wept.   But, good Pisanio,
When shall we hear from him?
    Pis.   Be assured, madam,
With his next vantage.
    Imo. I did not take my leave of him, but had
Most pretty things to say: ere I could tell him
How I would think on him at certain hours
Such thoughts and such, or I could make him swear
The shes of Italy should not betray
Mine interest and his honour, or have charged him,   3c
At the sixth hour of morn, at noon, at midnight,
To encounter me with orisons, for then
I am in heaven for him; or ere I could
Give him that parting kiss which I had set
Betwixt two charming words, comes in my father
And like the tyrannous breathing of the north
Shakes all our buds from growing.

Enter a Lady.

    Lady.   The queen, madam,
Desires your highness' company.
    Imo. Those things I bid you do, get them dispatch'd.
I will attend the queen.
    Pis.   Madam, I shall.   [*Exeunt.* 40

SCENE IV.   *Rome.   Philario's house.*

Enter PHILARIO, IACHIMO, *a* Frenchman, *a* Dutchman,
and a Spaniard.

    Iach. Believe it, sir, I have seen him in Britain: he was
then of a crescent note, expected to prove so worthy as since
he hath been allowed the name of; but I could then have
looked on him without the help of admiration, though the
catalogue of his endowments had been tabled by his side and
I to peruse him by items.
    Phi. You speak of him when he was less furnished than
now he is with that which makes him both without and
within.
    French. I have seen him in France: we had very many
there could behold the sun with as firm eyes as he.   11
    Iach. This matter of marrying his king's daughter, wherein

he must be weighed rather by her value than his own, words him, I doubt not, a great deal from the matter.

French. And then his banishment.

Iach. Ay, and the approbation of those that weep this lamentable divorce under her colours are wonderfully to extend him; be it but to fortify her judgement, which else an easy battery might lay flat, for taking a beggar without less quality.   But how comes it he is to sojourn with you?   How creeps acquaintance?   21

Phi. His father and I were soldiers together; to whom I have been often bound for no less than my life.   Here comes the Briton: let him be so entertained amongst you as suits, with gentlemen of your knowing, to a stranger of his quality.

Enter POSTHUMUS.

I beseech you all, be better known to this gentleman, whom I commend to you as a noble friend of mine: how worthy he is I will leave to appear hereafter, rather than story him in his own hearing.

French. Sir, we have known together in Orleans.   30

Post. Since when I have been debtor to you for courtesies, which I will be ever to pay and yet pay still.

French. Sir, you o'er-rate my poor kindness: I was glad I did atone my countryman and you; it had been pity you should have been put together with so mortal a purpose as then each bore, upon importance of so slight and trivial a nature.

Post. By your pardon, sir, I was then a young traveller; rather shunned to go even with what I heard than in my every action to be guided by others' experiences: but upon my mended judgement—if I offend not to say it is mended—my quarrel was not altogether slight.   42

French. Faith, yes, to be put to the arbitrement of swords, and by such two that would by all likelihood have confounded one the other, or have fallen both.

Iach. Can we, with manners, ask what was the difference?

French. Safely, I think: 't was a contention in public, which may, without contradiction, suffer the report.   It was much like an argument that fell out last night, where each of us fell in praise of our country mistresses; this gentleman at that time vouching—and upon warrant of bloody affirmation—his to be more fair, virtuous, wise, chaste, constant-qualified and less attemptable than any the rarest of our ladies in France.

Iach. That lady is not now living, or this gentleman's opinion by this worn out.   55

Post. She holds her virtue still and I my mind.

Iach. You must not so far prefer her 'fore ours of Italy.

Post. Being so far provoked as I was in France, I would abate her nothing, though I profess myself her adorer, not her friend.   60

Iach. As fair and as good—a kind of hand-in-hand comparison—had been something too fair and too good for any lady in Britain. If she went before others I have seen, as that diamond of yours outlustres many I have beheld, I could not but believe she excelled many: but I have not seen the most precious diamond that is, nor you the lady.

Post. I praised her as I rated her: so do I my stone.

Iach. What do you esteem it at?

Post. More than the world enjoys.

Iach. Either your unparagoned mistress is, dead, or she's outprized by a trifle.   71

Post. You are mistaken: the one may be sold, or given, if there were wealth enough for the purchase, or merit for the gift: the other is not a thing for sale, and only the gift of the gods.

Iach. Which the gods have given you?

Post. Which, by their graces, I will keep.

Iach. You may wear her in title yours: but, you know, strange fowl light upon neighbouring ponds. Your ring may be stolen too. So your brace of unprizable estimations, the one is but frail and the other casual; a cunning thief, or a that way accomplished courtier, would hazard the winning both of first and last.   83

Post. Your Italy contains none so accomplished a courtier to convince the honour of my mistress, if, in the holding or loss of that, you term her frail. I do nothing doubt you have store of thieves; notwithstanding, I fear not my ring.

Phi. Let us leave here, gentlemen.

Post. Sir, with all my heart. This worthy signior, I thank him, makes no stranger of me; we are familiar at first.   90

Iach. With five times so much conversation, I should get ground of your fair mistress, make her go back, even to the yielding, had I admittance and opportunity to friend.

Post. No, no.

Iach. I dare thereupon pawn the moiety of my estate to your ring; which, in my opinion, o'ervalues it something: but I make my wager rather against your confidence than her reputation: and, to bar your offence herein too, I durst attempt it against any lady in the world.   99

Post. You are a great deal abused in too bold a persuasion;

and I doubt not you sustain what you're worthy of by your attempt.

Iach. What's that?

Post. A repulse: though your attempt, as you call it, deserve more; a punishment too.

Phi. Gentlemen, enough of this: it came in too suddenly; let it die as it was born, and, I pray you, be better acquainted.

Iach. Would I had put my estate and my neighbour's on the approbation of what I have spoke!

Post. What lady would you choose to assail?   110

Iach. Yours; whom in constancy you think stands so safe. I will lay you ten thousand ducats to your ring, that, commend me to the court where your lady is, with no more advantage than the opportunity of a second conference, and I will bring from thence that honour of hers which you imagine so reserved.   .

Post. I will wage against your gold, gold to it: my ring I hold dear as my finger; 'tis part of it.

Iach. You are afraid, and therein the wiser. If you buy ladies' flesh at a million a dram, you cannot preserve it from tainting: but I see you have some religion in you, that you fear.   122

Post. This is but a custom in your tongue; you bear a graver purpose, I hope.

Iach. I am the master of my speeches, and would undergo what's spoken, I swear.

Post. Will you? I shall but lend my diamond till your return: let there be covenants drawn between 's: my mistress exceeds in goodness the hugeness of your unworthy thinking: I dare you to this match: here's my ring.   130

Phi. I will have it no lay.

Iach. By the gods, it is one. If I bring you no sufficient testimony, my ten thousand ducats are yours; so is your diamond too: if I come off, and leave her in such honour as you have trust in, she your jewel, this your jewel, and my gold are yours: provided I have your commendation for my more free entertainment.

Post. I embrace these conditions; let us have articles betwixt us. Only, thus far you shall answer: if you make your voyage upon her and give me directly to understand you have prevailed, I am no further your enemy; she is not worth our debate: if she remain unseduced, you not making it appear otherwise, for your ill opinion and the assault you have made to her chastity you shall answer me with your sword.   145

Iach. Your hand ; a covenant : we will have these things set down by lawful counsel, and straight away for Britain, lest the bargain should catch cold and starve : I will fetch my gold and have our two wagers recorded. 149
Post. Agreed. [*Exeunt Posthumus and Iachimo.*
French. Will this hold, think you?
Phi. Signior Iachimo will not from it. Pray, let us follow 'em. [*Exeunt.*

SCENE V. *Britain. A room in Cymbeline's palace.*

Enter QUEEN, Ladies, *and* CORNELIUS.

Queen. Whiles yet the dew's on ground, gather those flowers: Make haste : who has the note of them?
First Lady. I, madam.
Queen. Dispatch. [*Exeunt Ladies.*
Now, master doctor have you brought those drugs?
Cor. Pleaseth your highness, ay : here they are, madam :
[*Presenting a small box.*
But I beseech your grace, without offence,—
My conscience bids me ask—wherefore you have
Commanded of me these most poisonous compounds,
Which are the movers of a languishing death,
But, though slow, deadly.
Queen. I wonder, doctor, 10
Thou ask'st me such a question. Have I not been
Thy pupil long? Hast thou not learn'd me how
To make perfumes? distil? preserve? yea, so
That our great king himself doth woo me oft
For my confections? Having thus far proceeded,—
Unless thou think'st me devilish—is 't not meet
That I did amplify my judgement in
Other conclusions? I will try the forces
Of these thy compounds on such creatures as
We count not worth the hanging, but none human, 20
To try the vigour of them and apply
Allayments to their act, and by them gather
Their several virtues and effects.
Cor. Your highness
Shall from this practice but make hard your heart :
Besides, the seeing these effects will be
Both noisome and infectious.
Queen. O, content thee.

Enter PISANIO.

[*Aside*] Here comes a flattering rascal; upon him
Will I first work: he 's for his master,
And enemy to my son.   How now, Pisanio!
Doctor, your service for this time is ended;   30
Take your own way.
    Cor.   [*Aside*] I do suspect you, madam;
But you shall do no harm.
    Queen.   [*To Pisanio*] Hark thee, a word.
    Cor. [*Aside*] I do not like her.   She doth think she has
Strange lingering poisons: I do know her spirit,
And will not trust one of her malice with
A drug of such damn'd nature.   Those she has
Will stupefy and dull the sense awhile;
Which first, perchance, she'll prove on cats and dogs,
Then afterward up higher: but there is
No danger in what show of death it makes,   40
More than the locking-up the spirits a time,
To be more fresh, reviving.   She is fool'd
With a most false effect; and I the truer,
So to be false with her.
    Queen.   ·   No further service, doctor,
Until I send for thee.
    Cor.   I humbly take my leave.   [*Exit.*
    Queen. Weeps she still, say'st thou?   Dost thou think in time
She will not quench and let instructions enter
Where folly now possesses?   Do thou work:
When thou shalt bring me word she loves my son,
I'll tell thee on the instant thou art then   50
As great as is thy master, greater, for
His fortunes all lie speechless and his name
Is at last gasp: return he cannot, nor
Continue where he is: to shift his being
Is to exchange one misery with another,
And every day that comes comes to decay
A day's work in him.   What shalt thou expect,
To be depender on a thing that leans,
Who cannot be new built, nor has no friends,   59
So much as but to prop him? [*The Queen drops the box:
    Pisanio takes it up.*] Thou takest up
Thou know'st not what; but take it for thy labour:
It is a thing I made, which hath the king
Five times redeem'd from death: I do not know
What is more cordial.   Nay, I prithee, take it;

It is an earnest of a farther good
That I mean to thee.   Tell thy mistress how
The case stands with her; do 't as from thyself.
Think what a chance thou changest on; but think
Thou hast thy mistress still, to boot, my son,
Who shall take notice of thee: I 'll move the king   70
To any shape of thy preferment such
As thou 'lt desire; and then myself, I chiefly,
That set thee on to this desert, am bound
To load thy merit richly.   Call my women:
Think on my words.   [*Exit Pisanio.*
                A sly and constant knave,
Not to be shaked; the agent for his master
And the remembrancer of her to hold
The hand-fast to her lord.   I have given him that
Which, if he take, shall quite unpeople her
Of liegers for her sweet, and which she after,   80
Except she bend her humour, shall be assured
To taste of too.

Re-enter PISANIO *and* Ladies.

                So, so: well done, well done:
The violets, cowslips, and the primroses,
Bear to my closet.   Fare thee well, Pisanio;
Think on my words.   [*Exeunt Queen and Ladies.*
   Pis.   And shall do:
But when to my good lord I prove untrue,
I 'll choke myself: there 's all I 'll do for you.   [*Exit.*

SCENE VI. *The same.   Another room in the palace.*

Enter IMOGEN.

   Imo. A father cruel, and a step-dame false;
A foolish suitor to a wedded lady,
That hath her husband banish'd;—O, that husband!
My supreme crown of grief! and those repeated
Vexations of it!   Had I been thief-stol'n,
As my two brothers, happy! but most miserable
Is the desire that 's glorious: blest be those,
How mean soe'er, that have their honest wills,
Which seasons comfort.   Who may this be?   Fie!

Enter PISANIO *and* IACHIMO.

   Pis. Madam, a noble gentleman of Rome,   10
Comes from my lord with letters.

Iach.   Change you, madam?
The worthy Leonatus is in safety
And greets your highness dearly.   [*Presents a letter.*
    Imo.   Thanks, good sir:
You 're kindly welcome.
    Iach. [*Aside*] All of her that is out of door most rich!
If she be furnish'd with a mind so rare,
She is alone the Arabian bird, and I
Have lost the wager.   Boldness be my friend!
Arm me, audacity, from head to foot!
Or, like the Parthian, I shall flying fight;   20
Rather, directly fly.
    Imo. [*Reads*] '. . . He is one of the noblest note, to whose
kindnesses I am most infinitely tied.   Reflect upon him
accordingly, as you value your trust. . . .   LEONATUS.'
So far I read aloud:
But even the very middle of my heart
Is warm'd by the rest, and takes it thankfully.
You are as welcome, worthy sir, as I
Have words to bid you, and shall find it so
In all that I can do.
    Iach.   Thanks, fairest lady.   30
What, are men mad?   Hath nature given them eyes
To see this vaulted arch, and the rich crop
Of sea and land, which can distinguish 'twixt
The fiery orbs above and the twinn'd stones
Upon the number'd beach? and can we not
Partition make with spectacles so precious
'Twixt fair and foul?
    Imo.   What makes your admiration?
    Iach. It cannot be i' the eye, for apes and monkeys
'Twixt two such shes would chatter this way and
Contemn with mows the other; nor i' the judgement;   40
For idiots in this case of favour would
Be wisely definite; nor i' the appetite;
Sluttery to such neat excellence opposed
Should make desire vomit emptiness,
Not so allured to feed.
    Imo. What is the matter, trow?
    Iach.   The cloyed will,
That satiate yet unsatisfied desire, that tub
Both fill'd and running, ravening first the lamb
Longs after for the garbage.
    Imo.   What, dear sir,
Thus raps you?   Are you well?   50

Iach. Thanks, madam ; well. [*To Pisanio*] Beseech you,
  sir,
Desire my man's abode where I did leave him :
He 's strange and peevish.
  Pis.   I was going, sir,
To give him welcome.   [*Exit.*
  Imo. Continues well my lord?   His health, beseech you?
  Iach. Well, madam.
  Imo. Is he dispos'd to mirth? I hope he is.
  Iach. Exceeding pleasant ; none a stranger there
So merry and so gamesome : he is call'd
The Briton reveller.
  Imo.   When he was here,   60
He did incline to sadness, and oft-times
Not knowing why.
  Iach.   I never saw him sad.
There is a Frenchman his companion, one
An eminent monsieur, that, it seems, much loves
A Gallian girl at home ; he furnaces
The thick sighs from him, whiles the jolly Briton—
Your lord, I mean—laughs from 's free lungs, cries ' O,
Can my sides hold, to think that man, who knows
By history, report, or his own proof,
What woman is, yea, what she cannot choose   70
But must be, will his free hours languish for
Assured bondage?'
  Imo.   Will my lord say so?
  Iach. Ay, madam, with his eyes in flood with laughter :
It is a recreation to be by
And hear him mock the Frenchman.   But, heavens know,
Some men are much to blame.
  Imo.   Not he, I hope.
  Iach. Not he : but yet heaven's bounty towards him might
Be used more thankfully.   In himself, 't is much ;
In you, which I account his beyond all talents,
Whilst I am bound to wonder, I am bound   80
To pity too.
  Imo.   What do you pity, sir?
  Iach. Two creatures heartily.
  Imo.   Am I one, sir?
You look on me : what wreck discern you in me
Deserves your pity?
  Iach.   Lamentable!   What,
To hide me from the radiant sun and solace
I' the dungeon by a snuff?

Imo.   I pray you, sir,
Deliver with more openness your answers
To my demands.   Why do you pity me?
   Iach. That others do—
I was about to say—enjoy your——But   90
It is an office of the gods to venge it,
Not mine to speak on 't.
   Imo.   You do seem to know
Something of me, or what concerns me: pray you,—
Since doubting things go ill often hurts more
Than to be sure they do; for certainties
Either are past remedies, or, timely knowing,
The remedy then born—discover to me
What both you spur and stop.
   Iach.   Had I this cheek
To bathe my lips upon; this hand, whose touch,
Whose every touch, would force the feeler's soul   100
To the oath of loyalty; this object, which
Takes prisoner the wild motion of mine eye,
Fixing it only here; should I, damn'd then,
Slaver with lips as common as the stairs
That mount the Capitol; join gripes with hands
Made hard with hourly falsehood—falsehood, as
With labour; then by-peeping in an eye
Base and unlustrous as the smoky light
That 's fed with stinking tallow; it were fit
That all the plagues of hell should at one time   110
Encounter such revolt.
   Imo.   My lord, I fear,
Has forgot Britain.
   Iach.   And himself.   Not I,
Inclined to this intelligence, pronounce
The beggary of his change; but 't is your graces
That from my mutest conscience to my tongue
Charms this report out.
   Imo.   Let me hear no more.
   Iach. O dearest soul! your cause doth strike my heart
With pity, that doth make me sick.   A lady
So fair, and fasten'd to an empery,
Would make the great'st king double,—to be partner'd   120
With tomboys hired with that self-exhibition
Which your own coffers yield!   Be revenged;
Or she that bore you was no queen, and you
Recoil from your great stock.
   Imo.   Revenged!

How should I be revenged?   If this be true,—
As I have such a heart that both mine ears
Must not in haste abuse—if it be true,
How should I be revenged?
 Iach. I dedicate myself to your sweet pleasure,
More noble than that runagate to your bed,   130
And will continue fast to your affection,
Still close as sure.
 Imo.   What, ho, Pisanio!
 Iach. Let me my service tender on your lips.
 Imo. Away!   I do condemn mine ears that have
So long attended thee.   If thou wert honourable,
Thou wouldst have told this tale for virtue, not
For such an end thou seek'st,—as base as strange.
Thou wrong'st a gentleman, who is as far
From thy report as thou from honour, and
Solicit'st here a lady that disdains   140
Thee and the devil alike.   What ho, Pisanio!
The king my father shall be made acquainted
Of thy assault: if he shall think it fit,
A saucy stranger in his court to expound
His beastly mind to us, he hath a court
He little cares for and a daughter who
He not respects at all.   What, ho, Pisanio!
 Iach. O happy Leonatus! I may say:
The credit that thy lady hath of thee
Deserves thy trust, and thy most perfect goodness 150
Her assured credit.   Blessed live you long!
A lady to the worthiest sir that ever
Country call'd his! and you his mistress, only
For the most worthiest fit!   Give me your pardon.
I have spoke this, to know if your affiance
Were deeply rooted; and shall make your lord,
That which he is, new o'er: and he is one
The truest manner'd; such a holy witch
That he enchants societies into him;
Half all men's hearts are his.
 Imo.   You make amends.   160
 Iach. He sits 'mongst men like a descended god:
He hath a kind of honour sets him off,
More than a mortal seeming.   Be not angry,
Most mighty princess, that I have adventured
To try your taking of a false report; which hath
Honour'd with confirmation your great judgement
In the election of a sir so rare,

Which you know cannot err: the love I bear him
Made me to fan you thus, but the gods made you,
Unlike all others, chaffless.   Pray, your pardon.   170
    Imo. All's well, sir: take my power i' the court for yours.
    Iach. My humble thanks.   I had almost forgot
To entreat your grace but in a small request,
And yet of moment too, for it concerns
Your lord; myself and other noble friends
Are partners in the business.
    Imo.   Pray, what is't?
    Iach. Some dozen Romans of us and your lord—
The best feather of our wing—have mingled sums
To buy a present for the emperor;
Which I, the factor for the rest, have done   180
In France: 't is plate of rare device, and jewels
Of rich and exquisite form; their values great;
And I am something curious, being strange,
To have them in safe stowage: may it please you
To take them in protection?
    Imo.   Willingly;
And pawn mine honour for their safety: since
My lord hath interest in them, I will keep them
In my bedchamber.
    Iach.   They are in a trunk,
Attended by my men: I will make bold
To send them to you, only for this night;   190
I must aboard to-morrow.
    Imo.   O, no, no.
    Iach. Yes, I beseech; or I shall short my word
By lengthening my return.   From Gallia
I cross'd the seas on purpose and on promise
To see your grace.
    Imo.   I thank you for your pains:
But not away to-morrow!
    Iach.   O, I must, madam:
Therefore I shall beseech you, if you please
To greet your lord with writing, do 't to-night:
I have outstood my time; which is material
To the tender of our present.
    Imo.   I will write.   200
Send your trunk to me; it shall safe be kept,
And truly yielded you.   You're very welcome.   [*Exeunt.*

ACT II.

SCENE I. *Britain. Before Cymbeline's palace.*

Enter CLOTEN *and two* Lords.

Clo. Was there ever man had such luck! when I kissed the jack, upon an up-cast to be hit away! I had a hundred pound on 't: and then a whoreson jackanapes must take me up for swearing; as if I borrowed mine oaths of him and might not spend them at my pleasure.

First Lord. What got he by that? You have broke his pate with your bowl.

Sec. Lord. [*Aside*] If his wit had been like him that broke it, it would have run all out. 9

Clo. When a gentleman is disposed to swear, it is not for any standers-by to curtail his oaths, ha?

Sec. Lord. No, my lord; [*Aside*] nor crop the ears of them.

Clo. Whoreson dog! I give him satisfaction? Would he had been one of my rank!

Sec. Lord. [*Aside*] To have smelt like a fool.

Clo. I am not vexed more at anything in the earth: a pox on 't! I had rather not be so noble as I am; they dare not fight with me, because of the queen my mother: every Jack-slave hath his bellyful of fighting, and I must go up and down like a cock that nobody can match. 20

Sec. Lord. [*Aside*] You are cock and capon too; and you crow, cock, with your comb on.

Clo. Sayest thou?

Sec. Lord. It is not fit your lordship should undertake every companion that you give offence to.

Clo. No, I know that: but it is fit I should commit offence to my inferiors.

Sec. Lord. Ay, it is fit for your lordship only.

Clo. Why, so I say.

First Lord. Did you hear of a stranger that 's come to court to-night? ·31

Clo. A stranger, and I not know on 't!

Sec. Lord. [*Aside*] He 's a strange fellow himself, and knows it not.

First Lord. There 's an Italian come; and, 't is thought, one of Leonatus' friends.

Clo. Leonatus! a banished rascal; and he 's another, what-soever he be. Who told you of this stranger?

First Lord. One of your lordship's pages.

Clo. Is it fit I went to look upon him? is there no deroga-
tion in 't?   41
  Sec. Lord. You cannot derogate, my lord.
  Clo. Not easily, I think.
  Sec. Lord. [*Aside*] You are a fool granted: therefore your
issues, being foolish, do not derogate.
  Clo. Come, I 'll go see this Italian: what I have lost to-day
at bowls I 'll win to-night of him. Come, go.
  Sec. Lord. I 'll attend your lordship.
                           [*Exeunt Cloten and First Lord.*
That such a crafty devil as is his mother
Should yield the world this ass! a woman that   50
Bears all down with her brain; and this her son
Cannot take two from twenty, for his heart,
And leave eighteen. Alas, poor princess,
Thou divine Imogen, what thou endurest,
Betwixt a father by thy step-dame govern'd,
A mother hourly coining plots, a wooer
More hateful than the foul expulsion is
Of thy dear husband, than that horrid act
Of the divorce he 'ld make! The heavens hold firm
The walls of thy dear honour, keep unshaked   60
That temple, thy fair mind, that thou mayst stand,
To enjoy thy banish'd lord and this great land.   [*Exit.*

SCENE II. *Imogen's bedchamber in Cymbeline's palace:
            a trunk in one corner of it.*

IMOGEN *in bed, reading; a* Lady *attending.*

Imo. Who 's there? my woman Helen?
Lady.   Please you, madam.
Imo. What hour is it?
Lady.   Almost midnight, madam.
Imo. I have read three hours then: mine eyes are weak:
Fold down the leaf where I have left: to bed:
Take not away the taper, leave it burning;
And if thou canst awake by four o' the clock,
I prithee, call me. Sleep hath seized me wholly.
                                          [*Exit Lady.*
To your protection I commend me, gods.
From fairies and the tempters of the night
Guard me, beseech ye.   10
            [*Sleeps. Iachimo comes from the trunk.*
Iach. The crickets sing, and man's o'er-labour'd sense

Repairs itself by rest.   Our Tarquin thus
Did softly press the rushes, ere he waken'd
The chastity he wounded.   Cytherea,
How bravely thou becomest thy bed, fresh lily,
And whiter than the sheets!   That I might touch!
But kiss; one kiss.   Rubies unparagon'd,
How dearly they do't!   'T is her breathing that
Perfumes the chamber thus: the flame o' the taper
Bows toward her, and would under-peep her lids,   20
To see the enclosed lights, now canopied
Under these windows, white and azure, laced
With blue of heaven's own tinct.   But my design,
To note the chamber: I will write all down:
Such and such pictures; there the window; such
The adornment of her bed; the arras; figures,
Why, such and such; and the contents o' the story.
Ah, but some natural notes about her body
Above ten thousand meaner movables
Would testify, to enrich mine inventory.   30
O sleep, thou ape of death, lie dull upon her!
And be her sense but as a monument,
Thus in a chapel lying!   Come off, come off:
                                [*Taking off her bracelet.*
As slippery as the Gordian knot was hard!
'T is mine; and this will witness outwardly,
As strongly as the conscience does within,
To the madding of her lord.   On her left breast
A mole cinque-spotted, like the crimson drops
I' the bottom of a cowslip: here's a voucher,
Stronger than ever law could make: this secret   40
Will force him think I have pick'd the lock and ta'en
The treasure of her honour.   No more.   To what end?
Why should I write this down, that's riveted,
Screw'd to my memory?   She hath been reading late
The tale of Tereus; here the leaf's turn'd down
Where Philomel gave up.   I have enough:
To the trunk again, and shut the spring of it.
Swift, swift, you dragons of the night, that dawning
May bare the raven's eye! I lodge in fear;
Though this a heavenly angel, hell is here. [*Clock strikes.* 50
One, two, three: time, time!
                        [*Goes into the trunk.   The scene closes.*

SCENE III. *An ante-chamber adjoining Imogen's apartments.*

Enter CLOTEN *and* Lords.

First Lord. Your lordship is the most patient man in loss, the most coldest that ever turned up ace.

Clo. It would make any man cold to lose.

First Lord. But not every man patient after the noble temper of your lordship. You are most hot and furious when you win.

Clo. Winning will put any man into courage. If I could get this foolish Imogen, I should have gold enough. It's almost morning, is 't not?

First Lord. Day, my lord.　　　　　　　　　　　10

Clo. I would this music would come: I am advised to give her music o' mornings; they say it will penetrate.

Enter Musicians.

Come on; tune: if you can penetrate her with your fingering, so; we'll try with tongue too: if none will do, let her remain; but I'll never give o'er. First, a very excellent good conceited thing; after, a wonderful sweet air, with admirable rich words to it: and then let her consider.

SONG.

Hark, hark! the lark at heaven's gate sings,
　　And Phœbus 'gins arise,
His steeds to water at those springs　　　　　20
　　On chaliced flowers that lies;
And winking Mary-buds begin
　　To ope their golden eyes:
With every thing that pretty is,
　　My lady sweet, arise:
　　Arise, arise.

Clo. So, get you gone. If this penetrate, I will consider your music the better: if it do not, it is a vice in her ears, which horse-hairs and calves'-guts, nor the voice of eunuch to boot, can never amend.　　　　　　*[Exeunt Musicians.*　30

Sec. Lord. Here comes the king.

Clo. I am glad I was up so late; for that's the reason I was up so early: he cannot choose but take this service I have done fatherly.

Enter CYMBELINE *and* QUEEN.

Good morrow to your majesty and to my gracious mother.

Cym. Attend you here the door of our stern daughter?
Will she not forth?

Clo. I have assailed her with music, but she vouchsafes no
notice.

Cym. The exile of her minion is too new;   40
She hath not yet forgot him: some more time
Must wear the print of his remembrance out,
And then she's yours.

Queen.   You are most bound to the king,
Who lets go by no vantages that may
Prefer you to his daughter. Frame yourself
To orderly soliciting, and be friended
With aptness of the season; make denials
Increase your services; so seem as if
You were inspired to do those duties which
You tender to her; that you in all obey her,   50
Save when command to your dismission tends,
And therein you are senseless.

Clo.   Senseless! not so.

Enter a Messenger.

Mess. So like you, sir, ambassadors from Rome;
The one is Caius Lucius.

Cym.   A worthy fellow,
Albeit he comes on angry purpose now;
But that's no fault of his: we must receive him
According to the honour of his sender;
And towards himself, his goodness forespent on us,
We must extend our notice. Our dear son,
When you have given good morning to your mistress,   60
Attend the queen and us; we shall have need
To employ you towards this Roman. Come, our queen.
                    [*Exeunt all but Cloten.*

Clo. If she be up, I'll speak with her; if not,
Let her lie still and dream. [*Knocks*] By your leave, ho!
I know her women are about her: what
If I do line one of their hands? 'T is gold
Which buys admittance; oft it doth; yea, and makes
Diana's rangers false themselves, yield up
Their deer to the stand o' the stealer; and 't is gold
Which makes the true man kill'd and saves the thief;   70
Nay, sometime hangs both thief and true man: what

Can it not do and undo? I will make
One of her women lawyer to me, for
I yet not understand the case myself.
[*Knocks*] By your leave.

Enter a Lady.

Lady. Who's there that knocks?
Clo.　　　　　　　　　　A gentleman.
Lady.　　　　　　　　　　　　　　No more?
Clo. Yes, and a gentlewoman's son.
Lady.　　　　　　　　　　That's more
Than some, whose tailors are as dear as yours,
Can justly boast of.　What's your lordship's pleasure?
　Clo. Your lady's person : is she ready?
　Lady.　　　　　　　　　Ay,　　　　　80
To keep her chamber.
　Clo.　　　　　There is gold for you ;
Sell me your good report.
　Lady. How! my good name? or to report of you
What I shall think is good?—The princess !

Enter IMOGEN.

　Clo. Good morrow, fairest : sister, your sweet hand.
　　　　　　　　　　　　　　　[*Exit Lady.*
　Imo. Good morrow, sir.　You lay out too much pains
For purchasing but trouble : the thanks I give
Is telling you that I am poor of thanks
And scarce can spare them.
　Clo.　　　　　　　Still, I swear I love you.
　Imo. If you but said so, 't were as deep with me :　　90
If you swear still, your recompense is still
That I regard it not.
　Clo.　　　　　This is no answer.
　Imo. But that you shall not say I yield being silent,
I would not speak.　I pray you, spare me : faith,
I shall unfold equal discourtesy
To your best kindness : one of your great knowing
Should learn, being taught, forbearance.
　Clo. To leave you in your madness, 't were my sin :
I will not.
　Imo. Fools cure not mad folks.
　Clo.　　　　　　　　Do you call me fool?　　100
　Imo. As I am mad, I do :
If you 'll be patient, I 'll no more be mad ;
That cures us both.　I am much sorry, sir,

You put me to forget a lady's manners,
By being so verbal: and learn now, for all,
That I, which know my heart, do here pronounce,
By the very truth of it, I care not for you,
And am so near the lack of charity—
To accuse myself—I hate you; which I had rather
You felt than make 't my boast.
  Clo.   You sin against 110
Obedience, which you owe your father. For
The contract you pretend with that base wretch,
One bred of alms and foster'd with cold dishes,
With scraps o' the court, it is no contract, none:
And though it be allow'd in meaner parties—
Yet who than he more mean?—to knit their souls,
On whom there is no more dependency
But brats and beggary, in self-figured knot;
Yet you are curb'd from that enlargement by
The consequence o' the crown, and must not soil 120
The precious note of it with a base slave,
A hilding for a livery, a squire's cloth,
A pantler, not so eminent.
  Imo.   Profane fellow!
Wert thou the son of Jupiter and no more
But what thou art besides, thou wert too base
To be his groom: thou wert dignified enough,
Even to the point of envy, if 't were made
Comparative for your virtues to be styled
The under-hangman of his kingdom, and hated
For being preferr'd so well.
  Clo.   The south-fog rot him! 130
  Imo. He never can meet more mischance than come
To be but named of thee. His meanest garment,
That ever hath but clipp'd his body, is dearer
In my respect than all the hairs above thee,
Were they all made such men. How now, Pisanio!

      Enter PISANIO.

  Clo. ' His garment!' Now the devil—
  Imo. To Dorothy my woman hie thee presently—
  Clo. ' His garment!'
  Imo.   I am sprited with a fool,
Frighted, and anger'd worse: go bid my woman
Search for a jewel that too casually 140
Hath left mine arm: it was thy master s: 'shrew me,
If I would lose it for a revenue

Of any king's in Europe.   I do think
I saw 't this morning : confident I am
Last night 't was on mine arm ; I kiss'd it :
I hope it be not gone to tell my lord
That I kiss aught but he.
  Pis.   'T will not be lost.
  Imo. I hope so : go and search. [*Exit Pisanio.*
  Clo.   You have abused me :
' His meanest garment ! '
  Imo.   Ay, I said so, sir :
If you will make 't an action, call witness to 't. 150
  Clo. I will inform your father.
  Imo.   Your mother too :
She 's my good lady, and will conceive, I hope,
But the worst of me.   So, I leave you, sir,
To the worst of discontent.   [*Exit.*
  Clo.   I 'll be revenged :
' His meanest garment ! '   Well.   [*Exit.*

SCENE IV.   *Rome.   Philario's house.*

Enter POSTHUMUS *and* PHILARIO.

 Post. Fear it not, sir : I would I were so sure
To win the king as I am bold her honour
Will remain hers.
  Phi.   What means do you make to him?
 Post. Not any, but abide the change of time,
Quake in the present winter's state and wish
That warmer days would come : in these fear'd hopes,
I barely gratify your love; they failing,
I must die much your debtor.
  Phi. Your very goodness and your company
O'erpays all I can do.   By this, your king 10
Hath heard of great Augustus : Caius Lucius
Will do 's commission throughly : and I think
He 'll grant the tribute, send the arrearages,
Or look upon our Romans, whose remembrance
Is yet fresh in their grief.
  Post.   I do believe,
Statist though I am none, nor like to be,
That this will prove a war; and you shall hear
The legions now in Gallia sooner landed
In our not-fearing Britain than have tidings
Of any penny tribute paid.   Our countrymen 20

Are men more order'd than when Julius Cæsar
Smiled at their lack of skill, but found their courage
Worthy his frowning at: their discipline,
Now mingled with their courage, will make known
To their approvers they are people such
That mend upon the world.

Enter IACHIMO.

Phi.   See! Iachimo!
Post. The swiftest harts have posted you by land;
And winds of all the corners kiss'd your sails,
To make your vessel nimble.
Phi.   Welcome, sir.
Post. I hope the briefness of your answer made   30
The speediness of your return.
Iach.   Your lady
Is one of the fairest that I have look'd upon.
Post. And therewithal the best; or let her beauty
Look through a casement to allure false hearts
And be false with them.
Iach.   Here are letters for you.
Post. Their tenour good, I trust.
Iach.   'T is very like.
Phi. Was Caius Lucius in the Britain court
When you were there?
Iach.   He was expected then,
But not approach'd.
Post.   All is well yet.
Sparkles this stone as it was wont? or is 't not   40
Too dull for your good wearing?
Iach.   If I had lost it,
I should have lost the worth of it in gold.
I 'll make a journey twice as far, to enjoy
A second night of such sweet shortness which
Was mine in Britain, for the ring is won.
Post. The stone 's too hard to come by.
Iach.   Not a whit,
Your lady being so easy.
Post.   Make not, sir,
Your loss your sport: I hope you know that we
Must not continue friends.
Iach.   Good sir, we must,
If you keep covenant. Had I not brought   50
The knowledge of your mistress home, I grant
We were to question further: but I now

Profess myself the winner of her honour,
Together with your ring; and not the wronger
Of her or you, having proceeded but
By both your wills.
 Post.   If you can make 't apparent,
My hand
And ring is yours; if not, the foul opinion
You had of her pure honour gains or loses
Your sword or mine, or masterless leaves both 60
To who shall find them.
 Iach.   Sir, my circumstances,
Being so near the truth as I will make them,
Must first induce you to believe: whose strength
I will confirm with oath; which, I doubt not,
You 'll give me leave to spare, when you shall find
You need it not.
 Post.   Proceed.
 Iach.   First, her bedchamber,—
Where, I confess, I slept not, but profess
Had that was well worth watching—it was hang'd
With tapestry of silk and silver; the story
Proud Cleopatra, when she met her Roman, 70
And Cydnus swell'd above the banks, or for
The press of boats or pride: a piece of work
So bravely done, so rich, that it did strive
In workmanship and value; which I wonder'd
Could be so rarely and exactly wrought,
Since the true life on 't was—
 Post.   This is true;
And this you might have heard of here, by me,
Or by some other.
 Iach.   More particulars
Must justify my knowledge.
 Post.   So they must,
Or do your honour injury.
 Iach.   The chimney 80
Is south the chamber, and the chimney-piece
Chaste Dian bathing: never saw I figures
So likely to report themselves: the cutter
Was as another nature, dumb; outwent her,
Motion and breath left out.
 Post.   This is a thing
Which you might from relation likewise reap,
Being, as it is, much spoke of.
 Iach.   The roof o' the chamber

With golden cherubins is fretted: her andirons—
I had forgot them—were two winking Cupids
Of silver, each on one foot standing, nicely   90
Depending on their brands.
   Post.   This is her honour!
Let it be granted you have seen all this—and praise
Be given to your remembrance—the description
Of what is in her chamber nothing saves
The wager you have laid.
   Iach.   Then, if you can,
                         [Showing the bracelet.
Be pale: I beg you leave to air this jewel; see!
And now 't is up again: it must be married
To that your diamond; I 'll keep them.
   Post.   Jove!
Once more let me behold it: is it that
Which I left with her?
   Iach.   Sir—I thank her—that: 100
She stripp'd it from her arm; I see her yet;
Her pretty action did outsell her gift,
And yet enrich'd it too: she gave it me, and said
She prized it once.
   Post.   May be she pluck'd it off,
To send it me.
   Iach.   She writes so to you, doth she?
   Post. O, no, no, no! 't is true.   Here, take this too;
                       [Gives the ring.
It is a basilisk unto mine eye,
Kills me to look on 't.   Let there be no honour
Where there is beauty; truth, where semblance; love,
Where there 's another man: the vows of women   110
Of no more bondage be, to where they are made,
Than they are to their virtues; which is nothing.
O, above measure false!
   Phi.   Have patience, sir,
And take your ring again: 't is not yet won:
It may be probable she lost it; or
Who knows if one of her women, being corrupted,
Hath stol'n it from her?
   Post.   Very true;
And so, I hope, he came by 't.   Back my ring:
Render to me some corporal sign about her,
More evident than this; for this was stolen.   120
   Iach. By Jupiter, I had it from her arm.
   Post. Hark you, he swears; by Jupiter he swears.

'T is true:—nay, keep the ring—'t is true: I am sure
She would not lose it: her attendants are
All sworn and honourable:—they induced to steal it!
And by a stranger!—No, he hath enjoy'd her.
There, take thy hire; and all the fiends of hell
Divide themselves between you!
 Phi.   Sir, be patient:
This is not strong enough to be believed
Of one persuaded well of—   130
 Post. Never talk on 't.
 Iach.   If you seek
For further satisfying, under her breast—
Worthy the pressing—lies a mole, right proud
Of that most delicate lodging: by my life,
I kiss'd it; and it gave me present hunger
To feed again, though full. You do remember
This stain upon her?
 Post.   Ay, and it doth confirm
Another stain, as big as hell can hold,
Were there no more but it.
 Iach.   Will you hear more?
 Post. Spare your arithmetic: never count the turns; 140
Once, and a million!
 Iach.   I 'll be sworn—
 Post.   No swearing.
If you will swear you have not done 't, you lie.
O, that I had her here, to tear her limb-meal!
I will go there and do 't—i' the court—before
Her father. I 'll do something—   *[Exit.*
 Phi.   Quite besides
The government of patience! You have won:
Let 's follow him, and pervert the present wrath
He hath against himself.
 Iach.   With all my heart. *[Exeunt.*

  SCENE V. *Another room in Philario's house.*

Enter POSTHUMUS.

 Post. Could I find out
The woman's part in me! For there 's no motion
That tends to vice in man, but I affirm
It is the woman's part: be it lying, note it,
The woman's; flattering, hers; deceiving, hers;
Lust and rank thoughts, hers, hers; revenges, hers:

Ambitions, covetings, change of prides, disdain,
Nice longing, slanders, mutability,
All faults that may be named, nay, that hell knows,
Why, hers, in part or all; but rather, all;   10
For even to vice
They are not constant, but are changing still
One vice, but of a minute old, for one
Not half so old as that. I 'll write against them,
Detest them, curse them: yet 't is greater skill
In a true hate, to pray they have their will:
The very devils cannot plague them better.   [Exit.

ACT III.

SCENE I. *Britain. A hall in Cymbeline's palace.*

Enter in state, CYMBELINE, QUEEN, CLOTEN, *and* Lords,
    at one door, and at another, CAIUS LUCIUS *and* Atten-
    dants.

Cym. Now say, what would Augustus Cæsar with us?
Luc. When Julius Cæsar, whose remembrance yet
Lives in men's eyes, and will to ears and tongues
Be theme and hearing ever, was in this Britain
And conquer'd it, Cassibelan, thine uncle,—
Famous in Cæsar's praises, no whit less
Than in his feats deserving it—for him
And his succession granted Rome a tribute,
Yearly three thousand pounds, which by thee lately
Is left untender'd.
Queen.   And, to kill the marvel,   1C
Shall be so ever.
Clo.   There be many Cæsars,
Ere such another Julius. Britain is
A world by itself; and we will nothing pay
For wearing our own noses.
Queen.   That opportunity
Which then they had to take from 's, to resume
We have again. Remember, sir, my liege,
The kings your ancestors, together with
The natural bravery of your isle, which stands
As Neptune's park, ribbed and paled in
With rocks unscalable and roaring waters,   20

With sands that will not bear your enemies' boats,
But suck them up to the topmast. A kind of conquest
Cæsar made here ; but made not here his brag
Of ' Came' and 'saw' and 'overcame': with shame—
The first that ever touch'd him—he was carried
From off our coast, twice beaten ; and his shipping—
Poor ignorant baubles !—on our terrible seas,
Like egg-shells moved upon their surges, crack'd
As easily 'gainst our rocks : for joy whereof
The famed Cassibelan, who was once at point—   30
O giglot fortune !—to master Cæsar's sword,
Made Lud's town with rejoicing fires bright
And Britons strut with courage.

Clo. Come, there's no more tribute to be paid : our kingdom is stronger than it was at that time ; and, as I said, there
is no moe such Cæsars : other of them may have crook'd
noses, but to owe such straight arms, none.

Cym. Son, let your mother end.   38

Clo. We have yet many among us can gripe as hard as
Cassibelan : I do not say I am one ; but I have a hand. Why
tribute? why should we pay tribute? If Cæsar can hide the
sun from us with a blanket, or put the moon in his pocket, we
will pay him tribute for light; else, sir, no more tribute, pray
you now.

Cym. You must know,
Till the injurious Romans did extort
This tribute from us, we were free: Cæsar's ambition,
Which swell'd so much that it did almost stretch
The sides o' the world, against all colour here
Did put the yoke upon 's; which to shake off   50
Becomes a warlike people, whom we reckon
Ourselves to be.

Clo.   We do.

Cym.   Say, then, to Cæsar,
Our ancestor was that Mulmutius which
Ordain'd our laws, whose use the sword of Cæsar
Hath too much mangled; whose repair and franchise
Shall, by the power we hold, be our good deed,
Though Rome be therefore angry: Mulmutius made our laws,
Who was the first of Britain which did put
His brows within a golden crown and call'd
Himself a king.

Luc.   I am sorry, Cymbeline,   60
That I am to pronounce Augustus Cæsar
Cæsar, that hath more kings his servants than

Thyself domestic officers—thine enemy;
Receive it from me, then: war and confusion
In Cæsar's name pronounce I 'gainst thee: look
For fury not to be resisted.   Thus defied,
I thank thee for myself.
    Cym.   Thou art welcome, Caius
Thy Cæsar knighted me; my youth I spent
Much under him; of him I gather'd honour;
Which he to seek of me again, perforce,   70
Behoves me keep at utterance.   I am perfect
That the Pannonians and Dalmatians for
Their liberties are now in arms; a precedent
Which not to read would show the Britons cold:
So Cæsar shall not find them.
    Luc.   Let proof speak.
    Clo. His majesty bids you welcome.   Make pastime with
us a day or two, or longer: if you seek us afterwards in other
terms, you shall find us in our salt-water girdle: if you beat
us out of it, it is yours; if you fall in the adventure, our crows
shall fare the better for you; and there's an end.   80
    Luc. So, sir.
    Cym. I know your master's pleasure and he mine:
All the remain is ' Welcome!'   [*Exeunt.*

SCENE II.   *Another room in the palace.*

Enter PISANIO, *with a letter.*

    Pis. How! of adultery?   Wherefore write you not
What monster's her accuser?   Leonatus!
O master! what a strange infection
Is fall'n into thy ear!   What false Italian,
As poisonous-tongued as handed, hath prevail'd
On thy too ready hearing?   Disloyal!   No:
She's punish'd for her truth, and undergoes,
More goddess-like than wife-like, such assaults
As would take in some virtue.   O my master!
Thy mind to her is now as low as were   10
Thy fortunes.   How! that I should murder her,
Upon the love and truth and vows which I
Have made to thy command?   I, her? her blood?
If it be so to do good service, never
Let me be counted serviceable.   How look I,
That I should seem to lack humanity
So much as this fact comes to?   " Do't: the letter

That I have sent her, by her own command
Shall give thee opportunity." O damn'd paper!
Black as the ink that's on thee! Senseless bauble,　　20
Art thou a feodary for this act, and look'st
So virgin-like without? Lo, here she comes.
I am ignorant in what I am commanded.

Enter IMOGEN.

Imo. How now, Pisanio!
Pis. Madam, here is a letter from my lord.
Imo. Who? thy lord? that is my lord, Leonatus!
O, learn'd indeed were that astronomer
That knew the stars as I his characters,
He 'ld lay the future open. You good gods,
Let what is here contain'd relish of love,　　30
Of my lord's health, of his content, yet not
That we two are asunder; let that grieve him:
Some griefs are med'cinable; that is one of them,
For it doth physic love: of his content,
All but in that! Good wax, thy leave. Blest be
You bees that make these locks of counsel! Lovers
And men in dangerous bonds pray not alike:
Though forfeiters you cast in prison, yet
You clasp young Cupid's tables. Good news, gods!　　39

[*Reads*] 'Justice, and your father's wrath, should he take
me in his dominion, could not be so cruel to me, as you, O
the dearest of creatures, would even renew me with your eyes.
Take notice that I am in Cambria, at Milford-Haven: what
your own love will out of this advise you, follow. So he
wishes you all happiness, that remains loyal to his vow, and
your, increasing in love,　　　　LEONATUS-POSTHUMUS.'

O, for a horse with wings! Hear'st thou, Pisanio?
He is at Milford-Haven: read, and tell me
How far 't is thither. If one of mean affairs
May plod it in a week, why may not I　　50
Glide thither in a day? Then, true Pisanio,—
Who long'st, like me, to see thy lord; who long'st,—
O, let me bate,—but not like me—yet long'st,
But in a fainter kind:—O, not like me;
For mine's beyond beyond: say, and speak thick—
Love's counsellor should fill the bores of hearing,
To the smothering of the sense—how far it is
To this same blessed Milford: and by the way
Tell me how Wales was made so happy as
(M 332)　　　　　　　　　　　　　　　　　E

To inherit such a haven: but first of all,　　　　　　60
How we may steal from hence, and for the gap
That we shall make in time, from our hencegoing
And our return, to excuse: but first, how get hence:
Why should excuse be born or ere begot?
We'll talk of that hereafter.　Prithee, speak,
How many score of miles may we well ride
'Twixt hour and hour?
　　Pis.　　　　　　　　　One score 'twixt sun and sun,
Madam, 's enough for you: [*Aside*] and too much too.
　　Imo. Why, one that rode to's execution, man,
Could never go so slow: I have heard of riding wagers,　70
Where horses have been nimbler than the sands
That run i' the clock's behalf.　But this is foolery:
Go bid my woman feign a sickness; say
She'll home to her father: and provide me presently
A riding-suit, no costlier than would fit
A franklin's housewife.
　　Pis.　　　　　　　　Madam, you're best consider.
　　Imo. I see before me, man: nor here, nor here,
Nor what ensues, but have a fog in them,
That I cannot look through.　Away, I prithee;
Do as I bid thee: there's no more to say;　　　　80
Accessible is none but Milford way.　　　　[*Exeunt.*

SCENE III.　*Wales: a mountainous country with a cave.*

Enter, from the cave, BELARIUS; GUIDERIUS,
and ARVIRAGUS *following.*

　　Bel. A goodly day not to keep house, with such
Whose roof's as low as ours!　Stoop, boys; this gate
Instructs you how to adore the heavens and bows you
To a morning's holy office: the gates of monarchs
Are arch'd so high that giants may jet through
And keep their impious turbans on, without
Good morrow to the sun.　Hail, thou fair heaven!
We house i' the rock, yet use thee not so hardly
As prouder livers do.
　　Gui.　　　　　　Hail, heaven!
　　Arv.　　　　　　　　　　　Hail, heaven!
　　Bel. Now for our mountain sport: up to yond hill;　10
Your legs are young; I'll tread these flats.　Consider,
When you above perceive me like a crow,
That it is place which lessens and sets off:

And you may then revolve what tales I have told you
Of courts, of princes, of the tricks in war:
This service is not service, so being done,
But being so allow'd: to apprehend thus,
Draws us a profit from all things we see;
And often, to our comfort, shall we find
The sharded beetle in a safer hold   20
Than is the full-wing'd eagle.   O, this life
Is nobler than attending for a check,
Richer than doing nothing for a bribe,   ′
Prouder than rustling in unpaid-for silk:
Such gain the cap of him that makes 'em fine,
Yet keeps his book uncross'd: no life to ours.
  Gui. Out of your proof you speak: we, poor unfledged,
Have never wing'd from view o' the nest, nor know not
What air's from home.   Haply this life is best,
If quiet life be best; sweeter to you   30
That have a sharper known; well corresponding
With your stiff age: ′but unto us it is
A cell of ignorance; travelling a-bed;
A prison for a debtor, that not dares
To stride a limit. ′
  Arv.   What should we speak of
When we are old as you?   When we shall hear
The rain and wind beat dark December, how,
In this our pinching cave, shall we discourse
The freezing hours away?   We have seen nothing;
We are beastly, subtle as the fox for prey,   40
Like warlike as the wolf for what we eat;
Our valour is to chase what flies; our cage
We make a quire, as doth the prison'd bird,
And sing our bondage freely.
  Bel.   How you speak!
Did you but know the city's usuries
And felt them knowingly; the art o' the court,
As hard to leave as keep; whose top to climb
Is certain falling, or so slippery that
The fear's as bad as falling; the toil o' the war,
A pain that only seems to seek out danger   50
I' the name of fame and honour, which dies i' the search,
And hath as oft a slanderous epitaph
As record of fair act; nay, many times,
Doth ill deserve by doing well; what's worse,
Must court'sy at the censure:—O boys, this story
The world may read in me: my body's mark'd

With Roman swords, and my report was once
First with the best of note: Cymbeline loved me,
And when a soldier was the theme, my name
Was not far off: then was I as a tree   60
Whose boughs did bend with fruit: but in one night,
A storm or robbery, call it what you will,
Shook down my mellow hangings, nay, my leaves,
And left me bare to weather.
   Gui.   Uncertain favour!
   Bel. My fault being nothing—as I have told you oft—
But that two villains, whose false oaths prevail'd
Before my perfect honour, swore to Cymbeline
I was confederate with the Romans: so
Follow'd my banishment, and this twenty years
This rock and these demesnes have been my world;   70
Where I have lived at honest freedom, paid
More pious debts to heaven than in all
The fore-end of my time.   But up to the mountains!
This is not hunters' language: he that strikes
The venison first shall be the lord o' the feast;
To him the other two shall minister;
And we will fear no poison, which attends
In place of greater state.   I 'll meet you in the valleys.
             [*Exeunt Guiderius and Arviragus.*
How hard it is to hide the sparks of nature!
These boys know little they are sons to the king;   80
Nor Cymbeline dreams that they are alive.
They think they are mine; and though train'd up thus meanly
I' the cave wherein they bow, their thoughts do hit
The roofs of palaces, and nature prompts them
In simple and low things to prince it much
Beyond the trick of others.   This Polydore,
The heir of Cymbeline and Britain, who
The king his father call'd Guiderius,—Jove!
When on my three-foot stool I sit and tell
The warlike feats I have done, his spirits fly out   90
Into my story: say 'Thus mine enemy fell,
And thus I set my foot on 's neck'; even then
The princely blood flows in his cheek, he sweats,
Strains his young nerves and puts himself in posture
That acts my words.   The younger brother, Cadwal,
Once Arviragus, in as like a figure,
Strikes life into my speech and shows much more
His own conceiving.—Hark, the game is roused!—
O Cymbeline! heaven and my conscience knows

Thou didst unjustly banish me: whereon,   100
At three and two years old, I stole these babes:
Thinking to bar thee of succession, as
Thou reft'st me of my lands.   Euriphile,
Thou wast their nurse; they took thee for their mother,
And every day do honour to her grave:
Myself, Belarius, that am Morgan call'd,
They take for natural father.   The game is up.   [*Exit.*

SCENE IV.   *Country near Milford-Haven.*

Enter PISANIO *and* IMOGEN.

Imo. Thou told'st me, when we came from horse, the place
Was near at hand: ne'er long'd my mother so
To see me first, as I have now.   Pisanio! man!
Where is Posthumus?   What is in thy mind,
That makes thee stare thus?   Wherefore breaks that sigh
From the inward of thee?   One, but painted thus,
Would be interpreted a thing perplex'd
Beyond self-explication: put thyself
Into a haviour of less fear, ere wildness
Vanquish my staider senses.   What's the matter?   10
Why tender'st thou that paper to me, with
A look untender?   If't be summer news,
Smile to't before; if winterly, thou need'st
But keep that countenance still.   My husband's hand!
That drug-damn'd Italy hath out-crafted him,
And he's at some hard point.   Speak, man: thy tongue
May take off some extremity, which to read
Would be even mortal to me.
Pis.   Please you, read;
And you shall find me, wretched man, a thing
The most disdain'd of fortune.   20
Imo. [*Reads*] 'Thy mistress, Pisanio, hath played the
strumpet in my bed; the testimonies whereof lie bleeding in
me.   I speak not out of weak surmises, but from proof as
strong as my grief and as certain as I expect my revenge.
That part thou, Pisanio, must act for me, if thy faith be not
tainted with the breach of hers.   Let thine own hands take
away her life: I shall give thee opportunity at Milford-Haven.
She hath my letter for the purpose: where if thou fear to
strike and to make me certain it is done, thou art the pandar
to her dishonour and equally to me disloyal.'   30
Pis. What shall I need to draw my sword? the paper

Hath cut her throat already.   No, 't is slander,
Whose edge is sharper than the sword, whose tongue
Outvenoms all the worms of Nile, whose breath
Rides on the posting winds and doth belie
All corners of the world : kings, queens and states,
Maids, matrons, nay, the secrets of the grave
This viperous slander enters.   What cheer, madam?
   Imo. False to his bed!   What is it to be false?
To lie in watch there and to think on him?   40
To weep 'twixt clock and clock? if sleep charge nature,
To break it with a fearful dream of him
And cry myself awake? that 's false to 's bed, is it?
   Pis. Alas, good lady!
   Imo. I false!   Thy conscience witness.   Iachimo,
Thou didst accuse him of incontinency;
Thou then look'dst like a villain ; now methinks
Thy favour 's good enough.   Some jay of Italy,
Whose mother was her painting, hath betray'd him :
Poor I am stale, a garment out of fashion ;   50
And, for I am richer than to hang by the walls,
I must be ripp'd :—to pieces with me!—O,
Men's vows are women's traitors!   All good seeming,
By thy revolt, O husband, shall be thought
Put on for villany; not born where 't grows,
But worn a bait for ladies.
   Pis.   Good madam, hear me.
   Imo. True honest men being heard, like false Æneas,
Were in his time thought false, and Sinon's weeping
Did scandal many a holy tear, took pity
From most true wretchedness : so thou, Posthumus,   60
Wilt lay the leaven on all proper men ;
Goodly and gallant shall be false and perjured
From thy great fail.   Come, fellow, be thou honest:
Do thou thy master's bidding : when thou see'st him,
A little witness my obedience: look!
I draw the sword myself: take it, and hit
The innocent mansion of my love, my heart :
Fear not; 't is empty of all things but grief:
Thy master is not there, who was indeed
The riches of it: do his bidding; strike.   70
Thou mayst be valiant in a better cause;
But now thou seem'st a coward.
   Pis.   Hence, vile instrument!
Thou shalt not damn my hand.
   Imo.   Why, I must die :

And if I do not by thy hand, thou art
No servant of thy master's.   Against self-slaughter
There is a prohibition so divine
That cravens my weak hand.   Come, here's my heart,
Something's afore't.   Soft, soft! we'll no defence;
Obedient as the scabbard.   What is here?
The scriptures of the loyal Leonatus,   80
All turn'd to heresy?   Away, away,
Corrupters of my faith! you shall no more
Be stomachers to my heart.   Thus may poor fools
Believe false teachers.   Though those that are betray'd
Do feel the treason sharply, yet the traitor
Stands in worse case of woe.
And thou, Posthumus, thou that didst set up
My disobedience 'gainst the king my father,
And make me put into contempt the suits
Of princely fellows, shalt hereafter find   90
It is no act of common passage, but
A strain of rareness: and I grieve myself
To think, when thou shalt be disedged by her
That now thou tirest on, how thy memory
Will then be pang'd by me.   Prithee, dispatch:
The lamb entreats the butcher: where's thy knife?
Thou art too slow to do thy master's bidding,
When I desire it too.
  Pis.   O gracious lady,
Since I received command to do this business
I have not slept one wink.
  Imo.   Do't, and to bed then.   100
  Pis. I'll wake mine eye-balls blind first.
  Imo.   Wherefore then
Didst undertake it?   Why hast thou abused
So many miles with a pretence? this place?
Mine action and thine own? our horses' labour?
The time inviting thee? the perturb'd court
For my being absent? whereunto I never
Purpose return.   Why hast thou gone so far,
To be unbent when thou hast ta'en thy stand,
The elected deer before thee?
  Pis.   But to win time
To lose so bad employment; in the which   110
I have consider'd of a course.   Good lady,
Hear me with patience.
  Imo.   Talk thy tongue weary; speak:
I have heard I am a strumpet; and mine ear,

Therein false struck, can take no greater wound,
Nor tent to bottom that.   But speak.
 Pis.   Then, madam,
I thought you would not back again.
 Imo.   Most like,
Bringing me here to kill me.
 Pis.   Not so, neither:
But if I were as wise as honest, then
My purpose would prove well.   It cannot be
But that my master is abused: 120
Some villain, ay, and singular in his art,
Hath done you both this cursed injury.
 Imo. Some Roman courtezan.
 Pis.   No, on my life.
I 'll give but notice you are dead and send him
Some bloody sign of it; for 't is commanded
I should do so: you shall be miss'd at court,
And that will well confirm it;—
 Imo.   Why, good fellow,
What shall I do the while? where bide? how live?
Or in my life what comfort, when I am
Dead to my husband?
 Pis.   If you 'll back to the court—   130
 Imo. No court, no father; nor no more ado
With that harsh, noble, simple nothing,
That Cloten, whose love-suit hath been to me
As fearful as a siege.
 Pis.   If not at court,
Then not in Britain must you bide.
 Imo.   Where then?
Hath Britain all the sun that shines?   Day, night,
Are they not but in Britain?   I' the world's volume
Our Britain seems as of it, but not in 't;
In a great pool a swan's nest: prithee, think
There 's livers out of Britain.
 Pis.   I am most glad   140
You think of other place.   The ambassador,
Lucius the Roman, comes to Milford-Haven
To-morrow: now, if you could wear a mind
Dark as your fortune is, and but disguise
That which, to appear itself, must not yet be
But by self-danger, you should tread a course
Pretty and full of view; yea, haply, near
The residence of Posthumus; so nigh at least
That though his actions were not visible, yet

Report should render him hourly to your ear   150
As truly as he moves.
   Imo.   O, for such means!
Though peril to my modesty, not death on 't,
I would adventure.
   Pis.   Well, then, here's the point:
You must forget to be a woman; change
Command into obedience: fear and niceness—
The handmaids of all women, or, more truly,
Woman it pretty self—into a waggish courage;
Ready in gibes, quick-answer'd, saucy and
As quarrelous as the weasel; nay, you must
Forget that rarest treasure of your cheek,   160
Exposing it—but, O, the harder heart!
Alack, no remedy!—to the greedy touch
Of common-kissing Titan, and forget
Your laboursome and dainty trims, wherein
You made great Juno angry.
   Imo.   Nay, be brief
I see into thy end, and am almost
A man already.
   Pis.   First, make yourself but like one.
Fore-thinking this, I have already fit—
'T is in my cloak-bag—doublet, hat, hose, all
That answer to them: would you in their serving,   170
And with what imitation you can borrow
From youth of such a season, 'fore noble Lucius
Present yourself, desire his service, tell him
Wherein you're happy,—which you'll make him know,
If that his head have ear in music,—doubtless
With joy he will embrace you, for he's honourable,
And doubling that, most holy. Your means abroad,
You have me, rich; and I will never fail
Beginning nor supplyment.
   Imo.   Thou art all the comfort
The gods will diet me with. Prithee, away: 18c
There's more to be consider'd; but we'll even
All that good time will give us: this attempt
I am soldier to, and will abide it with
A prince's courage. Away, I prithee.
   Pis. Well, madam, we must take a short farewell,
Lest, being miss'd, I be suspected of
Your carriage from the court. My noble mistress,
Here is a box; I had it from the queen:
What's in 't is precious; if you are sick at sea,

Or stomach-qualm'd at land, a dram of this   190
Will drive away distemper.   To some shade,
And fit you to your manhood.   May the gods
Direct you to the best!
   Imo. Amen: I thank thee.   [*Exeunt, severally.*

   SCENE V. *A room in Cymbeline's palace.*

Enter CYMBELINE, QUEEN, CLOTEN, LUCIUS, Lord, *and*
               Attendants.

   Cym. Thus far; and so farewell.
   Luc.   Thanks, royal sir.
My emperor hath wrote, I must from hence;
And am right sorry that I must report ye
My master's enemy.
   Cym.   Our subjects, sir,
Will not endure his yoke; and for ourself
To show less sovereignty than they, must needs
Appear unkinglike.
   Luc.   So, sir; I desire of you
A conduct over-land to Milford-Haven.
Madam, all joy befal your grace and you!
   Cym. My lords, you are appointed for that office;   10
The due of honour in no point omit.
So farewell, noble Lucius.
   Luc.   Your hand, my lord.
   Clo. Receive it friendly; but from this time forth
I wear it as your enemy.
   Luc.   Sir, the event
Is yet to name the winner: fare you well.
   Cym. Leave not the worthy Lucius, good my lords,
Till he have cross'd the Severn.   Happiness!
                 [*Exeunt Lucius and Lords.*
   Queen. He goes hence frowning: but it honours us
That we have given him cause.
   Clo.   'T is all the better;
Your valiant Britons have their wishes in it.   20
   Cym. Lucius hath wrote already to the emperor
How it goes here.   It fits us therefore ripely
Our chariots and our horsemen be in readiness:
The powers that he already hath in Gallia
Will soon be drawn to head, from whence he moves
His war for Britain.

Queen.   'T is not sleepy business;
But must be look'd to speedily and strongly.
    Cym. Our expectation that it would be thus
Hath made us forward.   But, my gentle queen,
Where is our daughter?   She hath not appear'd   30
Before the Roman, nor to us hath tender'd
The duty of the day: she looks us like
A thing more made of malice than of duty:
We have noted it.   Call her before us; for
We have been too slight in sufferance. [*Exit an Attendant.*
    Queen.   Royal sir,
Since the exile of Posthumus, most retired
Hath her life been; the cure whereof, my lord,
'T is time must do.   Beseech your majesty,
Forbear sharp speeches to her: she's a lady
So tender of rebukes that words are strokes   40
And strokes death to her.

                  Re-enter Attendant.

    Cym.   Where is she, sir?   How
Can her contempt be answer'd?
    Atten.   Please you, sir,
Her chambers are all lock'd; and there's no answer
That will be given to the loud'st of noise we make.
    Queen. My lord, when last I went to visit her,
She pray'd me to excuse her keeping close,
Whereto constrain'd by her infirmity,
She should that duty leave unpaid to you,
Which daily she was bound to proffer: this
She wish'd me to make known; but our great court   50
Made me to blame in memory.
    Cym.   Her doors lock'd?
Not seen of late?   Grant, heavens, that which I fear
Prove false!   [*Exit.*
    Queen.   Son, I say, follow the king.
    Clo. That man of hers, Pisanio, her old servant,
I have not seen these two days.
    Queen.   Go, look after. [*Exit Cloten.*
Pisanio, thou that stand'st so for Posthumus!
He hath a drug of mine; I pray his absence
Proceed by swallowing that, for he believes
It is a thing most precious.   But for her,
Where is she gone?   Haply, despair hath seized her,   60
Or, wing'd with fervour of her love, she's flown
To her desired Posthumus: gone she is

To death or to dishonour; and my end
Can make good use of either: she being down,
I have the placing of the British crown.

Re-enter CLOTEN.

How now, my son?
  Clo.   'T is certain she is fled.
Go in and cheer the king: he rages; none
Dare come about him.
  Queen.   [*Aside*]   All the better: may
This night forestall him of the coming day!   [*Exit.*
  Clo. I love and hate her: for she 's fair and royal,   70
And that she hath all courtly parts more exquisite
Than lady, ladies, woman; from every one
The best she hath, and she, of all compounded,
Outsells them all; I love her therefore: but
Disdaining me and throwing favours on
The low Posthumus slanders so her judgement
That what 's else rare is choked; and in that point
I will conclude to hate her, nay, indeed,
To be revenged upon her. For when fools
Shall—

Enter PISANIO.

         Who is here? What, are you packing, sirrah?   80
Come hither: ah, you precious pandar! | Villain,
Where is thy lady? In a word; or else|
Thou art straightway with the fiends.
  Pis.   O, good my lord!
  Clo. Where is thy lady? or, by Jupiter,—
I will not ask again. Close villain,
I 'll have this secret from thy heart, or rip
Thy heart to find it. Is she with Posthumus?
From whose so many weights of baseness cannot
A dram of worth be drawn.）
  Pis.   Alas, my lord,
How can she be with him? When was she miss'd?   90
He is in Rome.
  Clo.   Where is she, sir? Come nearer;
No farther halting: satisfy me home
What is become of her.
  Pis. O, my all-worthy lord!
  Clo.   All-worthy villain
Discover where thy mistress is at once,
At the next word: no more of 'worthy lord'!

Speak, or thy silence on the instant is
Thy condemnation and thy death.
  Pis.   Then, sir,
This paper is the history of my knowledge
Touching her flight.   [*Presenting a letter.*
  Clo.   Let's see 't. I will pursue her   100
Even to Augustus' throne.
  Pis.   [*Aside*] Or this, or perish.
She's far enough; and what he learns by this
May prove his travel, not her danger.
  Clo.   Hum!
  Pis. [*Aside*] I'll write to my lord she's dead. O Imogen,
Safe mayst thou wander, safe return again!
  Clo. Sirrah, is this letter true!
  Pis. Sir, as I think.   107
  Clo. It is Posthumus' hand; I know't. Sirrah, if thou
wouldst not be a villain, but do me true service, undergo
those employments wherein I should have cause to use thee
with a serious industry, that is, what villany soe'er I bid thee
do, to perform it directly and truly, I would think thee an
honest man: thou shouldst neither want my means for thy
relief nor my voice for thy preferment.   114
  Pis. Well, my good lord.
  Clo. Wilt thou serve me? for since patiently and constantly
thou hast stuck to the bare fortune of that beggar Posthumus,
thou canst not, in the course of gratitude, but be a diligent
follower of mine: wilt thou serve me?
  Pis. Sir, I will.   120
  Clo. Give me thy hand; here's my purse. Hast any of thy
late master's garments in thy possession?
  Pis. I have, my lord, at my lodging, the same suit he wore
when he took leave of my lady and mistress.
  Clo. The first service thou dost me, fetch that suit hither:
let it be thy first service; go.
  Pis. I shall, my lord.   [*Exit.* 127
  Clo. Meet thee at Milford-Haven!—I forgot to ask him
one thing: I'll remember't anon:—even there, thou villain
Posthumus, will I kill thee. I would these garments were
come. She said upon a time—the bitterness of it I now
belch from my heart—that she held the very garment of
Posthumus in more respect than my noble and natural person,
together with the adornment of my qualities. With that suit
upon my back, will I ravish her: first kill him, and in her eyes;
there shall she see my valour, which will then be a torment
to her contempt. He on the ground, my speech of insultment

ended on his dead body, to the court I'll knock her back, foot
her home again. She hath despised me rejoicingly, and I'll
be merry in my revenge.   140

Re-enter PISANIO, *with the clothes.*

Be those the garments?
  Pis. Ay, my noble lord.
  Clo. How long is't since she went to Milford-Haven?
  Pis. She can scarce be there yet.
  Clo. Bring this apparel to my chamber; that is the second
thing that I have commanded thee: the third is, that thou wilt
be a voluntary mute to my design. Be but duteous, and true
preferment shall tender itself to thee. My revenge is now at
Milford: would I had wings to follow it! Come, and be
true.   [*Exit.* 150
  Pis. Thou bid'st me to my loss: for true to thee
Were to prove false, which I will never be,
To him that is most true. To Milford go,
And find not her whom thou pursuest. Flow, flow,
You heavenly blessings, on her! This fool's speed
Be cross'd with slowness; labour be his meed!   [*Exit.*

SCENE VI. *Wales. Before the cave of Belarius.*

Enter IMOGEN, *in boy's clothes.*

  Imo. I see a man's life is a tedious one:
I have tired myself, and for two nights together
Have made the ground my bed. I should be sick,
But that my resolution helps me. Milford,
When from the mountain-top Pisanio show'd thee,
Thou wast within a ken: O Jove! I think
Foundations fly the wretched; such, I mean,
Where they should be relieved. Two beggars told me
I could not miss my way: will poor folks lie,
That have afflictions on them, knowing 't is   10
A punishment or trial? Yes; no wonder,
When rich ones scarce tell true. To lapse in fulness
Is sorer than to lie for need, and falsehood
Is worse in kings than beggars. My dear lord!
Thou art one o' the false ones. Now I think on thee,
My hunger's gone; but even before, I was
At point to sink for food. But what is this?
Here is a path to 't: 't is some savage hold:
I were best not call; I dare not call: yet famine,

Ere clean it o'erthrow nature, makes it valiant.　20
Plenty and peace breeds cowards: hardness ever
Of hardiness is mother.　Ho! who's here?
If any thing that's civil, speak; if savage,
Take or lend.　Ho!　No answer?　Then I'll enter.
Best draw my sword; and if mine enemy
But fear the sword like me, he'll scarcely look on't.
Such a foe, good heavens!　　　　*[Exit, to the cave.*

Enter BELARIUS, GUIDERIUS, *and* ARVIRAGUS.

Bel. You, Polydore, have proved best woodman and
Are master of the feast: Cadwal and I
Will play the cook and servant; 'tis our match:　30
The sweat of industry would dry and die,
But for the end it works to.　Come; our stomachs
Will make what's homely savoury: weariness
Can snore upon the flint, when resty sloth
Finds the down pillow hard.　Now peace be here,
Poor house, that keep'st thyself!
　　Gui.　　　　　　　　I am throughly weary.
　　Arv. I am weak with toil, yet strong in appetite.
　　Gui. There is cold meat i' the cave; we'll browse on that,
Whilst what we have kill'd be cook'd.
　　Bel. [*Looking into the cave*] Stay; come not in.　40
But that it eats our victuals, I should think
Here were a fairy.
　　Gui.　　　　　　What's the matter, sir?
　　Bel. By Jupiter, an angel! or, if not,
An earthly paragon!　Behold divineness
No elder than a boy!

Re-enter IMOGEN.

　　Imo. Good masters, harm me not:
Before I enter'd here, I call'd; and thought
To have begg'd or bought what I have took: good troth,
I have stol'n nought, nor would not, though I had found
Gold strew'd i' the floor.　Here's money for my meat:　50
I would have left it on the board so soon
As I had made my meal, and parted
With prayers for the provider.
　　Gui.　　　　　　　Money, youth?
　　Arv. All gold and silver rather turn to dirt!
As 'tis no better reckon'd, but of those
Who worship dirty gods.
　　Imo.　　　　　　I see you're angry:

Know, if you kill me for my fault, I should
Have died had I not made it.
 Bel.   Whither bound?
 Imo. To Milford-Haven.
 Bel. What's your name?   60
 Imo. Fidele, sir. I have a kinsman who
Is bound for Italy; he embark'd at Milford;
To whom being going, almost spent with hunger,
I am fall'n in this offence.
 Bel.   Prithee, fair youth,
Think us no churls, nor measure our good minds
By this rude place we live in. Well encounter'd!
'T is almost night: you shall have better cheer
Ere you depart; and thanks to stay and eat it.
Boys, bid him welcome.
 Gui.   Were you a woman, youth,
I should woo hard but be your groom in honesty. 70
I bid for you as I do buy.
 Arv.   I'll make't my comfort
He is a man; I'll love him as my brother:
And such a welcome as I'ld give to him
After long absence, such is yours: most welcome!
Be sprightly, for you fall 'mongst friends.
 Imo.   'Mongst friends,
If brothers. [*Aside*] Would it had been so, that they
Had been my father's sons! then had my prize
Been less, and so more equal ballasting
To thee, Posthumus.
 Bel.   He wrings at some distress.
 Gui. Would I could free't!
 Arv.   Or I, whate'er it be, 80
What pain it cost, what danger. Gods!
 Bel.   Hark, boys.
          [*Whispering.*
 Imo. Great men,
That had a court no bigger than this cave,
That did attend themselves and had the virtue
Which their own conscience seal'd them—laying by
That nothing-gift of differing multitudes—
Could not out-peer these twain. Pardon me, gods!
I'ld change my sex to be companion with them,
Since Leonatus's false.
 Bel.   It shall be so.
Boys, we'll go dress our hunt. Fair youth, come in: 90
Discourse is heavy, fasting; when we have supp'd,

We'll mannerly demand thee of thy story,
So far as thou wilt speak it.
 Gui.   Pray, draw near.
 Arv. The night to the owl and morn to the lark less welcome.
 Imo. Thanks, sir.
 Arv. I pray, draw near.   [*Exeunt.*

SCENE VII. *Rome. A public place.*

Enter two Senators *and* Tribunes.

 First Sen. This is the tenour of the emperor's writ:
That since the common men are now in action
'Gainst the Pannonians and Dalmatians,
And that the legions now in Gallia are
Full weak to undertake our wars against
The fall'n-off Britons, that we do incite
The gentry to this business. He creates
Lucius proconsul: and to you the tribunes,
For this immediate levy, he commends
His absolute commission. Long live Cæsar!   10
 First Tri. Is Lucius general of the forces?
 Sec. Sen.   Ay.
 First Tri. Remaining now in Gallia?
 First Sen.   With those legions
Which I have spoke of, whereunto your levy
Must be supplyant: the words of your commission
Will tie you to the numbers and the time
Of their dispatch.
 First Tri. We will discharge our duty.   [*Exeunt.*

ACT IV.

SCENE I. *Wales: near the cave of Belarius.*

Enter CLOTEN.

 Clo. I am near to the place where they should meet, if
Pisanio have mapped it truly. How fit his garments serve
me! Why should his mistress, who was made by him that
made the tailor, not be fit too? the rather—saving reverence
of the word—for 't is said a woman's fitness comes by fits.
Therein I must play the workman. I dare speak it to myself
—for it is not vain-glory for a man and his glass to confer in

his own chamber—I mean, the lines of my body are as well
drawn as his; no less young, more strong, not beneath him
in fortunes, beyond him in the advantage of the time, above
him in birth, alike conversant in general services, and more
remarkable in single oppositions: yet this imperceiverant
thing loves him in my despite. What mortality is! Posthumus,
thy head, which now is growing upon thy shoulders, shall
within this hour be off; thy mistress enforced; thy garments
cut to pieces before thy face: and all this done, spurn her
home to her father; who may haply be a little angry for my
so rough usage; but my mother, having power of his testiness,
shall turn all into my commendations.   My horse is tied up
safe: out, sword, and to a sore purpose!   Fortune, put them
into my hand!   This is the very description of their meeting-
place; and the fellow dares not deceive me.   [*Exit.*   22

SCENE II.   *Before the cave of Belarius.*

Enter, from the cave, BELARIUS, GUIDERIUS, ARVIRAGUS,
and IMOGEN.

Bel. [*To Imogen*] You are not well: remain here in the cave;
We'll come to you after hunting.
   Arv.   [*To Imogen*]   Brother, stay here:
Are we not brothers?
   Imo.   So man and man should be;
But clay and clay differs in dignity,
Whose dust is both alike.   I am very sick.
   Gui. Go you to hunting; I'll abide with him.
   Imo. So sick I am not, yet I am not well;
But not so citizen a wanton as
To seem to die ere sick: so please you, leave me,
Stick to your journal course: the breach of custom
Is breach of all.   I am ill, but your being by me
Cannot amend me; society is no comfort
To one not sociable: I am not very sick,
Since I can reason of it.   Pray you, trust me here:
I'll rob none but myself; and let me die,
Stealing so poorly.
   Gui.   I love thee; I have spoke it:
How much the quantity, the weight as much,
As I do love my father.
   Bel.   What! how! how!
   Arv. If it be sin to say so, sir, I yoke me
In my good brother's fault: I know not why   20

I love this youth; and I have heard you say,
Love's reason's without reason : the bier at door,
And a demand who is 't shall die, I 'ld say
' My father, not this youth'.
    Bel.   [*Aside*] O noble strain !
O worthiness of nature ! breed of greatness !
Cowards father cowards and base things sire base :
Nature hath meal and bran, contempt and grace.
I 'm not their father; yet who this should be,
Doth miracle itself, loved before me.
'T is the ninth hour o' the morn.
    Arv.   Brother, farewell.   30
    Imo. I wish ye sport.
    Arv.   You health. So please you, sir.
    Imo. [*Aside*] These are kind creatures. Gods, what lies I
    have heard !
Our courtiers say all 's savage but at court:
Experience, O, thou disprovest report !
The imperious seas breed monsters, for the dish
Poor tributary rivers as sweet fish.
I am sick still; heart-sick. Pisanio,
I 'll now taste of thy drug.
    Gui.   I could not stir him:
He said he was gentle, but unfortunate;
Dishonestly afflicted, but yet honest.   40
    Arv. Thus did he answer me : yet said, hereafter
I might know more.
    Bel.   To the field, to the field !
We 'll leave you for this time : go in and rest.
    Arv. We 'll not be long away.
    Bel.   Pray, be not sick,
For you must be our housewife.
    Imo.   Well or ill,
I am bound to you.
    Bel.   And shalt be ever.
                    [*Exit Imogen, to the cave.*
This youth, howe'er distress'd, appears he hath had
Good ancestors.
    Arv.   How angel-like he sings !
    Gui. But his neat cookery ! he cut our roots in characters
And sauced our broths, as Juno had been sick   50
And he her dieter.
    Arv.   Nobly he yokes
A smiling with a sigh, as if the sigh
Was that it was, for not being such a smile;

The smile mocking the sigh, that it would fly
From so divine a temple, to commix
With winds that sailors rail at.
   Gui.   I do note
That grief and patience, rooted in him both,
Mingle their spurs together.
   Arv.   Grow, patience!
And let the stinking elder, grief, untwine
His perishing root with the increasing vine!   60
   Bel. It is great morning. Come, away!—Who's there?

Enter CLOTEN.

   Clo. I cannot find those runagates; that villain
Hath mock'd me. I am faint.
   Bel.   'Those runagates!'
Means he not us! I partly know him: 't is
Cloten, the son o' the queen. I fear some ambush.
I saw him not these many years, and yet
I know 't is he. We are held as outlaws: hence!
   Gui. He is but one: you and my brother search
What companies are near: pray you, away;
Let me alone with him.   [*Exeunt Belarius and Arviragus.*
   Clo.   Soft! What are you   70
That fly me thus? some villain mountaineers?
I have heard of such. What slave art thou?
   Gui.   A thing
More slavish did I ne'er than answering
A slave without a knock.
   Clo.   Thou art a robber,
A law-breaker, a villain: yield thee, thief.
   Gui. To who? to thee? What art thou? Have not I
An arm as big as thine? a heart as big?
Thy words, I grant, are bigger, for I wear not
My dagger in my mouth. Say what thou art,
Why I should yield to thee?
   Clo.   Thou villain base,   80
Know'st me not by my clothes?
   Gui.   No, nor thy tailor, rascal,
Who is thy grandfather: he made those clothes,
Which, as it seems, make thee.
   Clo.   Thou precious varlet,
My tailor made them not.
   Gui.   Hence, then, and thank
The man that gave them thee. Thou art some fool·
I am loath to beat thee.

Clo.   Thou injurious thief,
Hear but my name, and tremble.
   Gui.   What's thy name?
   Clo. Cloten, thou villain.
   Gui. Cloten, thou double-villain, be thy name,
I cannot tremble at it: were it Toad, or Adder, Spider, 90
'T would move me sooner.
   Clo.   To thy further fear,
Nay, to thy mere confusion, thou shalt know
I am son to the queen.
   Gui.   I am sorry for 't; not seeming
So worthy as thy birth.
   Clo.   Art not afeard?
   Gui. Those that I reverence those I fear, the wise:
At fools I laugh, not fear them.
   Clo.   Die the death:
When I have slain thee with my proper hand,
I 'll follow those that even now fled hence,
And on the gates of Lud's town set your heads:
Yield, rustic mountaineer.   [*Exeunt fighting.* 100

    Re-enter BELARIUS *and* ARVIRAGUS.

   Bel. No company 's abroad?
   Arv. None in the world: you did mistake him, sure.
   Bel. I cannot tell: long is it since I saw him,
But time hath nothing blurr'd those lines of favour
Which then he wore; the snatches in his voice,
And burst of speaking, were as his: I am absolute
'T was very Cloten.
   Arv.   In this place we left them:
I wish my brother make good time with him,
You say he is so fell.
   Bel.   Being scarce made up,
I mean, to man, he had not apprehension   110
Of roaring terrors; for the effect of judgement
Is oft the cause of fear. But, see, thy brother.

    Re-enter GUIDERIUS, *with* CLOTEN'S *head.*

   Gui. This Cloten was a fool, an empty purse;
There was no money in 't: not Hercules
Could have knock'd out his brains, for he had none:
Yet I not doing this, the fool had borne
My head as I do his.
   Bel.   What hast thou done?
   Gui. I am perfect what: cut off one Cloten's head,

Son to the queen, after his own report;
Who call'd me traitor, mountaineer, and swore   120
With his own single hand he'ld take us in,
Displace our heads where—thank the gods!—they grow,
And set them on Lud's town.
   Bel.   We are all undone.
   Gui. Why, worthy father, what have we to lose,
But that he swore to take, our lives?   The law
Protects not us: then why should we be tender
To let an arrogant piece of flesh threat us,
Play judge and executioner all himself,
For we do fear the law?   What company
Discover you abroad?
   Bel.   No single soul   130
Can we set eye on; but in all safe reason
He must have some attendants.   Though his humour
Was nothing but mutation, ay, and that
From one bad thing to worse; not frenzy, not
Absolute madness could so far have raved
To bring him here alone; although perhaps
It may be heard at court that such as we
Cave here, hunt here, are outlaws, and in time
May make some stronger head; the which he hearing—
As it is like him—might break out, and swear   140
He'ld fetch us in; yet is't not probable
To come alone, either he so undertaking,
Or they so suffering: then on good ground we fear,
If we do fear this body hath a tail
More perilous than the head.
   Arv.   Let ordinance
Come as the gods foresay it: howsoe'er,
My brother hath done well.
   Bel.   I had no mind
To hunt this day: the boy Fidele's sickness
Did make my way long forth.
   Gui.   With his own sword,
Which he did wave against my throat, I have ta'en   150
His head from him: I'll throw't into the creek
Behind our rock; and let it to the sea,
And tell the fishes he's the queen's son, Cloten:
That's all I reck.   [*Exit*
   Bel.   I fear 't will be revenged:
Would, Polydore, thou hadst not done't! though valour
Becomes thee well enough.
   Arv.   Would I had done't,

So the revenge alone pursued me!   Polydore,
I love thee brotherly, but envy much
Thou hast robb'd me of this deed: I would revenges,
That possible strength might meet, would seek us through
And put us to our answer.
 Bel.   Well, 't is done: 161
We 'll hunt no more to-day, nor seek for danger
Where there 's no profit.   I prithee, to our rock;
You and Fidele play the cooks: I 'll stay
Till hasty Polydore return, and bring him
To dinner presently.
 Arv.   Poor sick Fidele!
I 'll willingly to him: to gain his colour
I 'ld let a parish of such Clotens blood,
And praise myself for charity.   [*Exit.*
 Bel.   O thou goddess,
Thou divine Nature, how thyself thou blazon'st 170
In these two princely boys!   They are as gentle
As zephyrs blowing below the violet,
Not wagging his sweet head; and yet as rough,
Their royal blood enchafed, as the rudest wind,
That by the top doth take the mountain pine,
And make him stoop to the vale.   'T is wonder
That an invisible instinct should frame them
To royalty unlearn'd, honour untaught,
Civility not seen from other, valour
That wildly grows in them, but yields a crop 180
As if it had been sow'd. Yet still it 's strange
What Cloten's being here to us portends,
Or what his death will bring us.

    Re-enter GUIDERIUS.

 Gui.   Where 's my brother?
I have sent Cloten's clotpoll down the stream,
In embassy to his mother: his body 's hostage
For his return.   [*Solemn music.*
 Bel.   My ingenious instrument!
Hark, Polydore, it sounds!   But what occasion
Hath Cadwal now to give it motion?   Hark!
 Gui. Is he at home?
 Bel.   He went hence even now.
 Gui. What does he mean? since death of my dear'st mother
It did not speak before.   All solemn things 191
Should answer solemn accidents.   The matter?
Triumphs for nothing and lamenting toys

Is jollity for apes and grief for boys.
Is Cadwal mad?

Re-enter ARVIRAGUS, *with* IMOGEN *as dead, bearing her in his arms.*

Bel.   Look, here he comes,
And brings the dire occasion in his arms
Of what we blame him for.
Arv.   The bird is dead
That we have made so much on.   I had rather
Have skipp'd from sixteen years of age to sixty,
To have turn'd my leaping-time into a crutch,   200
Than have seen this.
Gui.   O sweetest, fairest lily!
My brother wears thee not th' one half so well
As when thou grew'st thyself.
Bel.   O melancholy!
Who ever yet could sound thy bottom? find
The ooze, to show what coast thy sluggish crare
Might easiliest harbour in?   Thou blessed thing!
Jove knows what man thou mightst have made; but I,
Thou diedst, a most rare boy, of melancholy.
How found you him?
Arv.   Stark, as you see:
Thus smiling, as some fly had tickled slumber,   210
Not as death's dart, being laugh'd at; his right cheek
Reposing on a cushion.
Gui.   Where?
Arv.   O' the floor;
His arms thus leagued: I thought he slept, and put
My clouted brogues from off my feet, whose rudeness
Answer'd my steps too loud.
Gui.   Why, he but sleeps:
If he be gone, he'll make his grave a bed;
With female fairies will his tomb be haunted,
And worms will not come to thee.
Arv.   With fairest flowers
Whilst summer lasts and I live here, Fidele,
I'll sweeten thy sad grave: thou shalt not lack   220
The flower that's like thy face, pale primrose, nor
The azured harebell, like thy veins, no, nor
The leaf of eglantine, whom not to slander,
Out-sweeten'd not thy breath: the ruddock would,
With charitable bill,—O bill, sore-shaming
Those rich-left heirs that let their fathers lie

Without a monument!—bring thee all this;
Yea, and furr'd moss besides, when flowers are none,
To winter-ground thy corse.
 Gui. Prithee, have done;
And do not play in wench-like words with that 230
Which is so serious. Let us bury him,
And not protract with admiration what
Is now due debt. To the grave!
 Arv. Say, where shall's lay him?
 Gui. By good Euriphile, our mother.
 Arv. Be't so:
And let us, Polydore, though now our voices
Have got the mannish crack, sing him to the ground,
As once our mother; use like note and words,
Save that 'Euriphile' must be 'Fidele'.
 Gui. Cadwal,
I cannot sing: I'll weep, and word it with thee; 240
For notes of sorrow out of tune are worse
Than priests and fanes that lie.
 Arv. We'll speak it, then.
 Bel. Great griefs, I see, medicine the less; for Cloten
Is quite forgot. He was a queen's son, boys;
And though he came our enemy, remember
He was paid for that: though mean and mighty, rotting
Together, have one dust, yet reverence,
That angel of the world, doth make distinction
Of place 'tween high and low. Our foe was princely;
And though you took his life, as being our foe, 250
Yet bury him as a prince.
 Gui. Pray you, fetch him hither.
Thersites' body is as good as Ajax',
When neither are alive.
 Arv. If you'll go fetch him,
We'll say our song the whilst. Brother, begin.
         [*Exit Belarius.*
 Gui. Nay, Cadwal, we must lay his head to the east;
My father hath a reason for't.
 Arv. 'T is true.
 Gui. Come on then, and remove him.
 Arv. So. Begin.

SONG.

 Gui. Fear no more the heat o' the sun,
   Nor the furious winter's rages;

Thou thy worldly task hast done,   260
   Home art gone and ta'en thy wages:
Golden lads and girls all must,
As chimney-sweepers, come to dust.

Arv.   Fear no more the frown o' the great;
   Thou art past the tyrant's stroke;
Care no more to clothe and eat;
   To thee the reed is as the oak:
The sceptre, learning, physic, must
All follow this, and come to dust.

Gui.   Fear no more the lightning-flash,   270
Arv.   Nor the all-dreaded thunder-stone;
Gui.   Fear not slander, censure rash;
Arv.   Thou hast finish'd joy and moan:
Both.   All lovers young, all lovers must
Consign to thee, and come to dust.

Gui.   No exorciser harm thee!
Arv.   Nor no witchcraft charm thee!
Gui.   Ghost unlaid forbear thee!
Arv.   Nothing ill come near thee!
Both.   Quiet consummation have!   280
And renowned be thy grave!

Re-enter BELARIUS, *with the body of* CLOTEN.

Gui. We have done our obsequies: come, lay him down.
Bel. Here's a few flowers; but 'bout midnight, more:
The herbs that have on them cold dew o' the night
Are strewings fitt'st for graves.   Upon their faces.
You were as flowers, now wither'd: even so
These herblets shall, which we upon you strow.
Come on, away: apart upon your knees.
The ground that gave them first has them again:
Their pleasures here are past, so is their pain.   290
        [*Exeunt Belarius, Guiderius, and Arviragus.*
Imo. [*Awaking*] Yes, sir, to Milford-Haven; which is the
   way?—
I thank you—By yond bush?—Pray, how far thither?
'Ods pittikins! can it be six mile yet?—
I have gone all night.   'Faith, I'll lie down and sleep.
But, soft! no bedfellow!—O gods and goddesses!
        [*Seeing the body of Cloten.*
These flowers are like the pleasures of the world;
This bloody man, the care on 't.   I hope I dream;

For so I thought I was a cave-keeper,
And cook to honest creatures: but 't is not so;
'T was but a bolt of nothing, shot at nothing,   300
Which the brain makes of fumes: our very eyes
Are sometimes like our judgements, blind.   Good faith,
I tremble still with fear: but if there be
Yet left in heaven as small a drop of pity
As a wren's eye, fear'd gods, a part of it!
The dream 's here still: even when I wake, it is
Without me, as within me; not imagined, felt.
A headless man!   The garments of Posthumus!
I know the shape of 's leg: this is his hand;
His foot Mercurial; his Martial thigh;   310
The brawns of Hercules; but his Jovial face—
Murder in heaven?—How!—'T is gone.   Pisanio,
All curses madded Hecuba gave the Greeks,
And mine to boot, be darted on thee!   Thou,
Conspired with that irregulous devil, Cloten,
Hast here cut off my lord.   To write and read
Be henceforth treacherous!   Damn'd Pisanio
Hath with his forged letters,—damn'd Pisanio—
From this most bravest vessel of the world
Struck the main-top!   O Posthumus! alas,   320
Where is thy head? where 's that?   Ay me! where 's that?
Pisanio might have kill'd thee at the heart,
And left this head on.   How should this be?   Pisanio?
'T is he and Cloten: malice and lucre in them
Have laid this woe here.   O, 't is pregnant, pregnant!
The drug he gave me, which he said was precious
And cordial to me, have I not found it
Murderous to the senses?   That confirms it home:
This is Pisanio's deed, and Cloten's: O!
Give colour to my pale cheek with thy blood,   330
That we the horrider may seem to those
Which chance to find us: O, my lord, my lord!
                              [*Falls on the body.*

Enter LUCIUS, *a* Captain *and other* Officers, *and a*
                    Soothsayer.

Cap. To them the legions garrison'd in Gallia,
After your will, have cross'd the sea, attending
You here at Milford-Haven with your ships:
They are in readiness.
    Luc.   But what from Rome?
    Cap. The senate hath stirr'd up the confiners

And gentlemen of Italy, most willing spirits,
That promise noble service: and they come
Under the conduct of bold Iachimo,   340
Syenna's brother.
    Luc.   When expect you them?
    Cap. With the next benefit o' the wind.
    Luc.   This forwardness
Makes our hopes fair. Command our present numbers
Be muster'd: bid the captains look to 't. Now, sir,
What have you dream'd of late of this war's purpose?
    Sooth. Last night the very gods show'd me a vision—
I fast and pray'd for their intelligence—thus:
I saw Jove's bird, the Roman eagle, wing'd
From the spongy south to this part of the west,
There vanish'd in the sunbeams: which portends—   350
Unless my sins abuse my divination—
Success to the Roman host.
    Luc.   Dream often so,
And never false. Soft, ho! what trunk is here
Without his top? The ruin speaks that sometime
It was a worthy building. How! a page!
Or dead, or sleeping on him? But dead rather;
For nature doth abhor to make his bed
With the defunct, or sleep upon the dead.
Let 's see the boy's face.
    Cap.   He 's alive, my lord.
    Luc. He 'll then instruct us of this body. Young one, 360
Inform us of thy fortunes, for it seems
They crave to be demanded. Who is this
Thou makest thy bloody pillow? Or who was he
That, otherwise than noble nature did,
Hath alter'd that good picture? What 's thy interest
In this sad wreck? How came it? Who is it?
What art thou?
    Imo.   I am nothing: or if not,
Nothing to be were better. This was my master,
A very valiant Briton and a good,
That here by mountaineers lies slain. Alas!   370
There is no more such masters: I may wander
From east to occident, cry out for service,
Try many, all good, serve truly, never
Find such another master.
    Luc.   'Lack, good youth!
Thou movest no less with thy complaining than
Thy master in bleeding: say his name, good friend.

Imo. Richard du Champ. [*Aside*] If I do lie and do
No harm by it, though the gods hear, I hope
They 'll pardon it.—Say you, sir?
  Luc.   Thy name?
  Imo.   Fidele, sir.
  Luc. Thou dost approve thyself the very same: 380
Thy name well fits thy faith, thy faith thy name.
Wilt take thy chance with me?   I will not say
Thou shalt be so well master'd, but, be sure,
No less beloved.   The Roman emperor's letters,
Sent by a consul to me, should not sooner
Than thine own worth prefer thee: go with me.
  Imo. I 'll follow, sir.   But first, an 't please the gods,
I 'll hide my master from the flies, as deep
As these poor pickaxes can dig; and when
With wild wood-leaves and weeds I ha' strew'd his grave, 390
And on it said a century of prayers,
Such as I can, twice o'er, I 'll weep and sigh;
And leaving so his service, follow you,
So please you entertain me.
  Luc.   Ay, good youth;
And rather father thee than master thee.
My friends,   .
The boy hath taught us manly duties: let us
Find out the prettiest daisied plot we can,
And make him with our pikes and partisans
A grave: come, arm him.   Boy, he is preferr'd 400
By thee to us, and he shall be interr'd
As soldiers can.   Be cheerful; wipe thine eyes:
Some falls are means the happier to arise.   [*Exeunt.*

SCENE III.   *A room in Cymbeline's palace.*

Enter CYMBELINE, Lords, PISANIO, *and* Attendants.

Cym. Again; and bring me word how 't is with her.
             [*Exit an Attendant.*
A fever with the absence of her son,
A madness, of which her life's in danger.   Heavens,
How deeply you at once do touch me!   Imogen,
The great part of my comfort, gone; my queen
Upon a desperate bed, and in a time
When fearful wars point at me; her son gone,
So needful for this present: it strikes me, past
The hope of comfort.   But for thee, fellow,

Who needs must know of her departure and   10
Dost seem so ignorant, we'll enforce it from thee
By a sharp torture.
   Pis.   Sir, my life is yours ;
I humbly set it at your will ; but, for my mistress,
I nothing know where she remains, why gone,
Nor when she purposes return.   Beseech your highness,
Hold me your loyal servant.
   First Lord.   Good my liege,
The day that she was missing he was here :
I dare be bound he's true and shall perform
All parts of his subjection loyally.   For Cloten,
There wants no diligence in seeking him,   20
And will, no doubt, be found.
   Cym.   The time is troublesome.
[To Pisanio] We'll slip you for a season ; but our jealousy
Does yet depend.
   First Lord.   So please your majesty,
The Roman legions, all from Gallia drawn,
Are landed on your coast, with a supply
Of Roman gentlemen, by the senate sent.
   Cym. Now for the counsel of my son and queen !
I am amazed with matter.   .
   First Lord.   Good my liege,
Your preparation can affront no less
Than what you hear of : come more, for more you're ready:
The want is but to put those powers in motion   31
That long to move.
   Cym.   I thank you.   Let's withdraw ;
And meet the time as it seeks us.   We fear not
What can from Italy annoy us ; but
We grieve at chances here.   Away! *[Exeunt all but Pisanio.*
   Pis. I heard no letter from my master since
I wrote him Imogen was slain : 't is strange :
Nor hear I from my mistress, who did promise
To yield me often tidings ; neither know I
What is betid to Cloten ; but remain   40
Perplex'd in all.   The heavens still must work.
Wherein I am false I am honest ; not true, to be true.
These present wars shall find I love my country,
Even to the note o' the king, or I'll fall in them.
All other doubts, by time let them be clear'd :
Fortune brings in some boats that are not steer'd.   *[Exit.*

SCENE IV.   *Wales: before the cave of Belarius.*

Enter BELARIUS, GUIDERIUS, *and* ARVIRAGUS.

Gui. The noise is round about us.
Bel.   Let us from it.
Arv. What pleasure, sir, find we in life, to lock it
From action and adventure?
Gui.   Nay, what hope
Have we in hiding us?   This way, the Romans
Must or for Britons slay us, or receive us
For barbarous and unnatural revolts
During their use, and slay us after.
Bel.   Sons,
We'll higher to the mountains; there secure us.
To the king's party there's no going: newness
Of Cloten's death—we being not known, not muster'd   10
Among the bands—may drive us to a render
Where we have lived, and so extort from's that
Which we have done, whose answer would be death
Drawn on with torture.
Gui.   This is, sir, a doubt
In such a time nothing becoming you,
Nor satisfying us.
Arv.   It is not likely
That when they hear the Roman horses neigh,
Behold their quarter'd fires, have both their eyes
And ears so cloy'd importantly as now,
That they will waste their time upon our note,   20
To know from whence we are.
Bel.   O, I am known
Of many in the army: many years,
Though Cloten then but young, you see, not wore him
From my remembrance.   And, besides, the king
Hath not deserved my service nor your loves;
Who find in my exile the want of breeding,
The certainty of this hard life; aye hopeless
To have the courtesy your cradle promised,
But to be still hot summer's tanlings and
The shrinking slaves of winter.
Gui.   Than be so   30
Better to cease to be.   Pray, sir, to the army:
I and my brother are not known; yourself
So out of thought, and thereto so o'ergrown,
Cannot be question'd.   .

Arv.   By this sun that shines,
I 'll thither: what thing is it that I never
Did see man die! scarce ever look'd on blood,
But that of coward hares, hot goats, and venison!
Never bestrid a horse, save one that had
A rider like myself, who ne'er wore rowel
Nor iron on his heel!   I am ashamed   40
To look upon the holy sun, to have
The benefit of his blest beams, remaining
So long a poor unknown.
    Gui.   By heavens, I 'll go:
If you will bless me, sir, and give me leave,
I 'll take the better care, but if you will not,
The hazard therefore due fall on me by
The hands of Romans!
    Arv.   So say I: amen.
    Bel. No reason I, since of your lives you set
So slight a valuation, should reserve
My crack'd one to more care.   Have with you, boys!   50
If in your country wars you chance to die,
That is my bed too, lads, and there I 'll lie:
Lead, lead. [*Aside*] The time seems long; their blood
    thinks scorn,
Till it fly out and show them princes born.   [*Exeunt.*

ACT V.

SCENE I. *Britain.   The Roman camp.*

Enter POSTHUMUS, *with a bloody handkerchief.*

Post. Yea, bloody cloth, I 'll keep thee, for I wish'd
Thou shouldst be colour'd thus.   You married ones,
If each of you should take this course, how many
Must murder wives much better than themselves
For wrying but a little!   O Pisanio!
Every good servant does not all commands:
No bond but to do just ones.   Gods! if you
Should have ta'en vengeance on my faults, I never
Had lived to put on this: so had you saved
The noble Imogen to repent, and struck   10
Me, wretch more worth your vengeance.   But, alack,

You snatch some hence for little faults; that's love,
To have them fall no more: you some permit
To second ills with ills, each elder worse,
And make them dread it, to the doers' thrift.
But Imogen is your own: do your best wills,
And make me blest to obey!   I am brought hither
Among the Italian gentry, and to fight
Against my lady's kingdom: 't is enough
That, Britain, I have kill'd thy mistress; peace!   20
I 'll give no wound to thee.   Therefore, good heavens,
Hear patiently my purpose: I 'll disrobe me
Of these Italian weeds and suit myself
As does a Briton peasant: so I 'll fight
Against the part I come with; so I 'll die
For thee, O Imogen, even for whom my life
Is every breath a death; and thus, unknown,
Pitied nor hated, to the face of peril
Myself I 'll dedicate.   Let me make men know
More valour in me than my habits show.   30
Gods, put the strength o' the Leonati in me!
To shame the guise o' the world, I will begin
The fashion, less without and more within.   [*Exit.*

SCENE II.   *Field of battle between the British
and Roman camps.*

Enter, from one side, LUCIUS, IACHIMO, *and the* Roman
Army: *from the other side, the* British Army; LEONATUS
POSTHUMUS *following, like a poor soldier.   They march
over and go out.   Then enter again, in skirmish,*
IACHIMO *and* POSTHUMUS: *he vanquisheth and dis-
armeth* IACHIMO, *and then leaves him.*

Iach. The heaviness and guilt within my bosom
Takes off my manhood: I have belied a lady,
The princess of this country, and the air on 't
Revengingly enfeebles me; or could this carl,
A very drudge of nature's, have subdued me
In my profession?   Knighthoods and honours, borne
As I wear mine, are titles but of scorn.
If that thy gentry, Britain, go before
This lout as he exceeds our lords, the odds
Is that we scarce are men and you are gods.   [*Exit.* 10

The battle continues; the Britons *fly;* CYMBELINE *is taken:
then enter, to his rescue,* BELARIUS, GUIDERIUS, *and*
ARVIRAGUS.

Bel. Stand, stand! We have the advantage of the ground;
The lane is guarded: nothing routs us but
The villany of our fears.
   Gui. }
   Arv. }   Stand, stand, and fight!

Re-enter POSTHUMUS, *and seconds the* Britons; *they rescue*
CYMBELINE, *and exeunt. Then re-enter* LUCIUS, *and*
IACHIMO, *with* IMOGEN.

Luc. Away, boy, from the troops, and save thyself;
For friends kill friends, and the disorder's such
As war were hoodwink'd.
   Iach.   'T is their fresh supplies.
   Luc. It is a day turn'd strangely: or betimes
Let's re-inforce, or fly.   [*Exeunt.*

SCENE III.   *Another part of the field.*

Enter POSTHUMUS *and a* British Lord.

Lord. Camest thou from where they made the stand?
   Post.   I did:
Though you, it seems, come from the fliers.
   Lord.   I did.
   Post. No blame be to you, sir; for all was lost,
But that the heavens fought: the king himself
Of his wings destitute, the army broken,
And but the backs of Britons seen, all flying
Through a strait lane; the enemy full-hearted,
Lolling the tongue with slaughtering, having work
More plentiful than tools to do 't, struck down
Some mortally, some slightly touch'd, some falling   10
Merely through fear; that the strait pass was damm'd
With dead men hurt behind, and cowards living
To die with lengthen'd shame.
   Lord.   Where was this lane?
   Post. Close by the battle, ditch'd, and wall'd with **turf**;
Which gave advantage to an ancient soldier,
An honest one, I warrant; who deserved
So long a breeding as his white beard came to,
In doing this for 's country: athwart the lane,

He, with two striplings—lads more like to run
The country base than to commit such slaughter;   20
With faces fit for masks, or rather fairer
Than those for preservation cased, or shame,—
Made good the passage; cried to those that fled,
'Our Britain's harts die flying, not our men:
To darkness fleet souls that fly backwards.   Stand;
Or we are Romans and will give you that
Like beasts which you shun beastly, and may save,
But to look back in frown: stand, stand.'   These three,
Three thousand confident, in act as many—
For three performers are the file when all   30
The rest do nothing—with this word 'Stand, stand,'
Accommodated by the place, more charming
With their own nobleness, which could have turn'd
A distaff to a lance, gilded pale looks,
Part shame, part spirit renew'd; that some, turn'd coward
But by example—O, a sin in war,
Damn'd in the first beginners!—'gan to look
The way that they did, and to grin like lions
Upon the pikes o' the hunters.   Then began
A stop i' the chaser, a retire, anon   40
A rout, confusion thick; forthwith they fly
Chickens, the way which they stoop'd eagles; slaves,
The strides they victors made: and now our cowards,
Like fragments in hard voyages, became
The life o' the need: having found the back-door open
Of the unguarded hearts, heavens, how they wound
Some slain before, some dying; some, their friends
O'er-borne i' the former wave: ten, chased by one,
Are now each one the slaughter-man of twenty:
Those that would die or ere resist are grown   50
The mortal bugs o' the field.
  Lord.   This was strange chance:
A narrow lane, an old man, and two boys.
  Post. Nay, do not wonder at it: you are made
Rather to wonder at the things you hear
Than to work any.   Will you rhyme upon 't,
And vent it for a mockery?   Here is one:
'Two boys, an old man twice a boy, a lane,
Preserved the Britons, was the Romans' bane.'
  Lord. Nay, be not angry, sir.
  Post.   'Lack, to what end?
Who dares not stand his foe, I'll be his friend;   60
For if he'll do as he is made to do,

I know he 'll quickly fly my friendship too.
You have put me into rhyme.
    Lord.   Farewell; you 're angry.   [*Exit.*
    Post. Still going? This is a lord! O noble misery,
To be i' the field, and ask 'what news?' of me!
To-day how many would have given their honours
To have saved their carcases! took heel to do 't,
And yet died too! I, in mine own woe charm'd,
Could not find death where I did hear him groan,
Nor feel him where he struck: being an ugly monster,   70
'T is strange he hides him in fresh cups, soft beds,
Sweet words; or hath more ministers than we
That draw his knives i' the war. Well, I will find him:
For, being now a favourer to the Briton,
No more a Briton, I have resumed again
The part I came in: fight I will no more,
But yield me to the veriest hind that shall
Once touch my shoulder. Great the slaughter is
Here made by the Roman; great the answer be
Britons must take. For me, my ransom 's death;   80
On either side I come to spend my breath;
Which neither here I 'll keep nor bear again,
But end it by some means for Imogen.

    Enter two British Captains *and* Soldiers.

    First Cap. Great Jupiter be praised! Lucius is taken.
'T is thought the old man and his sons were angels.
    Sec. Cap. There was a fourth man, in a silly habit,
That gave the affront with them.
    First Cap.   So 't is reported:
But none of 'em can be found. Stand! who 's there?
    Post. A Roman,
Who had not now been drooping here, if seconds   90
Had answer'd him.
    Sec. Cap.   Lay hands on him; a dog!
A leg of Rome shall not return to tell
What crows have peck'd them here. He brags his service
As if he were of note: bring him to the king.

    Enter CYMBELINE, BELARIUS, GUIDERIUS, ARVIRAGUS,
        PISANIO, Soldiers, Attendants, *and* Roman Captives.
    The Captains *present* POSTHUMUS *to* CYMBELINE, *who*
    delivers him over to a Gaoler: *then exeunt omnes.*

SCENE IV. *A British prison.*

Enter POSTHUMUS *and two* Gaolers.

First Gaol. You shall not now be stol'n, you have locks
upon you ;
So graze as you find pasture.
  Sec. Gaol.   Ay, or a stomach.
                              [*Exeunt Gaolers.*
  Post. Most welcome, bondage ! for thou art a way,
I think, to liberty : yet am I better
Than one that 's sick o' the gout ; since he had rather
Groan so in perpetuity than be cured
By the sure physician, death, who is the key
To unbar these locks.   My conscience, thou art fetter'd
More than my shanks and wrists : you good gods, give me
The penitent instrument to pick that bolt,   10
Then, free for ever !   Is 't enough I am sorry?
So children temporal fathers do appease ;
Gods are more full of mercy.   Must I repent?
I cannot do it better than in gyves,
Desired more than constrain'd : to satisfy,
If of my freedom 't is the main part, take
No stricter render of me than my all.
I know you are more clement than vile men,
Who of their broken debtors take a third,
A sixth, a tenth, letting them thrive again   20
On their abatement : that 's not my desire :
For Imogen's dear life take mine ; and though
'T is not so dear, yet 't is a life ; you coin'd it :
'Tween man and man they weigh not every stamp ;
Though light, take pieces for the figure's sake :
You rather mine, being yours : and so, great powers,
If you will take this audit, take this life,
And cancel these cold bonds.   O Imogen !
I 'll speak to thee in silence.   [*Sleeps.*

Solemn music.   Enter, as in an apparition, SICILIUS LEON-
  ATUS, *father to Posthumus, an old man, attired like a
  warrior ; leading in his hand an ancient matron, his
  wife, and mother to Posthumus, with music before them :
  then, after other music, follow the two young* LEONATI,
  *brothers to Posthumus, with wounds as they died in the
  wars.   They circle* POSTHUMUS *round, as he lies sleeping.*

  Sici.   No more, thou thunder-master, show   30
          Thy spite on mortal flies :

With Mars fall out, with Juno chide,
  That thy adulteries
    Rates and revenges.
Hath my poor boy done aught but well,
  Whose face I never saw?
I died whilst in the womb he stay'd
  Attending nature's law:
Whose father then, as men report
  Thou orphans' father art,   40
Thou shouldst have been, and shielded him
  From this earth-vexing smart.

Moth. Lucina lent not me her aid,
  But took me in my throes;
That from me was Posthumus ript,
  Came crying 'mongst his foes,
    A thing of pity!

Sici. Great nature, like his ancestry,
  Moulded the stuff so fair,
That he deserved the praise o' the world,   50
  As great Sicilius' heir.

First Bro. When once he was mature for man,
  In Britain where was he
That could stand up his parallel;
  Or fruitful object be
In eye of Imogen, that best
  Could deem his dignity?

Moth. With marriage wherefore was he mock'd,
  To be exiled, and thrown
From Leonati seat, and cast   60
  From her his dearest one,
    Sweet Imogen?

Sici. Why did you suffer Iachimo,
  Slight thing of Italy,
To taint his nobler heart and brain
  With needless jealousy;
And to become the geck and scorn
  O' th' other's villany?   •

Sec. Bro. For this from stiller seats we came,
  Our parents and us twain,   70
That striking in our country's cause
  Fell bravely and were slain,
Our fealty and Tenantius' right
  With honour to maintain.

First Bro. Like hardiment Posthumus hath
　　　To Cymbeline perform'd :
　　　Then, Jupiter, thou king of gods,
　　　　Why hast thou thus adjourn'd
　　　The graces for his merits due,
　　　　Being all to dolours turn'd?　　　　80

Sici.　　Thy crystal window ope ; look out ;
　　　　No longer exercise
　　　Upon a valiant race thy harsh
　　　　And potent injuries.

Moth.　Since, Jupiter, our son is good,
　　　　Take off his miseries.

Sici.　　Peep through thy marble mansion ; help ;
　　　　Or we poor ghosts will cry
　　　To the shining synod of the rest
　　　　Against thy deity.　　　　90

Both Bro. Help, Jupiter ; or we appeal,
　　　　And from thy justice fly.

JUPITER *descends in thunder and lightning, sitting upon an
　　eagle : he throws a thunderbolt. The Ghosts fall on
　　their knees.*

Jup. No more, you petty spirits of region low,
　　　Offend our hearing ; hush ! How dare you ghosts
　　Accuse the thunderer, whose bolt, you know,
　　　Sky-planted batters all rebelling coasts?
　　Poor shadows of Elysium, hence, and rest
　　　Upon your never-withering banks of flowers :
　　Be not with mortal accidents opprest ;
　　　No care of yours it is ; you know 't is ours.　　　100
　　Whom best I love I cross ; to make my gift,
　　　The more delay'd, delighted. Be content ;
　　Your low-laid son our godhead will uplift :
　　　His comforts thrive, his trials well are spent.
　　Our Jovial star reign'd at his birth, and in
　　　Our temple was he married. Rise, and fade.
　　He shall be lord of lady Imogen,
　　　And happier much by his affliction made.
　　This tablet lay upon his breast, wherein
　　　Our pleasure his full fortune doth confine :　　　110
　　And so, away : no further with your din
　　　Express impatience, lest you stir up mine.
　　Mount, eagle, to my palace crystalline.　　　[*Ascends.*

Sici. He came in thunder; his celestial breath
Was sulphurous to smell: the holy eagle
Stoop'd, as to foot us: his ascension is
More sweet than our blest fields: his royal bird
Prunes the immortal wing and cloys his beak,
As when his god is pleased.
    All.   Thanks, Jupiter!
Sici. The marble pavement closes, he is enter'd   120
His radiant roof. Away! and, to be blest,
Let us with care perform his great behest.
                              [*The Ghosts vanish.*
    Post. [*Waking*] Sleep, thou hast been a grandsire, and
      begot
A father to me; and thou hast created
A mother and two brothers: but, O scorn!
Gone! they went hence so soon as they were born:
And so I am awake. Poor wretches that depend
On greatness' favour dream as I have done,
Wake and find nothing. But, alas, I swerve:
Many dream not to find, neither deserve,   130
And yet are steep'd in favours; so am I,
That have this golden chance and know not why.
What fairies haunt this ground? A book? O rare one!
Be not, as is our fangled world, a garment
Nobler than that it covers: let thy effects
So follow, to be most unlike our courtiers,
As good as promise.

    [*Reads*] 'Whenas a lion's whelp shall, to himself unknown,
without seeking find, and be embraced by a piece of tender
air; and when from a stately cedar shall be lopped branches,
which, being dead many years, shall after revive, be jointed
to the old stock and freshly grow; then shall Posthumus end
his miseries, Britain be fortunate and flourish in peace and
plenty.'   144

'T is still a dream, or else such stuff as madmen
Tongue and brain not; either both or nothing;
Or senseless speaking or a speaking such
As sense cannot untie. Be what it is,
The action of my life is like it, which
I'll keep, if but for sympathy.   150

                Re-enter Gaolers.

    First Gaol. Come, sir, are you ready for death?
    Post. Over-roasted rather; ready long ago.

First Gaol. Hanging is the word, sir: if you be ready for that, you are well cooked.

Post. So, if I prove a good repast to the spectators, the dish pays the shot. 156

First Gaol. A heavy reckoning for you, sir. But the comfort is, you shall be called to no more payments, fear no more tavern-bills; which are often the sadness of parting, as the procuring of mirth: you come in faint for want of meat, depart reeling with too much drink; sorry that you have paid too much, and sorry that you are paid too much; purse and brain both empty; the brain the heavier for being too light, the purse too light, being drawn of heaviness: of this contradiction you shall now be quit. O, the charity of a penny cord! it sums up thousands in a trice: you have no true debitor and creditor but it; of what's past, is, and to come, the discharge: your neck, sir, is pen, book and counters: so the acquittance follows.

Post. I am merrier to die than thou art to live. 170

First Gaol. Indeed, sir, he that sleeps feels not the tooth-ache: but a man that were to sleep your sleep, and a hangman to help him to bed, I think he would change places with his officer; for, look you, sir, you know not which way you shall go.

Post. Yes, indeed do I, fellow.

First Gaol. Your death has eyes in's head then; I have not seen him so pictured: you must either be directed by some that take upon them to know, or to take upon yourself that which I am sure you do not know, or jump the after inquiry on your own peril: and how you shall speed in your journey's end, I think you'll never return to tell one. 182

Post. I tell thee, fellow, there are none want eyes to direct them the way I am going, but such as wink and will not use them.

First Gaol. What an infinite mock is this, that a man should have the best of eyes to see the way of blindness! I am sure hanging's the way of winking.

Enter a Messenger.

Mess. Knock off his manacles; bring your prisoner to the king. 190

Post. Thou bring'st good news; I am called to be made free.

First Gaol. I'll be hang'd then.

Post. Thou shalt be then freer than a gaoler; no bolts for the dead. [*Exeunt all but the First Gaoler.*

First Gaol. Unless a man would marry a gallows and
beget young gibbets, I never saw one so prone. Yet, on
my conscience, there are verier knaves desire to live, for all
he be a Roman: and there be some of them too that die
against their wills; so should I, if I were one. I would we
were all of one mind, and one mind good; O, there were
desolation of gaolers and gallowses! I speak against my
present profit, but my wish hath a preferment in 't. [*Exit.* 203

SCENE V. *Cymbeline's tent.*

Enter CYMBELINE, BELARIUS, GUIDERIUS, ARVIRAGUS,
PISANIO, Lords, Officers, *and* Attendants.

Cym. Stand by my side, you whom the gods have made
Preservers of my throne. Woe is my heart
That the poor soldier that so richly fought,
Whose rags shamed gilded arms, whose naked breast
Stepp'd before targes of proof, cannot be found:
He shall be happy that can find him, if
Our grace can make him so.
　　　Bel. 　　　　　　　I never saw
Such noble fury in so poor a thing;
Such precious deeds in one that promised nought
But beggary and poor looks.
　　　Cym. 　　　　　　No tidings of him? 　　10
Pis. He hath been search'd among the dead and living,
But no trace of him.
　　　Cym. 　　　　To my grief, I am
The heir of his reward; [*To Belarius, Guiderius, and Arvi-
ragus*] which I will add
To you, the liver, heart and brain of Britain,
By whom I grant she lives. 'T is now the time
To ask of whence you are. Report it.
　　　Bel. 　　　　　　　Sir,
In Cambria are we born, and gentlemen:
Further to boast were neither true nor modest,
Unless I add, we are honest.
　　　Cym. 　　　　　　Bow your knees.
Arise my knights o' the battle: I create you 　　20
Companions to our person and will fit you
With dignities becoming your estates.

Enter CORNELIUS *and* Ladies.

There 's business in these faces. Why so sadly

Greet you our victory? you look like Romans,
And not o' the court of Britain.
   Cor.   Hail, great king!
To sour your happiness, I must report
The queen is dead.
   Cym.   Who worse than a physician
Would this report become?   But I consider,
By medicine life may be prolong'd, yet death
Will seize the doctor too.   How ended she?   30
   Cor. With horror, madly dying, like her life,
Which, being cruel to the world, concluded
Most cruel to herself.   What she confess'd
I will report, so please you: these her women
Can trip me, if I err; who with wet cheeks
Were present when she finish'd.
   Cym.   Prithee, say.
   Cor. First, she confess'd she never loved you, only
Affected greatness got by you, not you:
Married your royalty, was wife to your place;
Abhorr'd your person.
   Cym.   She alone knew this;   40
And, but she spoke it dying, I would not
Believe her lips in opening it.   Proceed.
   Cor. Your daughter, whom she bore in hand to love
With such integrity, she did confess
Was as a scorpion to her sight; whose life,
But that her flight prevented it, she had
Ta'en off by poison.
   Cym.   O most delicate fiend!
Who is 't can read a woman?   Is there more?
   Cor. More, sir, and worse.   She did confess she had
For you a mortal mineral; which, being took,   50
Should by the minute feed on life and lingering
By inches waste you: in which time she purposed,
By watching, weeping, tendance, kissing, to
O'ercome you with her show, and in time,
When she had fitted you with her craft, to work
Her son into the adoption of the crown:
But, failing of her end by his strange absence,
Grew shameless-desperate; open'd, in despite
Of heaven and men, her purposes; repented
The evils she hatch'd were not effected; so   60
Despairing died.
   Cym.   Heard you all this, her women?
  First Lady. We did, so please your highness.

Cym.   Mine eyes
Were not in fault, for she was beautiful; ·
Mine ears, that heard her flattery; nor my heart,
That thought her like her seeming; it had been vicious
To have mistrusted her: yet, O my daughter!
That it was folly in me, thou mayst say,
And prove it in thy feeling.   Heaven mend all!

Enter LUCIUS, IACHIMO, *the* Soothsayer, *and other* Roman
     Prisoners, *guarded*; POSTHUMUS *behind, and* IMOGEN.

Thou comest not, Caius, now for tribute; that
The Britons have razed out, though with the loss   70
Of many a bold one; whose kinsmen have made suit
That their good souls may be appeased with slaughter
Of you their captives, which ourself have granted:
So think of your estate.
     Luc. Consider, sir, the chance of war: the day
Was yours by accident; had it gone with us,
We should not, when the blood was cool, have threaten'd
Our prisoners with the sword.   But since the gods
Will have it thus, that nothing but our lives
May be call'd ransom, let it come: sufficeth   80
A Roman with a Roman's heart can suffer:
Augustus lives to think on 't: and so much
For my peculiar care.   This one thing only
I will entreat; my boy, a Briton born,
Let him be ransom'd: never master had
A page so kind, so duteous, diligent,
So tender over his occasions, true,
So feat, so nurse-like: let his virtue join
With my request, which I 'll make bold your highness
Cannot deny; he hath done no Briton harm,   90
Though he have served a Roman: save him, sir,
And spare no blood beside.
     Cym.   I have surely seen him:
His favour is familiar to me.   Boy,
Thou hast look'd thyself into my grace,
And art mine own.   I know not why nor wherefore
To say 'live, boy:' ne'er thank thy master; live:
And ask of Cymbeline what boon thou wilt,
Fitting my bounty and thy state, I 'll give it;
Yea, though thou do demand a prisoner,
The noblest ta'en.
     Imo.   I humbly thank your highness.   100

Luc. I do not bid thee beg my life, good lad;
And yet I know thou wilt.
Imo.   No, no: alack,
There's other work in hand: I see a thing
Bitter to me as death: your life, good master,
Must shuffle for itself.
Luc.   The boy disdains me,
He leaves me, scorns me: briefly die their joys
That place them on the truth of girls and boys.
Why stands he so perplex'd?
Cym.   What wouldst thou, boy?
I love thee more and more: think more and more
What's best to ask.   Know'st him thou look'st on? speak,
Wilt have him live?   Is he thy kin? thy friend?   111
Imo. He is a Roman; no more kin to me
Than I to your highness; who, being born your vassal,
Am something nearer.
Cym.   Wherefore eyest him so?
Imo. I 'll tell you, sir, in private, if you please
To give me hearing.
Cym.   Ay, with all my heart,
And lend my best attention.   What's thy name?
Imo. Fidele, sir.
Cym.   Thou 'rt my good youth, my page;
I 'll be thy master: walk with me; speak freely.
                         [*Cymbeline and Imogen converse apart.*
Bel. Is not this boy revived from death?
Arv.   One sand another
Not more resembles that sweet rosy lad   121
Who died, and was Fidele.   What think you?
Gui. The same dead thing alive.
Bel. Peace, peace! see further; he eyes us not; forbear;
Creatures may be alike: were 't he, I am sure
He would have spoke to us.
Gui.   But we saw him dead.
Bel. Be silent; let's see further.
Pis.   [*Aside*] It is my mistress:
Since she is living, let the time run on
To good or bad.   [*Cymbeline and Imogen come forward.*
Cym.   Come, stand thou by our side;
Make thy demand aloud. [*To Iachimo*] Sir, step you forth;
Give answer to this boy, and do it freely;   131
Or, by our greatness and the grace of it,
Which is our honour, bitter torture shall
Winnow the truth from falsehood.   On, speak to him.

Imo. My boon is, that this gentleman may render
Of whom he had this ring.
    Post.   [*Aside*] What's that to him?
    Cym. That diamond upon your finger, say
How came it yours?
    Iach. Thou'lt torture me to leave unspoken that
Which, to be spoke, would torture thee.
    Cym.   How! me?   140
    Iach. I am glad to be constrain'd to utter that
Which torments me to conceal. By villany
I got this ring: 't was Leonatus' jewel;
Whom thou didst banish; and—which more may grieve thee,
As it doth me—a nobler sir ne'er lived
'Twixt sky and ground. Wilt thou hear more, my lord?
    Cym. All that belongs to this.
    Iach.   That paragon, thy daughter,—
For whom my heart drops blood, and my false spirits
Quail to remember— Give me leave; I faint.
    Cym. My daughter! what of her? Renew thy strength.:
I had rather thou shouldst live while nature will   151
Than die ere I hear more: strive, man, and speak.
    Iach. Upon a time,—unhappy was the clock
That struck the hour!—it was in Rome,—accursed
The mansion where!—'t was at a feast,—O, would
Our viands had been poison'd, or at least
Those which I heaved to head!—the good Posthumus—
What should I say? he was too good to be
Where ill men were; and was the best of all
Amongst the rarest of good ones,—sitting sadly,   160
Hearing us praise our loves of Italy
For beauty that made barren the swell'd boast
Of him that best could speak, for feature, laming
The shrine of Venus, or straight-pight Minerva,
Postures beyond brief nature, for condition,
A shop of all the qualities that man
Loves woman for, besides that hook of wiving,
Fairness which strikes the eye—
    Cym.   I stand on fire:
Come to the matter.
    Iach.   All too soon I shall,
Unless thou wouldst grieve quickly. This Posthumus, 170
Most like a noble lord in love and one
That had a royal lover, took his hint;
And, not dispraising whom we praised,—therein
He was as calm as virtue—he began

His mistress' picture; which by his tongue being made,
And then a mind put in 't, either our brags
Were crack'd of kitchen-trulls, or his description
Proved us unspeaking sots.
　　Cym.　　　　　　　　Nay, nay, to the purpose.
　　Iach. Your daughter's chastity—there it begins.
He spake of her, as Dian had hot dreams,　　　　　180
And she alone were cold: whereat I, wretch,
Made scruple of his praise; and wager'd with him
Pieces of gold 'gainst this which then he wore
Upon his honour'd finger, to attain
In suit the place of 's bed and win this ring
By hers and mine adultery.　He, true knight,
No lesser of her honour confident
Than I did truly find her, stakes this ring;
And would so, had it been a carbuncle
Of Phœbus' wheel, and might so safely, had it　　　190
Been all the worth of 's car.　Away to Britain
Post I in this design: well may you, sir,
Remember me at court; where I was taught
Of your chaste daughter the wide difference
'Twixt amorous and villanous.　Being thus quench'd
Of hope, not longing, mine Italian brain
'Gan in your duller Britain operate
Most vilely; for my vantage, excellent:
And, to be brief, my practice so prevail'd,
That I return'd with simular proof enough　　　200
To make the noble Leonatus mad,
By wounding his belief in her renown
With tokens thus, and thus; averring notes
Of chamber-hanging, pictures, this her bracelet,—
O cunning, how I got it!—nay, some marks
Of secret on her person, that he could not
But think her bond of chastity quite crack'd,
I having ta'en the forfeit.　Whereupon—
Methinks, I see him now—
　　Post.　　　[*Advancing*]　Ay, so thou dost,
Italian fiend!　Ay me, most credulous fool,　　　210
Egregious murderer, thief, any thing
That 's due to all the villains past, in being,
To come!　O, give me cord, or knife, or poison,
Some upright justicer.　Thou, king, send out
For torturers ingenious: it is I
That all the abhorred things o' the earth amend
By being worse than they.　I am Posthumus,

That kill'd thy daughter:—villain-like, I lie—
That caused a lesser villain than myself,
A sacrilegious thief, to do 't: the temple   220
Of virtue was she; yea, and she herself.
Spit, and throw stones, cast mire upon me, set
The dogs o' the street to bay me: every villain
Be call'd Posthumus Leonatus; and
Be villany less than 't was! O Imogen!
My queen, my life, my wife! O Imogen,
Imogen, Imogen!
   Imo.   Peace, my lord; hear, hear—
   Post. Shall's have a play of this? Thou scornful page,
There lie thy part.   [*Striking her: she falls.*
   Pis.   O, gentlemen, help!
Mine and your mistress! O, my lord Posthumus!   230
You ne'er kill'd Imogen till now. Help, help!
Mine honour'd lady!
   Cym.   Does the world go round?
   Post. How come these staggers on me?
   Pis.   Wake, my mistress!
   Cym. If this be so, the gods do mean to strike me
To death with mortal joy.
   Pis.   How fares my mistress?
   Imo. O, get thee from my sight;
Thou gavest me poison: dangerous fellow, hence!
Breathe not where princes are.
   Cym.   The tune of Imogen!
   Pis. Lady,
The gods throw stones of sulphur on me, if   240
That box I gave you was not thought by me
A precious thing: I had it from the queen.
   Cym. New matter still?
   Imo.   It poison'd me.
   Cor.   O gods!
I left out one thing which the queen confess'd,
Which must approve thee honest: 'If Pisanio
Have' said she 'given his mistress that confection
Which I gave him for cordial, she is served
As I would serve a rat.'
   Cym.   What's this, Cornelius?
   Cor. The queen, sir, very oft importuned me
To temper poisons for her, still pretending   250
The satisfaction of her knowledge only
In killing creatures vile, as cats and dogs,
Of no esteem: I, dreading that her purpose

Was of more danger, did compound for her
A certain stuff, which, being ta'en, would cease
The present power of life, but in short time
All offices of nature should again
Do their due functions.   Have you ta'en of it?
  Imo. Most like I did, for I was dead.
  Bel.   My boys,
There was our error.
  Gui.   This is, sure, Fidele.   260
  Imo. Why did you throw your wedded lady from you?
Think that you are upon a rock; and now
Throw me again.   *[Embracing him.*
  Post.   Hang there like fruit, my soul,
Till the tree die!
  Cym.   How now, my flesh, my child!
What, makest thou me a dullard in this act?
Wilt thou not speak to me?
  Imo.   *[Kneeling]* Your blessing, sir.
  Bel. [*To Guiderius and Arviragus*] Though you did love
    this youth, I blame ye not;
You had a motive for't.
  Cym.   My tears that fall
Prove holy water on thee!   Imogen,
Thy mother's dead.
  Imo.   I am sorry for't, my lord.   270
  Cym. O, she was naught; and long of her it was
That we meet here so strangely: but her son
Is gone, we know not how nor where.
  Pis.   My lord,
Now fear is from me, I'll speak troth.   Lord Cloten,
Upon my lady's missing, came to me
With his sword drawn; foam'd at the mouth, and swore
If I discover'd not which way she was gone,
It was my instant death.   By accident,
I had a feigned letter of my master's
Then in my pocket; which directed him   280
To seek her on the mountains near to Milford;
Where, in a frenzy, in my master's garments,
Which he enforced from me, away he posts
With unchaste purpose and with oath to violate
My lady's honour: what became of him
I further know not.
  Gui.   Let me end the story:
I slew him there.
  Cym.   Marry, the gods forfend!

I would not thy good deeds should from my lips
Pluck a hard sentence: prithee, valiant youth,
Deny't again.
  Gui.   I have spoke it, and I did it.   290
  Cym. He was a prince.
  Gui. A most incivil one: the wrongs he did me
Were nothing prince-like; for he did provoke me
With language that would make me spurn the sea,
If it could so roar to me: I cut off's head;
And am right glad he is not standing here
To tell this tale of mine.
  Cym.   I am sorry for thee:
By thine own tongue thou art condemn'd, and must
Endure our law: thou 'rt dead.
  Imo.   That headless man
I thought had been my lord.
  Cym.   Bind the offender,   300
And take him from our presence.
  Bel.   Stay, sir king:
This man is better than the man he slew,
As well descended as thyself; and hath
More of thee merited than a band of Clotens
Had ever scar for. [*To the Guard*] Let his arms alone;
They were not born for bondage.
  Cym.   Why, old soldier,
Wilt thou undo the worth thou art unpaid for,
By tasting of our wrath? How of descent
As good as we?
  Arv.   In that he spake too far.
  Cym. And thou shalt die for't.
  Bel.   We will die all three, 310
But I will prove that two on's are as good
As I have given out him. My sons, I must,
For mine own part, unfold a dangerous speech,
Though, haply, well for you.
  Arv.   Your danger's ours.
  Gui. And our good his.
  Bel.   Have at it then, by leave.
Thou hadst, great king, a subject who
Was call'd Belarius.
  Cym.   What of him? he is
A banish'd traitor.
  Bel.   He it is that hath
Assumed this age; indeed a banish'd man;
I know not how a traitor.

Cym.						Take him hence:					320
The whole world shall not save him.
   Bel.						Not too hot:
First pay me for the nursing of thy sons;
And let it be confiscate all, so soon
As I have received it.
   Cym.					Nursing of my sons!
   Bel. I am too blunt and saucy: here's my knee:
Ere I arise, I will prefer my sons;
Then spare not the old father.	Mighty sir,
These two young gentlemen, that call me father
And think they are my sons, are none of mine;
They are the issue of your loins, my liege,					330
And blood of your begetting.
   Cym.					How! my issue!
   Bel. So sure as you your father's.	I, old Morgan,
Am that Belarius whom you sometime banish'd:
Your pleasure was my mere offence, my punishment
Itself, and all my treason; that I suffer'd
Was all the harm I did.	These gentle princes—
For such and so they are—these twenty years
Have I train'd up: those arts they have as I
Could put into them; my breeding was, sir, as
Your highness knows.	Their nurse, Euriphile,					340
Whom for the theft I wedded, stole these children
Upon my banishment: I moved her to 't,
Having received the punishment before,
For that which I did then: beaten for loyalty
Excited me to treason: their dear loss,
The more of you 't was felt, the more it shaped
Unto my end of stealing them.	But, gracious sir,
Here are your sons again; and I must lose
Two of the sweet'st companions in the world.
The benediction of these covering heavens					350
Fall on their heads like dew! for they are worthy
To inlay heaven with stars.
   Cym.					Thou weep'st, and speak'st.
The service that you three have done is more
Unlike than this thou tell'st.	I lost my children:
If these be they, I know not how to wish
A pair of worthier sons.
   Bel.					Be pleased awhile.
This gentleman, whom I call Polydore,
Most worthy prince, as yours, is true Guiderius:
This gentleman, my Cadwal, Arviragus,

Your younger princely son: he, sir, was lapp'd   360
In a most curious mantle, wrought by the hand
Of his queen mother, which for more probation
I can with ease produce.
  Cym.   Guiderius had
Upon his neck a mole, a sanguine star;
It was a mark of wonder.
  Bel.   This is he;
Who hath upon him still that natural stamp:
It was wise nature's end in the donation,
To be his evidence now.
  Cym.   O, what, am I
A mother to the birth of three? Ne'er mother
Rejoiced deliverance more. Blest pray you be,   370
That, after this strange starting from your orbs,
You may reign in them now! O Imogen,
Thou hast lost by this a kingdom.
  Imo.   No, my lord;
I have got two worlds by 't. O my gentle brothers,
Have we thus met? O, never say hereafter
But I am truest speaker: you call'd me brother,
When I was but your sister; I you brothers,
When ye were so indeed.
  Cym.   Did you e'er meet?
  Arv. Ay, my good lord.
  Gui.   And at first meeting loved;
Continued so, until we thought he died.   380
  Cor. By the queen's dram she swallow'd.
  Cym.   O rare instinct!
When shall I hear all through? This fierce abridgement
Hath to it circumstantial branches, which
Distinction should be rich in. Where? how lived you?
And when came you to serve our Roman captive?
How parted with your brothers? how first met them?
Why fled you from the court? and whither? These,
And your three motives to the battle, with
I know not how much more, should be demanded;
And all the other by-dependencies,   390
From chance to chance: but nor the time nor place
Will serve our long inter'gatories. See,
Posthumus anchors upon Imogen,
And she, like harmless lightning, throws her eye
On him, her brothers, me, her master, hitting
Each object with a joy: the counterchange
Is severally in all. Let's quit this ground,

And smoke the temple with our sacrifices.
[*To Belarius*] Thou art my brother; so we'll hold thee ever.
    Imo. You are my father too, and did relieve me,   400
To see this gracious season.
    Cym.   All o'erjoy'd,
Save these in bonds: let them be joyful too,
For they shall taste our comfort.
    Imo.   My good master,
I will yet do you service.
    Luc.   Happy be you!
    Cym. The forlorn soldier, that so nobly fought,
He would have well becomed this place, and graced
The thankings of a king.
    Post.   I am, sir,
The soldier that did company these three
In poor beseeming; 't was a fitment for
The purpose I then follow'd. That I was he,   410
Speak, Iachimo: I had you down and might
Have made you finish.
    Iach. [*Kneeling*] I am down again:
But now my heavy conscience sinks my knee,
As then your force did. Take that life, beseech you,
Which I so often owe: but your ring first;
And here the bracelet of the truest princess
That ever swore her faith.
    Post.   Kneel not to me:
The power that I have on you is to spare you;
The malice towards you to forgive you: live,
And deal with others better.
    Cym.   Nobly doom'd!   420
We'll learn our freeness of a son-in-law;
Pardon's the word to all.
    Arv.   You holp us, sir,
As you did mean indeed to be our brother;
Joy'd are we that you are.
    Post. Your servant, princes. Good my lord of Rome,
Call forth your soothsayer: as I slept, methought
Great Jupiter, upon his eagle back'd,
Appear'd to me, with other spritely shows
Of mine own kindred: when I waked, I found
This label on my bosom; whose containing   430
Is so from sense in hardness, that I can
Make no collection of it: let him show
His skill in the construction.
    Luc.   Philarmonus:

Sooth. Here, my good lord.
Luc.   Read, and declare the meaning.
Sooth. [*Reads*] 'When a lion's whelp shall, to himself
unknown, without seeking find, and be embraced by a piece
of tender air; and when from a stately cedar shall be lopped
branches, which, being dead many years, shall after revive,
be jointed to the old stock, and freshly grow; then shall
Posthumus end his miseries, Britain be fortunate and flourish
in peace and plenty.'   441
Thou, Leonatus, art the lion's whelp;
The fit and apt construction of thy name,
Being Leo-natus, doth impart so much.
[*To Cymbeline*] The piece of tender air, thy virtuous daughter,
Which we call 'mollis aer'; and 'mollis aer'
We term it 'mulier': which 'mulier' I divine
Is this most constant wife; who, even now,
Answering the letter of the oracle,
Unknown to you, unsought, were clipp'd about   450
With this most tender air.
Cym.   This hath some seeming.
Sooth. The lofty cedar, royal Cymbeline,
Personates thee: and thy lopp'd branches point
Thy two sons forth; who, by Belarius stol'n,
For many years thought dead, are now revived,
To the majestic cedar join'd, whose issue
Promises Britain peace and plenty.
Cym.   Well;
My peace we will begin. And, Caius Lucius,
Although the victor, we submit to Cæsar,
And to the Roman empire; promising   460
To pay our wonted tribute, from the which
We were dissuaded by our wicked queen;
Whom heavens, in justice, both on her and hers,
Have laid most heavy hand.
Sooth. The fingers of the powers above do tune
The harmony of this peace. The vision
Which I made known to Lucius, ere the stroke
Of this yet scarce-cold battle, at this instant
Is full accomplish'd; for the Roman eagle,
From south to west on wing soaring aloft,   470
Lessen'd herself, and in the beams o' the sun
So vanish'd: which foreshow'd our princely eagle,
The imperial Cæsar, should again unite
His favour with the radiant Cymbeline,
Which shines here in the west.

Cym.   Laud we the gods;
And let our crooked smokes climb to their nostrils
From our blest altars.   Publish we this peace
To all our subjects.   Set we forward: let
A Roman and a British ensign wave
Friendly together: so through Lud's town march: 480
And in the temple of great Jupiter
Our peace we'll ratify; seal it with feasts.
Set on there!   Never was a war did cease,
Ere bloody hands were wash'd, with such a peace.   [*Exeunt.*

NOTES

For single words, on which no note is given here, reference must be made to the Glossary. A word that occurs several times in the same sense is usually annotated only once, and the note on it can be found by reference to the Index. Students must bear in mind that no two words are synonymous; and therefore, rather than place too much reliance on the explanations here given, they should cultivate a sympathetic feeling for the meaning of words and passages.

"F 1" denotes a reading of the First Folio (1623); "Ff." the reading of *at least* the first two Folios. Only *verbal* emendations of the readings of the Folios are called attention to, not changes in spelling, punctuation, or arrangement of lines (see note on i. 1. 1). "*Abbott*" stands for the third edition of Dr. Abbott's *Shakespearian Grammar*. References to other plays of Shakespeare are to act, scene, and line of the Globe edition.

Time-analysis of the play by Mr. P. A. Daniel.[1]

"The time of the drama includes twelve days represented on the stage; with intervals.

Day 1. Act I. sc. i.–iii.
        An Interval.   Posthumus's journey to Rome.

„   2. Act I. sc. iv.
        An Interval.   Iachimo's journey to Britain.

„   3. Act I. sc. v. and vi., Act II. sc. i. and part of sc. ii.

„   4. Act II. sc. ii., in part, and sc. iii. [Act III. sc. i. also belongs to this day].
        An Interval.   Iachimo's return journey to Rome.

„   5. Act II. sc. iv. and v.
        An Interval.   Time for Posthumus's letters from Rome to arrive in Britain.
        [Act III. sc. i.   See Day No. 4.]

    6. Act III. sc. ii. and iii.
        An Interval, including one clear day.   Imogen and Pisanio journey to Wales.

„   7. Act III. sc. iv.
        An Interval, including one clear day.   Pisanio returns to court.

---

[1] *Transactions of New Shakspere Society*, 1877-79, p. 247.

Day 8. Act III. sc. v. and vi.
   [Act III. sc. vii. In Rome. Time, between Days 5 and 6.]
   An Interval, including one clear day. Cloten journeys
    to Wales.
„ 9. Act IV. sc. i. and ii.
   An Interval—a few days perhaps.
„ 10. Act IV. sc. iii.
„ 11. Act IV. sc. iv.
„ 12. Act V."

Title.   "The Tragedie of Cymbeline."   Ff.

DRAMATIS PERSONÆ

Cymbeline.   See Appendix B.

Cloten.   In *Holinshed,* Mulmucius (iii. 1. 53, 57) is "the son of Cloton ".   See Appendix B.

Posthúmus Leonatus. Posthumus is accented on the second syllable, except in iv. 2. 320, where the accent is on the first.   The name was given him by Cymbeline because he was a *posthumous* child, *i.e.* born after the death of his father.   See i. 1. 40 ff. Posthumus in Holinshed is another name of Ascanius, son of Æneas (edition of 1807–8, i. 437).   It is a singular fact that the opening stage-direction of *Much Ado,* in the quarto of 1600, runs: "Enter Leonato [and] Innogen his wife ".   Leonato is governor of Messina in that play, but his only feminine relatives are his daughter Hero and his niece Beatrice.   Shakespeare may have taken the name Leonatus from Sidney's *Arcadia.*

Guiderius.   } These names are taken from
Arvirágus (iii. 3. 96; v. 5. 359). }   Holinshed (see Appendix B), as are also, I have no doubt, the assumed names, *Polydore, Cadwal,* and *Morgan.*   Margan and Cunedag are nephews of "Cordeilla", youngest daughter of Lear.   "Cunedag came into Cambria, now called Wales, where the said Margan gave him eftsoons a new battle: but being too weak in number of men, he was there overcome and slain in the field, by reason whereof that country took name of him, being there slain, and so is called to this day Glau Margan, which is to mean in our English tongue, Margan's land" (*Holinshed,* 1807–8, i. 448).   Polydore Vergil, a Latin chronicler under the first Tudors, is one of Holinshed's authorities, and as such the name "Polydor" often occurs in the margin.   "Cadwallo" in Holinshed (*ib.* i. 610) is the British king Cadwalla, who slew Edwin, king of Northumbria, in 633 (see the *Anglo-Saxon Chronicle* under that year).   Shakespeare may have taken a hint from Holinshed for the characters of Guiderius and Arviragus, "This Guiderius being a man of stout courage" (*ib.* i. 480), and of Arviragus: "He bare himself right manfully against Claudius and his Romans" (*ib.* i. 484).

Lucius, in Holinshed (*ib.* i. 511), is the name of a king of Britain. The invasion of Caius Lucius is Shakespeare's invention.

Imogen.   In Holinshed, Innogen is the wife of Brute or Brutus, the great-grandson of Æneas (*ib.* i. 439).

Act I.—Scene I.

The date of the commencement of the play is A.D. 16, the twenty-fourth year of Cymbeline, the forty-second of Augustus.—*Fleay.*

"The two Gentlemen give us information while the action waits" (*Herford*).   They tell the audience and ourselves many things necessary for the understanding of the play: that Cymbeline, a widower with an only daughter, Imogen, has lately married a widow with an only son, Cloten; that their designs for securing the joint succession of this son and daughter by wedding them to each other have been frustrated by the marriage of Imogen and Posthumus Leonatus (a posthumous son of a famous British warrior, Sicilius Leonatus), who had been "bred as Imogen's playfellow" and made a gentleman of the bed-chamber; that in consequence of this marriage Posthumus is about to leave the court, a banished man; and that Cymbeline's only other children were two sons, who had been stolen twenty years ago, the elder being then three years old, and had never been heard of since.

Here the first scene ended in the Folios, and I should have adhered to this arrangement but for the inconvenience of departing from the Globe division.   It would then be a solitary instance, it is true, of a first scene in Shakespeare fulfilling the function of Prologue, giving information without action; but that might be merely one of the signs of the dramatic laxity referred to in the "History and Date of the Play" (Introduction, p. ix).

The remainder of the scene shows us Posthumus and Imogen taking a fond farewell and exchanging Mizpah-tokens, a ring and a bracelet; interrupted by the Queen, who is Imogen's jailer, and who, while feigning sympathetic indulgence for the young pair, reveals her true disposition by drawing the king to the spot, to dismiss Posthumus abruptly and rail at his daughter.

As already implied, this play is divided into acts and scenes in the Folios.

1–7.   The opening lines appear in F 1 as follows:—

> 1 *Gent.*
> You do not meet a man but Frownes.
> Our bloods no more obey the Heauens
> Then our Courtiers:
> Still seeme. as do's the Kings.
>   2 *Gent.*   But what's the matter?
>   1.   His daughter, and the heire of 's kingdome (whom
> He purpos'd to his wiues sole Sonne, a Widdow

> That late he married) hath referr'd her selfe
> Vnto a poore, but worthy Gentleman.

1. bloods, dispositions.

2. No, not. This is the key to the meaning of the sentence, as is clear from ll. 13, 14 below:

> " they wear their faces to the bent
> Of the king's looks ".

Every face reflects the frown on the king's brow (at his daughter's marriage) as unvaryingly as our dispositions are obedient to heavenly influences (in accordance with mediæval superstition).

An antithesis of the blood—which was supposed not to be in our own power, but to be dependent on the influences of the heavenly bodies—and the countenances, which are in our power really, though from flattery we bring them into a no less apparent dependence upon the sovereign, than the former are in actual dependence on the constellations.—*Coleridge.*

3. king, Tyrwhitt; *kings,* Ff.

6, 7. referr'd herself Unto, bestowed her hand upon; possibly an affectation of speech in keeping with much that follows.

10. touch'd at very heart, by the failure of his marriage scheme (ll. 4, 5).

22. In him that should compare, in the one that should be selected for comparison with Posthumus.

24. he. Cf. ii. 3. 145. Strict grammar requires *him,* which would be necessary in any completion of the sentence. In cases where the pronoun would be in the nominative in the completed sentence, modern grammar still hesitates between *he* and *him.* For a see *Abbott,* § 81.

25. My praise, however extensive, is within his merit (*Johnson*). For **extend** cf. i. 4. 18.

29. Sicilius, in *Holinshed* (iii. 5), is a king of Britain.

join. Jervis conjectured *gain. Join* yields good enough sense: he took an honourable part with Cassibelan against the Romans, but won his titles when serving under Tenantius.

31. Tenantius, father of Cymbeline, and son of Lud, whose younger brother Cassibelan had usurped the throne on Lud's death. See Appendix B.

37. fond of issue, doting on his children.

43. time, time of life, years.

47. This encomium is highly artful. To be at once in any great degree loved and praised is truly rare.—*Johnson.*

49. A glass that feated them, a mirror wherein they fashioned themselves. Cf. *2 Henry IV.*, ii. 3. 21, 22:

> "he [Hotspur] was indeed the glass
> Wherein the noble youth did dress themselves".

Unique instance of verb *feat* in Shakespeare. For the adjective, see v. 5. 88; and the Glossary.

50. to his mistress. The *to* is rendered redundant by the *anacoluthon* (the name given to the want of sequence in a sentence, when the latter part does not correspond in construction with the former).

51. For whom, because of his marriage with whom.

her own price, her own worth, not 'the price she put upon him'.

60. no guess [resulting] in knowledge.

63. convey'd, *sc.* away, made away with, kidnapped.

65. That, the relative pronoun, not the conjunction with the subject *it* omitted. See *Abbott*, § 279.

70. Scene 2 began with this line in the Ff. It was made a part of scene 1 by Rowe.

The Queen allows the interview to take place in order that she may bring the king to witness it, and so incense him further against Posthumus. See ll. 103–106.

71. After the slander, in accordance with the slanderous reputation of most stepmothers. Cf. i. 6. 1.

78. lean'd unto his sentence: cf. "to bow to the ruling of the court".

79. inform, suggest to.

84. This is the first indication given of the true character of the Queen, though of course Imogen does not suspect the depths of depravity afterwards revealed. The First Gentleman is too much of a courtier to express to an evident stranger any suspicions he may have had with reference to the Queen, though his scruples do not extend to her son.

88. me: you. The pronouns are emphatic. 'I have no fear for myself beyond what is implied in filial duty.'

104-106. The Queen is both parties in her quarrels with the King, first the offending party, and then receiving every satisfaction from the King, in order to be friends again, as if she were the injured party.

This "Aside" reveals much; the King is seen to be a mere tool in the hands of the Queen.

113. But, only. 'Keep it but till', no longer.

116. sear: probably only another spelling of *cere*, the "bonds of death" being the *cerecloth* (*Merchant of Venice*), or *cerements* (*Hamlet*), a waxed linen shroud. See Glossary.

118. it: by change of person for 'thee'. Other examples of change of person are: i. 6. 112–114; iii. 3. 104, 105; iv. 2. 217, 218; v. i. 3, 4.

119, 120. Cf. ll. 145–147:

> "and he is
> A man worth any woman, overbuys me
> Almost the sum he pays".

The lovers' generous estimate of each other's worth is very fine.

124. see: *sc.* one another. Cf. i. 4. 30: "Sir, we have known together in Orleans". See *Abbott*, § 382. Possibly the idiom is of great antiquity, for we find in the Old English poem of *Beowulf*, l. 1875:

> "ðæt hie seoððan geseon moston",

that they might see [one another] again; and the same expression is found again in an O.E. poem on St. Andrew (l. 1012).

126. fraught, burden. Cf. *Tempest*, i. 2. 13:

> "The fraughting souls within her".

Elsewhere in Shakespeare it is a perf. part. = freighted.

129. the good remainders of the court, the few good people left there.

135. senseless of, insensible to.

touch, feeling: the "sweet pain" of parting with Posthumus deadens her sensibility to all besides.

137. that way, past grace. This appears to me a theological play upon words. The sinner is beyond reach of grace as long as he despairs.

140. puttock, "the glede, a species of kite; also, sometimes, the common buzzard" (*Webster*); a useless bird of prey. See Glossary.

146, 147. overbuys me Almost the sum he pays, pays too much for worthless me by almost the whole of the purchase-money, his precious self.

156. advice, deliberation, reflection.
The Queen wishes to conciliate Imogen, in the hope that she will forget Posthumus and marry Cloten. See i. 5. 49.

157, 158. and, being aged, Die of this folly: which Imogen would no doubt very gladly do. The feebleness of this curse is characteristic.

162. Posthumus evidently *is* a hero to his valet.

167. in Afric, where there would be no one to part them.

172. **Of what commands I should be subject to,** as to the obedience I should render.

176. **walk awhile,** withdraw for a time.

177. **I,** Capell; Ff. omit.

Scene 2.

This scene is introduced to show up Cloten in a character which—to judge by his subsequent conduct—he hardly deserves, that of a conceited coward. The First Lord flatters him too grossly for human credulity, and the Second Lord, by "asides", lampoons him, for the benefit of the groundlings. The allusions are obscure, and the quibbles poor. It would be a relief to know that Shakespeare was not responsible for either this scene, or the first in Act II. Both, however, may be omitted without loss in reading this play.—*Ingleby.*

1-4. **You are reeking like a sacrifice,** and unwholesome cold air is pouring in to take the place of that with which you are favouring the atmosphere; therefore you had better change your shirt.

5, 6. **Have I hurt him?** *i.e.* Posthumus, in their late encounter.

8. **passable,** penetrable without being wounded.

9. **throughfare.** *Through* and *thorough* are variant spellings of the same word. Cf. *Matthew,* iii. 12: "and he will throughly purge his floor".

10, 11. Cloten's sword did not give as good as it got; it slunk away, like a debtor afraid to leave the back streets for fear of imprisonment.

23. **election,** choice; so also i. 1. 53, and i. 6. 167. Here there is probably another theological play upon words.

26. **sign.** (1) Possibly 'the sign of a house or inn', almost all of which, says Steevens, "had a motto or some attempt at a witticism" underneath them. (2) Possibly 'a constellation', in which case *wit* is used in its more common Elizabethan meaning of 'understanding', 'intellect'. This interpretation receives some support from *shines,* in line 28. (3) But *shines* may equally well be suggested by *reflection,* and this is quite in accordance with Shakespeare's way of punning, *reflection* being used by the Second Lord in a different sense from that in which it is used by the First (=radiance). In that case the First Lord simply repeats his first remark in other words—her mental equipments do not correspond with her fair exterior—which is quite as much as we have a right to expect from him.

34. Addressed to the Second Lord.

Scene 3.

Imogen's confidences to Pisanio show how utterly he is trusted by these married lovers; her pretty, clever talk about her husband reveals more fully than we have yet seen it the wonderfully beautiful union of heart and brain that we find in her throughout.

4. **offer'd mercy** has been explained as 'the pardon of a condemned criminal', which does not reach him. To me, the most probable reference is to the Divine mercy, offered and not accepted.

9. **this**, Warburton; *his*, Ff. No altogether satisfactory emendation has been proposed, but the sense seems to be: "As long as I was within ear-shot he called to me; when hearing failed he still waved me his farewells, till I could no longer distinguish him".

12. **fits and stirs**, impulses and movements.

15, 16. **ere left To after-eye him**, ere you ceased to gaze after him. With this sense of *leave*, not uncommon in Shakespeare, cf. Fr. *laisser*: "Ne laissez pas de le surveiller", do not cease to keep an eye on him. Cf. also the absolute use of *leave* in i. 4. 88, and ii. 2. 4.

17. **eye-strings.** These are supposed to be the tendons which move the eye-ball; but in this place the word is more applicable to the nerve-fibres which contract and expand the pupil.—*Ingleby*.

crack'd. To us, *crack'd* is something of an anti-climax after *broke*. But in Shakespeare *crack* was a stronger term than now, as in *Coriolanus*, i. 1. 72:
> "*Cracking* ten thousand curbs
> Of more strong link asunder".

Cf. its intransitive use in iii. 1. 28.

18, 19. **the diminution Of space**, *i.e.* of the space he filled to the eye.

24. **vantage**, opportunity.

29. Cf. iii. 4. 48, 49. For *she*=woman, cf. i. 6. 40, and see *Abbott*, § 224.

32. **encounter me with orisons**, join me in prayers.

33. **or ere**, or before. Here each word has its separate force, whereas in iii. 2. 64; v. 3. 50, and elsewhere in Shakespeare, *or ere* (often incorrectly written *or e'er*) is merely a reduplication of *ere*.

35. **charming words**, words which should have the power of a charm to ward off every kind of evil. The other passages in the play, in which the word occurs—i. 6. 116; iv. 2. 277; v. 3. 32, 68— should be compared with this. In Shakespeare it always retains something of the primary sense it has in this passage, even when it has moved so far towards its modern meaning as in *Twelfth Night*, ii. 2. 19: "Fortune forbid my outside have not charm'd her".

Scene 4.

Verse and Prose. Shakespeare's choice of these two modes of expression is noteworthy. It is mainly determined by two considerations: (*a*) the characters speaking; (*b*) the dominant sentiment or interest of the situation. Since prose is nearer to the language of ordinary life, it is used (*a*) by clowns, servants, and women in familiar conversation; (*b*) whenever the interest is mainly comic, intellectual, or commonplace. Verse is a more ceremonious and conventional mode of speech, and so is used (*a*) by noble persons; (*b*) wherever the interest is mainly emotional, passionate, or imaginative.—*J. C. Smith*, editor of *As You Like It* in the Arden Shakespeare.

This general statement must not be applied too rigidly to any particular play; but it is interesting to note that Cloten evidently finds talking in verse very hard work, for he loses no opportunity of slipping into prose. *The student must observe throughout the play what scenes are written in prose.*

Though the present scene must be felt by the spectator or reader to develop an almost tragic interest, it commences in very commonplace fashion, and would impress us as rather offhand than momentous throughout, were it not for the suspicion that much will depend upon it in the future. It should be compared with the sequel, Act II. sc. 4; there the intense interest demands verse; here the dramatist would have been seriously hampered by it.

Follow the scene carefully after reading the two criticisms below, and try to decide for yourself which critic is in the right. It will perhaps help you to decide if you turn to Iachimo's own account of the matter in v. 5. 153–209 (leave out of sight for the present that his account differs in some unimportant points of fact).

"It is a grievous fault that Posthumus accepts so disgraceful a challenge, and argues defective acumen that he does not discern base motive when it is put upon the footing of a wager for his priceless diamond."—*W. W. Lloyd.*

"The truth is, that Posthumus, under the first shock and provocation of this revolting encounter, behaves both modestly and patiently—'as calm as virtue', according to Iachimo's penitent admission. He does not propose the wager: it is forced upon him by the scoffs and taunts of the Italian; and is accepted at last with a view to punish them,—first, by the repulse which his addresses are sure to sustain,—secondly, by the loss of his property,—and thirdly, by the duel which is to follow. They who have so violently objected against the husband's procedure on this occasion, have judged of it according to the cool, calculating habits of feeling belonging to the modern time,—ignorant of, or overlooking the real character of that chivalric love, that truly religious faith and devotion of the heart, which Shakespeare found it here his business to paint."—*G. Fletcher.*

2. of a crescent note, &c., making his mark, giving promise of earning such a name as he has since been credited with (*unearned*,

Iachimo wishes to imply; observe his depreciatory tone from the first).   For *note* = distinction, cf. i. 6. 22; ii. 3. 121; iii. 3. 58.

4. **without the help of admiration,** without admiring him.

6. **I**: *sc.* had.

11. **could behold the sun**: a reference to the eagle, which, as Milton says in *Areopagitica*, "kindles her undazzl'd eyes at the full midday beam".

13, 14. **words him ... a great deal from the matter,** causes him to be spoken of in a way differing widely from the truth.   Cf. "story", l. 28.   For the pregnant use of *from* cf. v. 5. 431, and see *Abbott*, § 158.

16. This continued disparagement of Posthumus by Iachimo, who is envious of his reputation, makes the rest of the scene appear less forced and unnatural.

17. **under her colours,** of her party.

17, 18. **are wonderfully to extend him,** tend and are intended to give him a reputation far beyond his due.   I incline strongly to justify the plural *are* in the belief that Iachimo takes up the Frenchman's "banishment" into the subject by his approving "ay", and adds to it "the approbation, &c.".   Abbott regards it as an instance of "confusion of proximity"; see § 412.

18, 19. **an easy battery might lay flat,** might easily be impugned.

19, 20. **without less quality,** with no other than a beggar's position.   In support of the truth of Malone's observation, that "whenever *less* or *more* is to be joined with a verb denoting want, or a preposition of a similar import, Shakespeare never fails to be entangled in a grammatical inaccuracy, or rather, to use words that express the very contrary of what he means", many instances might be quoted, *e.g. Lear*, ii. 4. 140–142:

> "I have hope
> You less know how to value her desert
> Than she to scant her duty".

20, 21. **How creeps acquaintance?**   How do you come to be acquainted?

24. **Briton.**   *Britain*, Ff. always, as in Holinshed.

25. **knowing,** experience in society.   Cf. ii. 3. 96.

The stage-direction, "*Enter* POSTHUMUS", occurs in Ff. after "life"; it was shifted to its present position by Dyce.

30. The earlier meeting of the Frenchman and Posthumus in Orleans overcomes the awkwardness of an introduction to a party of strangers.   Besides, the Frenchman revives the memory of a former quarrel, and thus paves the way for the subsequent dispute on a similar ground.

32. **which I will be ever to pay and yet pay still,** for which I shall always be in your debt though never ceasing to return them (*Abbott*, § 405).

36. importance, import, cause.

39. to go even with what I heard is synonymous with 'to be guided by others' experiences'.   For *go even* in this sense cf. *Twelfth Night*, v. 246:

"Were you a woman, as the rest goes even".

The sense is: 'I was then a hot-headed young fellow: I preferred to go my own way rather than &c.'.

41. not.   Ff. omit; inserted by Rowe.

44. such two that.   See *Abbott*, §§ 279, 427.

confounded, destroyed; so often.   Cf. *confusion*, iii. 1. 64. 'One would have destroyed the other, or they would both have fallen.'

49, 50. fell in praise, fell to praising.

50. this gentleman, Posthumus, in the affair at Orleans. Shakespeare introduces the previous night's argument, in which Iachimo had taken part, as another means of easing the approach to the following quarrel.

52. constant-qualified, endowed with constancy: Capell's emendation for *constant, qualified*, Ff.   Ingleby defends the Folio reading, but his justificatory passages contain "*so* qualified", and are therefore not true parallels.

59, 60. though I profess myself her adorer, not her friend has afforded plenty of scope for discussion.   Friend = lover, and the usual explanation is: 'I regard her with the calm devotion of a worshipper, not with the rapt enthusiasm of a lover'; but it is easier to believe that Posthumus uses 'adorer' as a much stronger word than 'friend', and to regard the after-thought, "though... friend", as a concession to the enemy: 'I admit I'm anything but an unprejudiced champion'.

61–63.   The reference is to ll. 52, 53, and 58.   'If Posthumus had said [not "*more* fair", but] "*as* fair and *as* good [as any lady in Italy]"—a comparison wherein beauty and goodness go hand in hand —that would have been beyond the mark for any lady in Britain.'

65. but.   Ff. omit; inserted by Malone.

69.   The value of the ring is of course infinitely enhanced for Posthumus because it was Imogen's gift and the pledge of her love. Notice how the growing heat of the disputants is shown by the pointedness of their speeches, by the dropping of circumlocutions and affectations.

72. if; *or if*, Ff.; *or* omitted by Rowe.

73. purchase, Rowe; *purchases*, Ff.

80. unprizable estimations, things of priceless value.

81. casual, liable to mischance.

81, 82. a that way accomplished courtier. For other "phrase-compounds" see ii. 4. 19, and v. 5. 468, and *Abbott*, § 434.

85. convince, prevail against.

87. fear = fear for, is common in Shakespeare.

90. at first. See *Abbott*, § 90.

93. to friend, for my friend; *Abbott*, § 189.

96. it, your ring.

100. abused, deceived; cf. i. 6. 127; iii. 4. 102, 120.

109. approbation, proof, making good. So *approve* = prove, iv. 2. 380, and v. 5. 245. Cf. *Acts*, ii. 22: "A man approved of God among you by miracles".

111. whom, by a species of attraction, where modern grammar requires *who*. It is one of the numerous remnants of O. E. grammar in Shakespeare.

114. See Introduction, p. xviii.

119. afraid, Warburton; *a Friend*, Ff.

121. religion apparently means 'conscientious scruple' against putting your wife to a test which you can't expect her to stand.

125. undergo, carry out, take upon oneself. Cf. iii. 5. 109.

127. It will be seen, in ii. 3, that Imogen, under similar provocation—the defamation of her husband—loses her self-control in no more dignified fashion than he. It is almost a justification of Posthumus that his conduct on this occasion does not compare unfavourably with his wife's.

132. Observe Iachimo's artful statement of the conditions, something like "heads, you win; tails, I lose"; in reality he states only those conditions which will hold in case of his failure. Posthumus, however, while accepting them, makes the statement complete.

136, 137. your commendation for my more free entertainment, your recommendation to procure me a more cordial welcome.

148. lest the bargain should catch cold and starve, lest the wager which was laid in the heat of the dispute should be declared off, when the disputants have had time for cool reflection.—*Ingleby*.

Scene 5.

This scene is necessary to relieve the tension, and in order to allow Iachimo to reach the court of Cymbeline; otherwise it is rather important for subsequent developments than specially interesting in itself.

15. confections, drugs.   Again, v. 5. 246.

17. did.   For the sequence of tenses see *Abbott*, § 370.

18. conclusions, experiments; still preserved in "to try conclusions".

20. human: always spelt *humane* in the old editions, but with the accent on the first syllable.

22. act, action; often so used.

25. the seeing.   Here, and in l. 41, *the* is a remnant of the old verbal noun construction, "the seeing *of* these effects", from which our so-called gerundial construction was developed.   See *Abbott*, § 93.

26. noisome and infectious, both disgusting to you and dangerous in the way of infection, *i.e.* by their being taken up into her system.—*Deighton.*

32. Hark thee.   Abbott, § 212, regards this *thee*, not as a reflexive pronoun proper, but as a euphonic unemphatic reduction of *thou*, which we have still further reduced to nothing.

39–42.   If Shakespeare had not felt something akin to contempt for vulgar melodramatic effects, he would not have given us this premonition of the result of Imogen's swallowing the Queen's "confection".

42–44.   For passages of the same general tenor see Introduction, p. xxi, and cf. iii. 2. 14, 15.

44. So to be false, by (*or* for) thus being false.   The infinitive was used much more widely in Shakespeare's day than in ours, especially in contexts where we now employ, as here, a gerund governed by a preposition.   As Abbott points out, in Elizabethan English 'to walk' might also denote 'by walking', 'as regards walking', 'for walking', &c.   Thus in l. 58, "To be depender"= from being dependent; in iv. 4. 2, "to lock"=in locking; in v. 3. 28, "But to look back"=by merely looking back; while in iii. 1. 70, "to seek" is best represented by the present participle 'seeking'.
[The student should make for himself lists, which can afterwards be enlarged from other plays, of the chief grammatical and other anomalies, such as, words differently spelt or accented then and now, irregular past participles, &c.]

47. quench, grow cool, or let her grief be quenched.   Abbott says that in Elizabethan, as compared with Victorian English, "Clearness was preferred to grammatical correctness, and brevity both to correctness and clearness".   See the admirable summary of the chief differences between the "Queen's English" of the two periods in the Introduction to his *Shakespearian Grammar.*

54. being, all the conditions of life, including place of abode.

56. decay, spoil, *i.e.* either to prevent him from doing a day's work, or to undo the work of a day earlier in his life.

58. leans, is tottering to its fall.

64. What is more cordial, anything more spirit-reviving.

65. farther, Ff.; when used as an adjective modern editions often change the word to *further.*

68, 69. 'Think on what a chance [of promotion] thou changest (*or* wilt change) [masters]; remember too that thou hast thy same mistress still, and my son to boot.'

73. to this desert, to deserve this.

77, 78. And the remembrancer...lord, and one who reminds her to keep her plighted troth to her lord. *Remembrancer*, in law, was the name of an officer in the exchequer.

79, 80. shall quite unpeople her Of liegers for her sweet, shall deprive her of her husband's only ambassador at this court. "Liegers for her sweet" is a sarcastically exaggerated equivalent of "agent for his master" in l. 76, as if Imogen's "sweet" were a foreign power. For *lieger* see Glossary.

Scene 6.

Here we have Iachimo's sorry and foredoomed attempt to win the wager. He quails at the first sight of Imogen, but, calling "audacity" to his aid, makes a desperate bid for success. Up to a certain point all goes well for him. Starting with an enthusiastic recommendation from Posthumus, he first feigns a fit of abstraction, of which he takes advantage to reflect indirectly on the conduct of Posthumus, and thus awaken Imogen's anxiety, making his insinuations ever less vague; but the inevitable false step comes when he changes his tone to one of direct flattery, and proceeds to "expound his beastly mind" to her. Then her first thought is of her personal danger, her second—of resentment—shows her clear, practical intellect. Iachimo, however, is equal to the occasion, and beats a masterly retreat. His insidious eloquence and Imogen's behaviour deserve equally careful attention: the one is as diabolically clever as the other is magnificently natural.

4. My supreme crown of grief, the greatest and crowning sorrow of that grief, whose lesser tributaries are the three just specified—cruelty, falsity, and folly = "those repeated vexations of it" (*Ingleby*).

6, 7. most miserable Is the desire that's glorious, most miserable are those whose ambition is for glory.

9. Which seasons comfort, the fruition of which, having one's honest will, gives a zest to comfort.—*Abbott*, § 337.

Fie! Imogen is sorry to have her solitude broken in upon.

11. Change you, do you change colour? Imogen's colour changes rapidly from excitement, tremor, expectation of good or bad news.

17. She is alone the Arabian bird, she alone is the phœnix, of which Cynewulf says: "Himself is to himself both son and own dear father". *Alone*, because there was never more than one phœnix.

20. Parthian. The Parthians were a warlike Asiatic tribe living south-east of the Caspian. Their tactics in war became proverbial.

23. tied, bound by the ties of friendship, indebted

	Reflect upon, regard.

24. your trust is either 'my trust in you', or 'your position of trust as my wife'.

27. takes, Pope; *take,* Ff.

31–50. All this is a soliloquy in feigned abstraction; Imogen's interruptions being unheeded. Iachimo begins in the most impersonal way: "What, are *men* mad?" "and can *we* not?". But already in l. 39 he is particularizing, "two such shes", meaning, of course, Imogen and her imaginary rival.

32. crop. Crosby proposed *scope*; I retain *crop*, which I take to be a bold metaphor for the wide expanse or prospect of sea and land, suggesting the thought of a harvest. The general sense is: Cannot the eyes, which can take in the whole of heaven and earth at one sweep, and, on the other hand, can distinguish two objects, in heaven or earth, almost exactly alike,—cannot they distinguish fair and foul?

34. twinn'd stones refers to the likeness, as of twins, between the stones on the beach.

35. number'd, numerous, containing a great number. "It seems to be intended to bring the multitude of similar stones on the beach into comparison with the multitude of similar stars in the sky. Men's eyes can distinguish the stars from one another and the stones likewise, though both are so numerous and so much alike." Theobald proposed *th' unnumber'd* = the innumerable.

36. spectacles, organs of vision, eyes.

37. admiration, in its classical sense of 'wonder'.

38. It cannot be i' the eye, such perversity of choice cannot be the eye's fault.

41. in this case of favour, in judging of grace, charm. Beauty appeals to the eye, grace to the judgment, daintiness of appearance to the appetite. In iii. 4. 48 and iv. 2. 104 *favour* = personal appearance.

44, 45. 'Instead of tempting the appetite, would nauseate and produce retching from an empty stomach.' The sensation is familiar to bad sailors. *Should* and *would*, *shall* and *will*, are frequently interchanged, as here, in i. 4. 35, and iv. 3. 18.

46. trow: from *I trow* = I wonder, originally 'I believe'; thence the stages must have been 'I suppose', 'I guess', 'I doubt', 'I wonder'.

52. Desire, seek out. Iachimo takes the necessary precaution of getting Pisanio out of the way by sending him on a feigned errand.

53. strange and peevish, strange to the place and foolish. *Peevish* usually = foolish, simple, silly in Shakespeare; cf. *Richard III.*, iii. 1. 31:

　　"What an indirect and peevish course".

58. none a stranger there. Abbott (§§ 53, 85) considers that *none* here has adverbial force, = ne'er a stranger. To punctuate thus, "none, a stranger there", would be a simpler explanation.

65. furnaces. Abbott says that in Elizabethan English "almost any part of speech can be used as any other part of speech…Any noun, adjective, or neuter verb can be used as an active verb". Among nouns and adjectives used as transitive verbs in this play he mentions (§ 290): *furnace, foot* (iii. 5. 138), *tongue*, and *brain* (v. 4. 146).

67. from 's free lungs, freely, heartily.

71. his free hours, *sc.* during; accusative of duration of time.

78–81. In himself…pity too. 'As regards himself alone he is greatly to blame; as regards you, whom I must suppose to be irredeemably his, his conduct amazes me and fills me with pity.' This is, I believe, the meaning of this difficult sentence. Most recent editors punctuate line 79 thus:

　　"In you, which I account his, beyond all talents".

This makes the passage yield a totally different meaning, as in the following paraphrase (Deighton's): 'Heaven's bounty to him is abundant in regard to what is inherent in himself (*e.g.* noble descent, heroic character, manifold accomplishments), while in regard to you, whom I look upon as belonging to him, it is beyond all limit; but while I am on this account compelled to wonder, I am also compelled to pity'.

83. wreck: *wrack*, Ff. always.
For the omission of the relative pronoun see *Abbott*, § 244.

85. me, pleonastic.

94. doubting things go ill, the fear that things are going wrong. Cf. *doubt* in iv. 4. 14.

96. timely knowing, being known in time. *Knowing*, as if the subject of the sentence were 'we' or 'I', is a good example of an "unrelated participle".

98. What both you spur and stop, the information which (like a horse) you both urge onward and rein in.

101. this object, Imogen's beautiful self.

103. should I, damn'd then, were I (in that case damned) to. This begins the second protasis; the apodosis is in ll. 109–111.

104. Slaver with lips as common, exchange disgusting kisses with lips that are as much common property.

106, 107. Made hard ... labour, as hardened (figuratively) by constant falseness as if they had been hardened (literally) by toil.

107. by-peeping, casting sidelong glances, as at a companion sitting by one's side.

108. unlustrous, Rowe; *illustrious,* Ff.; *ill-lustrous,* Ingleby. Cf. *As You Like It,* ii. 7. 21: "lack-lustre eye".

111, 112. Notice the tender mildness of this reproach.

113. Inclined: causal use of the adjective; 'because I am inclined', 'because I am glad to convey'.

115. conscience, consciousness, inmost thoughts. Cf. ii. 2. 36.

116. Charms: see note on i. 3. 35. The singular verb after a relative pronoun with a plural antecedent Abbott connects with the fact that the relative has no inflection: see § 247 (but also § 333), and cf. ii. 3. 21.

The disgusting detail into which Iachimo immediately enters, as to the way in which, he says, her husband spends the money drawn from her own coffers, instead of strengthening her conviction and rousing her resentment, as he had anticipated, has precisely the contrary effects. It both affords her time to recover from the first stunning shock given to her mind by such a communication acting upon the unguarded confidence into which she had been betrayed, and, by the very overcharging of the picture which he draws, begins to awaken her incredulity as to the truth of the representation.—*Fletcher.*

118–122. 'For a lady, so fair and heir of such an empire, that she would make the greatest king himself twice over, to be put on an equality with wantons, hired with the very allowance that she herself pays!' *Exhibition* in Shakespeare has only this meaning, which is still retained at the universities.

124. Recoil, degenerate.

132. close, secret.

Imogen's call to Pisanio is a striking testimony to his worth and her confidence in him. Notice her sudden transition from dejection to vigour and animation, due partly to indignation, partly to her restored belief in her husband.

137. Note the omission after "end", of *as* correlative with *such.*

140. Solicit'st: *solicites,* Ff. So in iii. 3. 103, *refts,* Ff., for *reft'st.*   Abbott, § 340, says that in verbs ending with *t*, *-test* final in the second person singular often becomes *-ts* for euphony.

144. The clause is in apposition to *it* in the previous line. In present English we should either supply 'for'—'*for* a saucy stranger to expound'—or turn '*that...should* expound'.

146. who: cf. iii. 3. 87; iv. 2. 76 (*who* for *whom* interrogative), and see *Abbott*, § 274.

149–151. 'The trust that your lady has in you is worthy of your faith in her, and your perfect goodness deserves that confident trust of hers.'

155–170. Remember that this is not true, although Imogen believes it; and see with what subtle cunning Iachimo turns to good account his own previous slanders and insults, by making Imogen believe that "the love I bear him Made me to fan you thus"; in fact, that it was purely out of love for her husband he had designed this test, in order that he might carry back a report of her unalterable constancy.

157. That which he is, new o'er, over again and more than ever, that which he is already.

one: Abbott (§ 18) thinks that this word is emphatic, = above all, alone.

161. Cf. *Acts*, xiv. 11: "The gods are come down to us in the likeness of men".

163. seeming, a verbal noun—'a more than mortal bearing'.

168. Which ... cannot err: either (1) 'a judgment which is not liable to error', or (2) 'an election (=choice) in which you cannot be mistaken'.

169, 170. fan...chaffless. Cf. *Matthew*, iii. 12: "Whose *fan* is in his hand...but the chaff he will burn up".

171. The critics whose opinions I quoted at the head of this scene are equally opposed here. Imogen "is as inconsiderate in putting any trust in the beguiling Italian afterwards, as her husband in making covenants of honour with one so self-convicted of baseness and mean thoughts" (*Lloyd*).

She betrays no weakness of judgment in accepting this explanation from a man introduced to her, under her husband's own hand, as "one of the noblest note", to whose kindnesses he was most infinitely obliged. Overlooking, though not quite forgetting, the liberty taken with herself, the revulsion of feeling in her generous breast makes her welcome the insinuating stranger with hardly less cordiality than before, though with the added reserve of a dignity and a delicacy too lately wounded.—*Fletcher*.

172. When did Iachimo conceive the attempt to conceal his failure and win the wager by fraud? Did he devise it in case of failure before his arrival in Britain? or was it the fabrication of the few moments intervening since his defeat?

172. Observe how skilfully Shakespeare manages this incident in comparison with his sources. In *Boccaccio* Ambrogiuolo had to remain in the chest till the third day; in *Westward for Smelts* the villain concealed himself under the bed.

178. The best feather of our wing, the choicest spirit of our fellowship. For *feather* = 'bird' cf. *Twelfth Night*, iii. 1. 71:

> " And, like the haggard, check at every feather
> That comes before his eye".

For *wing* = 'fellowship' cf. Dekker's *Bellman of London* (1608): "Of all the mad rascals that are of this wing the Abraham-man is the most fantastic".

189. Attended, guarded. Shakespeare uses this transitive verb in several different senses, some of which are illustrated in this play: cf. i. 2. 35 and ii. 1. 48 (= accompany), i. 6. 135 (= attend to, listen to), ii. 3. 36 (= attend at, do homage at), iv. 2. 334 (= wait for). For its intransitive use see iii. 3. 22 (and note), 77.

Act II.—Scene I.

This scene is in many ways little more than a repetition of i. 2. (*q.v.*). It serves no special purpose, except to separate the two Imogen-Iachimo scenes. The Second Lord rises into verse when he is no longer playing to the groundlings with his *Asides*.

1, 2. In the game of bowls, to which Shakespeare has several allusions, the object of each player is to roll his bowls so that they come to rest as near as possible to the jack, the small bowl towards which aim is taken. The most successful stroke is to "kiss the jack", *i.e.* to play one's bowl alongside and touching the jack. From this position, however, one may be dislodged, as Cloten was, by the "up-cast" (delivery) of a following player's bowl.

8. like him, like his.

11. ha? eh?

18, 19. Jack-slave. See *jackanapes* in Glossary.

21, 22. How much Shakespeare intended to convey by this fooling is doubtful, but the danger of reading more into his words than he intended is exemplified by the following: "Ingleby says that Cloten is compared to a capon merely for his fatness; but surely there is an allusion to the want of courage of emasculated animals" (*Deighton*). It is certain that *comb on* is a pun on *capon*, and that the Second Lord meant that Cloten is a coxcomb. A cock's comb formed part of a fool's cap; hence *coxcomb* in Shakespeare meant (1) a fool's cap, (2) a fool. The puns on *curtail* and *crop the ears*, *rank* and *smelt* above, are sufficiently obvious.

25. companion, a term of contempt, 'low fellow'; often so used.

42. Foolish proceedings cannot be derogatory to an acknowledged fool.

56. It is plainly significant of the Queen's increasing daring and recklessness that even this courtier knows her to be "hourly coining plots". The Physician, we have seen, had the darkest suspicions; but, on the other hand, Imogen seems only to have vaguely mistrusted her as "false", while Pisanio did not even suspect the contents of the mysterious box.

Scene 2.

Was ever the victory of silent beauty, elegance, and purity, over the awe-struck spirit of a sensualist, so exquisitely painted or so nobly celebrated as in these lines! It is not "the flame o' the taper" that here "Bows toward her", but the unhallowed flames in a voluptuary and a treacherous breast, that render extorted yet grateful homage to the lovely, spotless, and fragrant soul!—*Fletcher.*

Iachimo's thoughts catch the delicacy and purity of their object, and he dare not utter a foul word even to himself.—*Hudson.*

The only stage-direction in the First Folio is, "*Enter Imogen, in her bed, and a Lady*". The bed must have been pushed on to the stage from behind the curtains at the back.

Ingleby's note (referred to on p. ix of my Introduction) is as follows: "In the course of this lovely scene one is frequently reminded of passages in the second act of *Macbeth*: a fact which may be of use in determining an earlier date (1606) for parts of this play. One would naturally infer that this scene was written while *Macbeth*, ii. 1, 2, and 3 were fresh in the writer's mind".

He then compares l. 2 with *Macbeth*, ii. 1. 1–3; ll. 7–10 with *Macbeth*, ii. 1. 6–9; ll. 11, 12 with *Macbeth*, ii. 2. 38 ("Sore labour's bath"); ll. 12–14 with *Macbeth*, ii. 1. 55, 56; ll. 22, 23 with *Macbeth*, ii. 3. 118 ("His silver skin laced with his golden blood"); l. 31 with *Macbeth*, ii. 3. 81 ("Shake off this downy sleep, death's counterfeit"). And concludes: "Add to these the slight resemblance in the mention of 'heaven' and 'hell' at the end both of this scene and of *Macbeth*, ii. 1".

Possibly this argument tells with equal force the other way: may not Shakespeare have been less liable to repeat himself when *Macbeth* had lately come white-hot from his brain?

8–10. Observe the fine dramatic contrast between the concluding wish of the Second Lord in the previous scene and Imogen's prayer on the one hand, and Iachimo's stealing from his trunk as if the prayer had been heard and answered by infernal deities.

13. The rushes are one of Shakespeare's many anachronisms, repeated in this case from his own poem *Lucrece* (l. 318). Floors of rooms and stages of theatres were strewn with rushes in Shake-speare's time.

14. **Cytherea**, Venus, so called because she was worshipped by the Phœnicians of Cythera, an island off the S. E. point of Laconia.

18. **How dearly they do 't**, how dearly do her lips kiss each other. Of course Iachimo does not kiss her.

22, 23. **windows...tinct.** Her eyelids were laced with deep-blue veins, which made them look "white and azure".

23. What a striking testimony to Imogen's beauty is the fact that even in this perilous situation it has detained Iachimo from his sole purpose.

31. **thou ape of death.** [Explain.]
    dull, heavy, almost 'dulling'.

34. **Gordian knot.** The pole of the wagon of Gordius, an ancient king of Phrygia, was fastened to the yoke in such a way that the ends of the cord could not be perceived. Hence the report went abroad that the empire of Asia was promised by an oracle to him who could untie it. Alexander the Great, on his arrival at Gordium, cut the knot with his sword, and applied the oracle to himself.

36. **conscience**, not of Posthumus, but of any guilty person.

37. **To the madding of,** with the result of maddening.

38. **cinque,** five, pronounced *sink*, as in the *Cinque* Ports.

crimson: not nearly the right colour, but the "drops i' the bottom of a cowslip" seem of a deeper colour in recollection than they actually are by contrast with the surrounding pale-yellow.
In the *Roman de la Violette* (Introduction, p. xiii) the traitor, while the lady is at her bath, "voit De sur sa destre mamelete Le semblant d'une violete" (sees on her right breast the mark of a violet).

45, 46. Tereus concealed his wife, Procne, that he might marry her sister, Philomela, whom he deceived with the report that Procne was dead. The tale is found in a collection of stories entitled, *A petite Pallace of Pettie his plesure*, compiled about 1576. It is the seventh of Chaucer's *Legends of Good Women*, and is in the fifth book of Gower's *Confessio Amantis* and the sixth of Ovid's *Metamorphoses*.

48. **you dragons**, that draw the chariot of the night.

49. **bare,** Theobald's conjecture; *beare*, Ff.; probably meaning 'bare'. It is said that the raven "catches the worm", and thus its eye is bared or opened by dawn.

51. Iachimo counts the strokes of the hour, and when he hears *four*, exclaims, "time", *i.e.* the time at which Imogen wished to be called. With reference to the notes of time in this scene, Mr. Daniel, whose time-analysis is quoted at the head of these notes, remarks: "Stage time is not measured by the glass, and to an expectant

audience the awful pause between the falling asleep of Imogen and the stealthy opening of the trunk from which Iachimo issues would be note and mark of time enough".

Scene 3.

Cloten does not shine in wooing, though he rises into verse for the occasion. But the scene is noteworthy for a perfect gem of song; for Imogen's anger at the abuse of her husband; for a magnificent example of tragic irony in ll. 146, 147; and for Cloten's threat of vengeance, because his stupid vanity is greater than his love.

2. most coldest. Double superlatives are not uncommon in Shakespeare; cf. i. 6. 154, and iv. 2. 319, and see *Abbott*, § 11.

ace. The game was evidently one in which the ace is the worst card.

3. lose, Rowe; *loose*, Ff. (not infrequently so).

12. o', Theobald; *a*, Ff.

15. excellent good-conceited, excellently well conceived, imagined, composed. *Excellent good* is not uncommon, *excellent* being used adverbially, as *wonderful* and *admirable* are below.

18–26. There are striking resemblances between this song and the 29th Sonnet, and a passage in Lyly's *Alexander and Campaspe*, from which Shakespeare may have derived a suggestion for the two former:

> "who is 't now we hear;
> None but the lark so shrill and clear;
> Now at heaven's gates she claps her wings,
> The morn not waking till she sings.
> Hark, hark".

Sonnet 29:

> "and then my state,
> Like to the lark at break of day arising
> From sullen earth, sings hymns at heaven's gate".

20, 21. The sun drinks up the dew lying in cup-shaped flowers.

22. Mary-buds, marigolds, which close at night. Cf. Sonnet 25:

> "Great princes' favourites their fair leaves spread
> But as the marigold at the sun's eye".

27, 28. consider your music the better, pay for it more liberally.

28. vice, Rowe; *voice*, Ff., an error probably due to "anticipation" of *voice* in the next line.

29. horse-hairs and calves'-guts, bow-strings and fiddle-strings. Shakespeare was much nearer the mark than some of his editors, who read *cats'-guts*, for catgut is made from sheep's intestines, never from those of the cat.

38. music, Hanmer; *musics*, Ff., for which cf. *All's Well*, iii. 7. 39, 40:

> "Every night he comes
> With musics of all sorts".

44, 45. vantages that may Prefer you, opportunities for endeavouring to ingratiate you. For *vantage* cf. i. 3. 24. *Prefer* has the same sense of 'recommend' in iv. 2. 386, 400, and = 'promote' in l. 130 and in v. 5. 326 (*q.v.*).

46. soliciting, Collier; *solicity*, F 1; *solicits*, F 2.

52. senseless. Senseless, insensible, devoid of sense: we have already had the word twice in the former meaning (i. 1. 135 and i. 3. 7), which Cloten here mistakes.

58, 59. his goodness ... notice, on account of his former kindness to us, we must show increased attention *or* regard. *His goodness ... us* is nominative absolute; or possibly *according to* is to be understood from the previous line.

68. Diana's rangers false themselves, Diana's huntresses perjure themselves, because they had taken vows against matrimony. It is possible that *false* is an adjective here, though that makes the construction very abrupt; there is no other certain instance of its use as a verb in Shakespeare, but it is common in Spenser.

69. stand, the station of the huntsman waiting for game. Cf. iii. 4. 108, 109.

74. Abbott, § 76, calls attention to the fact that *yet* is only used now after a negative.

95, 96. equal...kindness. Abbott (§ 419, *a*) and Schmidt take this to mean 'discourtesy equal to your best kindness', but it is at least equally likely that the more obvious meaning is the right one.

96, 97. one of your...forbearance, a man of your great knowledge, *or* experience, being taught forbearance should learn the lesson.

99. cure, Warburton; *are*, Ff. Steevens defends the Folio reading: "This, as Cloten very well understands it, is a covert mode of calling him fool. The meaning implied is this: If I am mad, as you tell me, I am what you can never be. 'Fools are not mad folks.'" If Cloten understood this, he must have been as clever as a Shakespearian commentator. It is certainly not the most obvious inference from "Fools are not mad folks", which rather is: 'Whether I am a fool may be a matter of question, but even fools are not necessarily mad'. I am compelled to adopt Warburton's conjecture, (1) because it makes Imogen's reply to Cloten perfectly apposite, and his following question most natural and pertinent; (2) because of the added force it gives to "That cures us both"; (3) because, though there are plenty of obscurities in the later plays, there is hardly a trace of obscurity in all Imogen's very plain speaking to Cloten.   To this I need only add, that when Imogen says she 'll "no more be mad", she does not refer to the madness that Cloten meant, that of her love, but to the madness which made her call him fool.

105. **By being so verbal**, by your repeated protestations. This is the obvious meaning, but several editors refer the expression to Imogen herself: 'by my expressing in words what is ordinarily understood by implication'.

109. **To accuse myself**: *sc.* of lack of charity.

117, 118. **no more dependency But**, nothing more depending than.

118. **self-figured knot**, a knot tied by themselves.

119, 120. **curb'd...crown**, restrained from such freedom of choice by the succession, by considerations of state.

120. **soil**, Hanmer; *foil*, Ff., which may be right, but *f* for *∫* (*s*) was an easy misprint.

122. **for a livery**, only fit for a livery. *A squire's cloth* is in apposition to *livery*.

123. **pantler**, the servant who had charge of the pantry. Cf. *2 Henry IV.*, ii. 4. 257–259: "'a' would have made a good pantler, a' would ha' chipped bread well".

124, 125. **and no more ... besides**, and in other respects no different from what you are at present.

126–130. 'It would be an enviable dignity for you, if the post of under-hangman of his kingdom were held to be sufficient recognition of your merits in comparison with his, and if you were hated for such excessive promotion.'

130. **south-fog**. Cf. "The spongy south" in iv. 2. 349. The moist south wind was supposed to be unhealthy.

138. **sprited with a fool**, haunted by a fool, as by a sprite.
The 'tragic irony'—"which consists in putting into the mouth of a speaker double-edged phrases, of which the hidden meaning is only apparent to the spectators"—of the rest of this speech will not escape notice.

148. **I hope so**=modern 'I hope not'.

150. Of course ironical.

154. Nothing in this scene becomes Cloten worse than "the leaving it".   His frequent repetition of this insult is perhaps the cause why he has not forgotten it even in iii. 5.   Cf. Dogberry in *Much Ado*,

Scene 4.

The fiendishly cruel and clever way in which Iachimo gradually enfolds Posthumus in the snare he has prepared for him requires the closest examination, step by step. The same eloquence, that spread its toils in vain for the seduction of Imogen, now serves the villain's purpose only too speedily and well.

Observe as you read the successive moves in the game—from Imogen's letters proving the visit to the court of Britain until Iachimo makes Posthumus see " her pretty action " of stripping the bracelet from her arm and reduces him to the last desperate suggestion, " May be she pluck'd it off to send it me "—by which Posthumus' reason and judgment are taken prisoner, so that at last he passes sentence, not like a judge, but in the temper of a raving madman.

3. What means do you make to him? What steps are you taking to win his favour?

6. fear'd hopes, hopes mingled with fear lest they should not be fulfilled. The *Globe* adopts Tyrwhitt's conjecture, *sear'd* = withered.

11. Hath heard of great Augustus, has received his message.

12. throughly, thoroughly; see note on i. 2. 9.

14. Or, ere. See Glossary.

14, 15. whose ... grief, the remembrance of whom is still kept fresh by the Britons' grief.

16. Statist, politician.

18. legions, Theobald; *legion,* Ff.; but cf. iii. 7. 4.

sooner qualifies *shall hear.*

24. courage, Dyce; *courages,* Ff. Shakespeare nowhere else uses the plural of this word.

25. their approvers, those who put them to the proof, make trial of them. Unique instance (*i.e.* the word occurs nowhere else in Shakespeare). See note on i. 4. 109. For such **That** see *Abbott,* § 279.

26. mend upon the world, earn and claim increasing recognition.

28. of all the corners, from every quarter.

34. through, Rowe; *thorough,* Ff. This preposition, when *dissyllabic*, is spelt both ways in Shakespeare, but here the metre requires a monosyllable. See note on l. 12 above.

36. tenour, Theobald; *tenure,* Ff. as usual.

37. *Phi.,* Capell; *Post.,* Ff. The assignment of the speech to Philario gives Posthumus time to glance through his letters.

40, 41. Referring to i. 4. 64. Posthumus means: Is it not a case of the fox and the grapes?

41. **had**, Singer; *have*, Ff., in support of which see *Abbott*, § 371: " The consequent does not always answer to the antecedent in mood or tense ".

58. **is.** *Abbott*, § 336: " The inflection in *s* is of frequent occurrence also when two or more singular nouns precede the verb ". Cf. l. 10; iii. 3. 99; iii. 6. 21; and v. 2. 2.

59, 60. **gains ... mine**, gains me your sword or loses mine.

60. **leaves**, Rowe; *leave*, Ff.

61. **circumstances**, circumstantial details.

68. **watching**, keeping awake for.

70. **her Roman**, Mark Antony.

71. **Cydnus**, a river in Cilicia, flowing into the Mediterranean.

73, 74. **it did strive In workmanship and value.** [What does this mean?]
Iachimo's language is such as a skilful villain would naturally use —a mixture of airy triumph and serious deposition.—*Johnson*.

82. **Chaste Dian.** Who is " Dian "? and why called " chaste "?

83. **So likely to report themselves**, *i.e.* to speak and say who they were.

83–85. ' The sculptor did all and more than all that nature could do, apart from speech, breathing, and movement.'

88. **andirons**, fire-dogs; to be seen in any good example of an old fireplace. See Glossary.

89. **winking**, with eyes closed or nearly so, because love is blind.

90, 91. **nicely Depending on their brands**, elegantly supported by their brands. Cf. i. 5. 58. *Brands* is explained in two ways: (1) =brand-irons, *i.e.* the horizontal bars at the back of the andirons on which the logs actually rest. The fact that the Cupids would not stand without the support of these " brands " favours this interpretation. (2) *Brands* = the Cupids' firebrands or torches, by resting on which they seemed to be maintaining their poise. Cupid's torch is a symbol of the inflaming power of love. This interpretation is supported by two passages in Sonnets 153 and 154:

"Cupid laid by his brand, and fell asleep".
" The little Love-god lying once asleep
Laid by his side his heart-inflaming brand."

These are the only passages in which Shakespeare has the word in either of the above meanings.

91. **This is her honour!** And the attainment of this knowledge is to pass for the corruption of her honour ! (*Johnson*).

(M 332)　　　　　　　　　　　　　　　　　　　　K

92. Let it be granted you have seen all this. This is a most damning and unforensic admission for Posthumus to make, but he is becoming exasperated with Iachimo's coolness and apparent mastery of the situation as well as with the flawless exactness of his "circumstances", which yet keep aloof from the real subject of the wager. But there is more than exasperation in the admission: Iachimo had actually seen all that he describes, and Posthumus must have felt that matters were taking an unpleasantly ominous turn, and his immediate impulse was to come to the crisis at once.

96, 97. Iachimo at first gives Posthumus but a tantalizing, maddening glimpse of the bracelet. To understand the tremendous effects of this sight upon Posthumus, we need to remember that it was the pledge of his wife's plighted troth, and must have recalled instantly and vividly to his mind the sacred endearments of their parting; that any shock to his trust in his wife's perfect fidelity would be all the greater because of the unassailably serene and confident nature of that trust; and that, though that trust still holds firm, he is now reduced to the excited and possibly vaguely alarmed state of mind in which he most easily falls a prey to the wiles of Iachimo.

98. I'll keep them, though your mistress and you have parted with them so easily—a perfectly Satanic thrust.

107. a basilisk, or cockatrice, was a fabulous creature supposed to be produced from a cock's egg hatched by a serpent; its breath and even its look were fatal to life.

109. semblance, a fair exterior.

110-112. the vows of women...virtues. 'Let the vows of women be held to have no more binding force towards those to whom they are made than there is binding force between them and their virtues.'

120. What is the meaning of *evident* here?

121. By Jupiter. This is here a very solemn asseveration. Iachimo uses it only this once, and in support of a statement which is literally true.

130. Of one persuaded well of [her virtue], by one convinced of.

133. the, Rowe; *her*, Ff.

145. besides (beside, by the side of, outside of), beyond.

146. Even the disinterested Philario, the friend of both parties, is convinced now.

147. pervert, turn aside; unique instance with this meaning.

Scene 5.

Shakespeare's dramatic purpose in this scene is evident and essential—to lay clearly open to us that stormy desolation, those volcanic heavings of a noble heart, our full conception of which can alone make us tolerate that purpose of sanguinary vengeance which is to be formed and pursued by his hero.—*Fletcher.*

Compare the whole behaviour and course of action of Posthumus, first with those of Imogen in somewhat similar circumstances, both (in i. 6) when Iachimo reports her husband's infidelity, and later when she convinces herself of his infidelity as the only explanation of his murderous commission to Pisanio (iii. 4. 48–52, 80 ff.); secondly, with his own opening speech in the 5th Act.

2. What a fall is here from the confident reply to Iachimo's " I durst attempt it against any lady in the world ": " You are a great deal abused in too bold a persuasion " (i. 4).

7. change of prides, pride on account of one thing at one time, of another at another.

8. Nice, fanciful, capricious.

14. I'll write against them : probably, with *against* emphatic, 'I'll join the "woman-hating crew"', certainly not 'I'll rush into print against them'. Cf. *Much Ado*, iv. 1. 57 : " Seeming ! I will write against it ".

17. *Exit*, with Iachimo, for two acts.

Act III.—Scene I.

This scene serves to carry on the political action and goes nearer than any other to justifying Skottowe's remark that Cloten "is a natural fool; yet he often talks with the wit of one of Shakespeare's professed fools ". After one short speech in verse he falls into the jocular, bantering vein for which prose is the fit medium. For Mulmutius (l. 53), the knighting of Cymbeline by Augustus (l. 68), and the mention of the Pannonians and Dalmatians (l. 72), see Appendix B.

5. uncle, great-uncle. Cassibelan was the younger brother of Lud, Cymbeline's grandfather.

6, 7. no whit less Than in his feats deserving it, no whit less famous than he deserved to be for his feats.

7, 8. for him And his succession, for himself and his successors.

12. Britain is, Pope, for the sake of the metre; *Britain's*, Ff.

13. A world by itself. Cf. Virgil's *Eclogues*, i. 68 :
      " Et penitus toto divisos orbe Britannos "
(and the Britons entirely cut off from the whole world).

14. For wearing our own noses, probably, 'for daring to have noses of our own not conformed to the Roman pattern'. See l. 37.

14-16. **That opportunity...have again.** Paraphrase this sentence.

20. **rocks,** Seward's conjecture; *oaks,* Ff.

27. **ignorant,** unacquainted with the nature of our boisterous seas (*Johnson*).

30. **at point,** on the point of.

30, 31. Told in *Holinshed* of Nenius, Cassibelan's brother. See Appendix B 2.

32. See Appendix B 3.

36. **other**: a remnant of the old plural form of the adjective, which had no *s*.

37. **to owe,** as regards owning (*Abbott*, § 357). See Glossary.

38. Cymbeline wishes the Queen to pronounce his ultimatum, but Cloten ignores the interruption. How full of meaning Shakespeare can make an apparently insignificant speech of five words!

46. **injurious,** insolent; cf. iv. 2. 86, and Fr. *injure* (insult).

48, 49. **Which swell'd...world.** What does this mean?

49. **against all colour,** without any pretence of right. Cf. *1 Henry IV.,* iii. 2. 100:
> "For of no right, nor colour like to right".

52. *Clo.* **We do.** So Dyce, following Collier's MS. Ff. assign the whole to Cymbeline, with a comma after *be*; but this is too feeble even for his majesty, and is quite foreign to Shakespeare's kingly style.

55. **franchise,** free exercise.

70, 71. **Which...utterance,** which [honour], he seeking it of me again by force, it behoves me to maintain to the uttermost, to the death. *At utterance*=Fr. *à outrance; un combat à outrance*=a fight to the death. Cf. *Macbeth,* iii. 1. 71, 72:
> "come fate into the list,
> And champion me to the utterance!"

"The phrase admits of no doubt" (as Ingleby says at the close of his impossible explanation).

71. **I am perfect,** I am perfectly informed, I know perfectly well; cf. iv. 2. 118.

72. **Pannonia** was a Roman province between the Danube and the Alps; Dalmatia, east of the Adriatic, nearly corresponded with the modern Dalmatia. The Pannonians joined the Dalmatians in their revolt from Rome in A.D. 7, but were finally conquered by Tiberius in A.D. 9.

83. **All the remain,** all that remains. The singular noun is rare; besides this passage Shakespeare has *remain* once, and *here remain* once, in each case in the sense of 'stay', 'sojourn'.

Scene 2.

The whole of this scene, after the entry of Imogen, is a prolonged example of tragic irony; this adds inexpressible pathos to her pretty talk: "Blest be you bees that make these locks of counsel"; "And by the way tell me how Wales was made so happy as to inherit such a haven".

2. **monster's her accuser,** Capell; *monsters her accuse,* Ff.

5. **As poisonous-tongued as handed,** with a tongue as ready for slander as his hands are to administer poison. The Italians had an evil reputation in Elizabeth's days as skilful poisoners. Cf. iii. 4. 15.

7. **truth** [meaning?].

undergoes, endures firmly, bears up against. [What meaning has it elsewhere in this play?]

9. **take in,** conquer, subdue, as in iv. 2. 121.

10, 11. **Thy mind...fortunes.** [Paraphrase this sentence.]

12. **Upon,** by; but we retain *upon* in 'upon my soul' and many similar phrases.

17. Pisanio is not actually reading from his master's letter which he has in his hand, and which is given in full in iii. 4. 21 ff., for the letter is of course prose; but he is giving its substance in two lines.

23. 'I know nothing (for the present) about these commands which have been laid upon me.'

33. **med'cinable,** medicinal; passive for active.

34. **doth physic love,** keeps love healthy and vigorous.

35. **All but in that,** in all but that, *i.e.* of his contentment with everything but our separation.

36. What are *these locks of counsel*?

36–39. The bees are not blessed by the man who forfeiting a bond is sent to prison, as they are by the lover for whom they perform the more pleasing office of sealing letters.—*Steevens.*
Verplanck points out that the seal was essential to the bond, though a signature was not; and that *forfeiters* was the technical term for those who had broken a contract and become liable to the legal penalty.

39. **tables,** tablets, letters.

40–43. Pope suggested *but* for *as*, and this probably gives the meaning: 'They could not be so cruel but that the sight of you would revive me'.

49. **of mean affairs,** bent on ordinary business.

50. May: in its etymological sense of 'can', as in *Psalms*, cxxv. 1 (Prayer-book version): "Mount Zion, which may not be removed". Cf. l. 66.

53. bate, abate, moderate, what I said: 'Who longest, as I do, but not like me'.

55. thick, fast.

63. And. Pope read *till*. But the irregularity is all of a piece with "the happy hurry of spirits and joyous impatience" of the whole speech.

to excuse, how to make excuse.

64. or ere begot, before the deed is done which it would be invented to excuse. For *or ere*=ere cf. v. 3. 50, and see *or* in Glossary.

69. With fine unconscious irony Imogen gives in the next line the very reason why twenty miles a day is "too much" in Pisanio's opinion.

71, 72. the sands That run i' the clock's behalf, the sands of the hour-glass: 'swifter than the flight of time'.

74. presently, immediately—its usual meaning. See ii. 3. 137; iv. 2. 166, and cf. *Matthew*, xxvi. 53: "and he shall presently give me more than twelve legions of angels".

76. franklin, originally 'a country gentleman whose estate consisted in *free* land, and was not subject to feudal services or payments'; this is the signification of the word in Chaucer. Johnson defines it as meaning 'a freeholder with a small estate'. Shakespeare uses the word only three times, apparently in the latter sense.

you're best, you were best, representing the old construction, *it were best for you*; but *you* is nominative in Shakespeare, because he has "I were best" (iii. 6. 19), "Thou 'rt best", &c.

77, 78. nor here, nor here, Nor what ensues, but have a fog in them, right and left (pointing) and behind me it is impenetrably foggy.

Scene 3.

This and the other scenes laid among the Welsh mountains bring with them, in addition to their intrinsic beauty, a sense of relief from the oppression of Cymbeline's court and the unsavoury nature of the main plot.

2. Stoop, Hanmer; *Sleep*, Ff.

6. turbans. The idea of a *giant* was, among the readers of romances, who were almost all the readers of those times, always confounded with that of a Saracen (*Johnson*).

12. Cf. i. 3. 15.

13. [Paraphrase this line.]

16, 17. This service...allow'd, it is not the doing of the deed, but the acknowledgment *or* approval of it [which may or may not follow], that makes it service. *Allow* in this sense (Fr. *allouer*, approve of = Lat. *allaudare*, praise) has a different etymology from *allow* = permit.

This line and a half is an illustration of the ways of courts, &c.; whereas "to apprehend thus" (= such moralizing) refers to the whole passage from l. **11.**

20. sharded, with scaly wing-cases. The *shards* are stretched out in flight; hence *Macbeth*, iii. 2. 42:

"The shard-borne beetle with his drowsy hums",

as if the shards supported the beetle. Notice the perfect contrast between "sharded beetle" and "full-wing'd eagle".

22. attending for a check, doing service, dancing attendance, only to be rebuked. Cf. l. 77.

23. bribe, Hanmer; *babe,* Ff.; *bauble,* Rowe. With the Folio reading *babe,* the line is explained either to mean 'dangling about in attendance on a youthful prince', or to be an allusion to court favourites administering the estates of infant wards and neglecting the children confided to their care. Neither explanation can be called obvious, if indeed they are not both forced. It has been objected to the emendation *bauble,* that the implied rebuke in "doing nothing for a bauble" (*i.e.* a decoration, title to a peerage, &c.) is pointless, because it is the recognized system to bestow them for "doing nothing". To *bribe* it has been objected that it gives *richer* a pecuniary sense, which, in the mouth of Belarius, is nonsense. But I cannot admit that the pecuniary sense of *richer* is a necessity. Just as he is speaking of true nobility and true pride, so he says in effect, 'Our life is more truly rich than if we took bribes for doing nothing'. In Spenser's *Mother Hubberd's Tale*, which is largely a satire on court life, there is a passage which well illustrates, if it does not support the reading adopted in the text. The Ape is a courtier, and the Fox is his servant, and we read of the latter:

"So would he work the silly man [a suitor] by treason
To buy his Master's frivolous good will,
That had not power to do him good or ill".

25. 'em, Capell; *him,* Ff. The tailor raises his cap to them politely, but does not get his money, and so cannot cross the debt out in his ledger.

28, 29. nor know not What air 's from home. Paraphrase. Quote other instances of double negative.

33. travelling: *travailing,* Ff., but the two forms were used indiscriminately.

34. for, Pope; *or*, Ff.

35. **To stride a limit,** to transgress his bounds.

40. **beastly** [meaning?].   Used as an adverb in v. 3. 27.

50. **pain,** toil, labour, trouble, like Fr. *peine.*

51. I take the antecedent of *which* to be "fame and honour"; but although *dies* undoubtedly suggested *epitaph* in the next line, I venture to think that the most satisfactory sense is got by putting a comma after "honour" (instead of the usual semicolon), reading "which dies i' the search" as parenthetical, and making "And hath &c." a parallel relative clause to "that only seems &c.", with antecedent "the toil o' the war, A pain".

54. **deserve,** earn, gain.

70. **demesnes** is merely another spelling of *domains.*

79 ff. In each of these [last] we can see Shakespeare, as it were, tenderly bending over the joys and sorrows of youth.   We recognize this rather through the total characterization, and through a feeling and a presence, than through definite incident or statement.   But some of this feeling escapes in the disinterested joy and admiration of old Belarius when he gazes at the princely youths.—*Dowden.*

83. **wherein they,** Warburton; *whereon the*, Ff.

85. **prince it.**   Shakespeare also uses "queen it" (*Winter's Tale*), and "dukes it" (*Measure for Measure*).   Abbott, § 226, says that "*it* is often added to nouns or words that are not generally used as verbs, in order to give them the force of verbs".

94. **nerves,** sinews, tendons.

96-98. **in as like...conceiving.**   Arviragus acts the words of Belarius as well as Guiderius, but in an even more lifelike way because he has a much clearer conception of what took place. Belarius here gives us the clue to the discrimination of the characters of the two youths, apparently so much alike—a clue that must be followed up in the succeeding scenes.

99 ff.   There are moments when Shakespeare was not wholly absorbed in his work as artist at this period; it is as if he were thinking of his own life, or of the fields and streams of Stratford, and still wrote on; it is as if the ties which bound him to his art were not severing with thrills of strong emotion, but were quietly growing slack.   The soliloquy of Belarius, at the end of the third scene of the third act of *Cymbeline*, and that of Imogen when she discovers the headless body of Cloten [iv. 2. 291 ff.], were written as if Shakespeare were now only moderately interested in certain portions of his dramatic work.   Such lines as the following [ll. 99-107], purporting to be part of a soliloquy, but being in fact an explanation addressed to the audience, could only have been written when the poet did not care to energize over the less interesting but still necessary passages of his drama.—*Dowden.*

Scene 4.

Here the pathetic tragedy of the play culminates. From this point matters tend on the whole to mend, although slowly and with apparent sets-back. The partial succumbing of Posthumus in the fiery ordeal by which he was tried—it must always be remembered that in actual fidelity he never wavered, any more than did Imogen—leads to the equally fearful testing of Imogen in this scene, a testing from which she emerges unscathed. In this she is helped by her splendidly healthy physical and moral nature, to which suicide is an impossibility (see also iv. 2. 330 ff.); and though she bids Pisanio execute his master's commands, and is in spirit faithful even unto death, she is quite ready to accept his way of escape, and to enter the service of Lucius with a view to prove the truth of Pisanio's surmise that "my master is abused". See also "Critical Comments".

3. **as I have now.** [Complete this elliptical sentence in two possible ways.]

9, 10. **ere...senses,** before madness takes possession of my hitherto composed senses. Unique instance of *staid*.

11, 12. **tender'st...untender.** The frequency of such plays upon words proves that they cannot have been esteemed in bad taste in Shakespeare's day.

15. Cowden Clarke says, with reference to this line: "And but once is she betrayed into an expression of anger". And Hudson says of Imogen: "The calm sweetness of her temper is ruffled but twice". Mention all the occasions on which Imogen speaks angrily.

17. **take off some extremity,** dull the sharpness of the blow.

22. **lie:** *lies,* Ff.

24. **as I expect my revenge,** as my expectation of revenge.

34. **worms,** serpents, snakes. In the Old English poem *Beowulf,* the dragon is called "the worm".

of Nile. Cf. *Antony and Cleopatra,* v. 2. 243, 244: "Hast thou the pretty worm of Nilus there, That kills and pains not?" *i.e.* the asp.

36. **states,** persons of the highest rank.

39-43. Observe the wonderful art that makes this speech express so much: the awful shock of the letter, the utter inability to comprehend for a time even the nature of the charge, the perfect sincerity of Imogen's innocence, the absolute purity of her nature.

45. **conscience,** consciousness, inmost thoughts. Cf. ii. 2. 36.
As soon as Imogen has sufficiently recovered from the first shock to be able to think of the cause of the charge, but one explanation occurs to her—that her husband himself is unfaithful; it is no *more*

difficult for her to believe in his infidelity than to find him capable
of believing in hers.   Therefore her interview with Iachimo at once
recurs to memory, and she now believes that he withdrew what were
true charges against her husband in order to allay her anger.   Do
not forget that Imogen is really wronging her husband in thought.
The true explanation—that Iachimo has slandered her to her husband,
as he tried to slander her husband to her—probably does not occur
to her because she could not conceive of such wickedness.

47. now, *sc.* I can no longer believe you were telling a lying tale.

48. Some jay of Italy = some Roman courtezan (l. 123).

49. Whose mother was her painting, the creature, not of
nature, but of painting (*Johnson*).   Cf. iv. 2. 81-83.

51, 52. for I am richer...ripp'd.   Steevens says that garments
no longer worn were hung up in a room devoted to the purpose,
and the richer ones were ripped up for domestic uses.

53-65. Compare this with Act ii. sc. 5, and see "Critical Comments" (Introduction, p. xxi).

57 ff. Just as Æneas, through his falsity to Dido, laid "true
honest men" under suspicion; just as Sinon, through the false
weeping which prevailed on the Trojans to receive the wooden
horse, cast a slur on holy tears and robbed the wretched of pity.
Being heard in l. 57 is in reply to *hear me* in l. 56.

61. the leaven.   Cf. *1 Corinthians*, v. 6: "Know ye not that a
little leaven leaveneth the whole lump?"

proper men, handsome gentlemen.

75, 76.   Cf. *Hamlet*, i. 2. 131, 132:

> "Or that the Everlasting had not fix'd
> His canon 'gainst self-slaughter!"

78. afore 't, Rowe; *afoot*, Ff.

79. Obedient as the scabbard.   [Explain.]

80, 81. scriptures...turn'd to heresy.   [Show that this expression has a double meaning.]

86-89. Capell inserted the second *thou* in l. 87 for the sake of the
metre.   Ff. make only three lines, ending, *Posthumus,...king...suits.*

89. make, Malone; *makes*, Ff.

90. fellows, equals in rank.
Even in Imogen's self-praise there is the utmost sweetness,
because of the disdained yet most devoted love which is expressed
in it.

91. passage, occurrence.

93. be disedged by her, have the keen edge of thy passion for
her blunted.   For *tirest* see Glossary.

101. blind, Hanmer; Ff. omit; *out*, Johnson. The last conjecture, though not so forcible as *blind*, derives support from two passages quoted by Steevens: "I shall watch my eyes out", from a MS. play called *The Bugbears*; and "I'll ride to Oxford and watch out mine eyes, but I'll hear the brazen head speak", from Middleton's *Roaring Girl*, 1611.

108. To be unbent, only to have your bow still unbent.

stand, cf. ii. 3. 69.

121, 122. Pisanio does not suspect Iachimo, because he knows nothing of the latter's imputations on his master's conduct in i. 6; his very ignorance also keeps his belief in his master's honour unimpaired.

125. See line 29: "to make me certain it is done".

135 ff. Imogen seems to think that Pisanio had meant that the court was the only place where she could live in Britain, and that any other country was out of the question (see ll. 136, 137), whereas she in reality takes his cue and pursues the train of thought he had wished to suggest (see ll. 137, 138).

137-140. 'Though Britain seems only like a swan's nest in a great pool—a small island in an ocean of waters—and though it is not *in* the world (cf. iii. 1. 13), yet there is a great world beyond *of* which it forms a part.'

140. There's livers. Abbott, § 335, says: "When the subject is as yet future and, as it were, unsettled, the third person singular might be regarded as the normal inflection. Such passages are very common, particularly in the case of 'There is'". See also iv. 2. 283, 371, and v. 5. 233.

143, 144. a mind Dark as your fortune is. Darkness applied to the mind is secrecy, applied to the fortune is obscurity (*Johnson*). Pisanio expounds his meaning in ll. 154 ff.

144-146. and but disguise...self-danger, and only disguise that (your sex and identity) the disclosure of which would for a time be full of danger.

147. Pretty is often glossed 'apt, suitable for the purpose'. The whole expression, "You should tread a pretty course", seems to me rather to mean: 'You would have a part to play that would be novel, full of interest, and likely to succeed'. Collier suggested the reading *privy*.

full of view, giving you a coign of vantage for observing unobserved. That this is the meaning is confirmed by the rest of the speech.

155. niceness, coyness, *or* dainty scrupulousness of attire (see l. 164). The adjective is common in the corresponding senses, but this is the unique instance of the noun.

157. it: a transitional form between *his*, the old genitive case singular neuter, and *its*, which came into common use in the 17th century. *It* (=its) is frequent in the early Quartos, and is found sixteen times in the First Folio. *Its* (spelt *it's* in every instance but one) occurs only ten times in the First Folio. In every other passage Shakespeare uses *his* (=its) in F 1. *Its* is not found in the Authorized Version of 1611; in the one passage in which it now occurs in the Authorized Version (*Leviticus*, xxv. 5) the edition of 1611 has "of *it* own accord". Milton uses the form *its* but three times in the whole of his poetry. *Abbott*, § 228.

159. As quarrelous as the weasel. It is said that weasels were formerly kept in houses for the destruction of vermin, as cats are now. They are very bloodthirsty, but there is no evidence to show that they are "quarrelous" (unique instance).

161. the harder heart. I am not certain of the meaning of these words, and therefore give three other interpretations before adding one of my own. (1) 'How more than hard his (Posthumus') heart', *i.e.* for compelling you to such hardships. (2) 'This too hard heart of mine', which urges you to such a course. (3) Pisanio apprehends that Imogen, in the part she is going to act, will feel the need of a man's harder, or tougher, heart. (4) I would suggest as possible: 'O, the danger of your heart becoming harder, more like a man's, when you don man's attire'! The following "Alack, no remedy!" at least seems to lend some countenance to this suggestion.

163. common-kissing Titan, the sun who kisses indiscriminately. The Titans were properly the sons and daughters of Uranus (Heaven) and Ge (Earth), but the name is also given to those divine or semi-divine beings who were descended from the Titans, especially Helios (the Sun).

168. fit, prepared. Cf. iv. 1. 4.

170. in their serving. [Explain.]

172. season, time of life.

174. Wherein you're happy, what your gifts are.

you'll, Hanmer; *will*, Ff.

176. embrace you, accept your offer.

177. holy, virtuous, righteous; so, often.

177, 178. Your means … rich, as to your means of support abroad, you have me to supply you, and I am rich.

179. supplyment, continual supply; unique instance.

181, 182. we'll even … give us, we'll make our achievements equal to our opportunities.

183. I am soldier to, I am as ready for as a soldier is for battle.

187. **Your carriage,** the conveying of you; *your*, objective genitive.

191. **distemper,** indisposition.

Scene 5.

Cloten rises into verse for the last time before, like the swan, he dies in melody in the next act. He is moved to do so by his patriotism, which is not unworthy, and by his unworthy passion for Imogen. When that passion degenerates into mere lust, Shakespeare rightly makes him speak it in prose.

2. **wrote.** *Abbott*, § 343. [Collect from the whole play all the verbal forms that are now anomalous.]

8. **conduct,** escort.

9. This is the reading of the Ff. The *Globe* assigns the words "And you!" to the Queen, but Mr. Aldis Wright returns to the original reading in the Cambridge edition. *You* then of course means Cymbeline.

22. **It fits us therefore ripely,** the time is ripe and fitting, the need is pressing.

25. **drawn to head,** collected for war, mobilised.

32. **looks us like.** [What should we now say?] See *Abbott*, § 220.

33. **thing.** [In what other passages of this play is the word "thing" applied to a person?]

35. **too slight in sufferance,** too lax in allowing such behaviour.

35–41. It is only in the Queen's soliloquies that we see her real character. On other occasions, like the true plotter, she is "all things to all men", attempting to conciliate everybody's good opinion by affected amiability.

44. **loud'st of,** Capell; *loud of*, Ff.

51. **Made me to blame in memory.** [Paraphrase.]

68, 69. **may This night...day!** This is usually taken to mean: 'May this night prevent his living to see another day'! But there is no sufficient reason for Cymbeline's dying that night, and the Queen's own method of getting rid of him was by slow poisoning (see v. 5. 49 ff.). It seems to me preferable, therefore, to give the sentence a figurative meaning: 'May this (night of) sorrow and despair caused by Imogen's disappearance deprive him of (the coming day of) her succession to the throne and happy reign!'

70. **for,** because.

71. **And that**=and for (that)=and because. *Abbott*, § 285.

72. **Than lady, ladies, woman,** than any lady, than all ladies, than all womankind (*Johnson*). Cf. *All's Well*, ii. 3. 202: "To any count, to all counts, to what is man".

73. **The best she hath, and she,** the best that she has, and *she* (Imogen). *Or*, the line may be read with a strong emphasis on " best ", and then each " she " = Imogen. [Discuss which meaning is the better.]

77. **choked,** as if by rank weeds.

in that point, *sc.* of view; on that account.

91. **Come nearer,** *sc.* to the point.

92. **home,** thoroughly; cf. iv. 2. 328. We still say "strike home", " drive it home ", " bring it home ", &c., in a similar sense.

99. This would seem to be the letter to Imogen (see sc. 2), for Pisanio says in v. 5. 278 ff.:

" By accident,
I had a feigned letter of my master's
Then in my pocket ".

See also l. 133 below. Pisanio could not have shown Cloten the letter to himself (sc. 4), which moreover was *not* a feigned letter.

101. **Or this, or perish.** [Explain.]

104, 105. Observe the riming couplet where verse is exchanged for prose.

128, 129. Observe how constantly Shakespeare's experience as an actor serves him in good stead; what a past master in the art of stagecraft he proves himself to be by his insertion of such natural touches as these, which, apparently insignificant in themselves, yet give the play an ever-present air of vivid reality.

129. **thou.** Observe carefully by whom, to whom, and on what occasions this pronoun is used in the play.

137. **insultment:** unique instance. The noun *insult* is not found in Shakespeare.

155. **speed,** success; with a play on the other meaning of the word.

Scene 6.

Julia, Jessica, Portia, Rosalind, and Viola had all assumed male disguise in earlier plays. Shakespeare doubtless adopted this device the more readily because female parts were played by boys in his day. The supreme charm of the scenes between Imogen and her brothers cannot need to be pointed out.

7. **Foundations,** firm, solid buildings. The following line hardly leaves it open to doubt that there is also a reference to charitable foundations.

10, 11. knowing 't is A punishment or trial, when they know that their afflictions are a punishment from heaven or a trial of their "patience".

12, 13. To lapse in fulness Is sorer, to fall from the truth is worse in a rich person. The verb *lapse* occurs only in one other passage, where it has the same meaning as here.

13, 14. falsehood reminds Imogen at once of Posthumus. How exquisitely pathetic is her tender reflection on his conduct.

17. At point to sink, on the point of sinking.

21. hardness, hardship. In v. 5. 431 it = difficulty.

23. civil, in contrast to *savage* = civilized.

24. Take or lend, take money in exchange for food, or give me food for hospitality's sake. This is the usual explanation, which is supported by ll. 47, 48: "and thought To have *begg'd or bought* what I have took". If *take* has this meaning, *lend* cannot have its usual modern sense, for a stranger could not proffer money and in the same breath suggest a loan: *lend* is frequently used by Shakespeare without the notion of return.

27. A prayer that she may encounter such a foe as she has just alluded to.
The Folios commence Scene 7 here, with "Enter Imogen" below. Rowe continued Scene 6.

28. woodman, hunter.

30. 't is our match. [Explain.]

32, 33. our stomachs, &c. 'Hunger is the best sauce.'

36. that keep'st thyself! Cf. *As You Like It*, iv. 3. 82, 83:
"But at this hour the house doth keep itself;
There's none within".

38. browse, a corruption of *broust* (O. F. *brouster*), etymologically 'to nibble off young shoots'; hence the very word for this context.

50. i' the floor. *In* for *on* was not uncommon. Cf. *Matthew*, vi. 10: "Thy will be done in earth", and see *Abbott*, § 160.

52. parted, departed; so, often.

61. Fidele. Characteristically enough she is obliged to conceal and preserve her fidelity under the false, but characteristic, name of Fidele (*Gervinus*).

62. embark'd. There is this to be said for Hanmer's emendation *embarks*, that it certainly makes Imogen's tale hang together better.

63. being going, going, being on the way. *Abbott*, § 295.

64. in = into, is common, and is preserved in "fall in love". *Abbott*, § 159.

70, 71. The reading in the text is that of the Ff. (except that they have only a colon at *honesty*), and I cannot see that any sufficiently good case has been made out for a change. I interpret the passage thus: ' I should woo hard rather than fail of being your bridegroom in an honourable way. I bid for your affection on my usual terms— in honourable exchange for mine.' *Groom* occurs only once in Shakespeare in the sense of ' bridegroom ', and then it immediately follows ' bride '—" like bride and groom ", *Othello*, ii. 3. 180—but this meaning is strongly suggested to me by the word ' woo ' here, and is confirmed by the following speech of Arviragus: " I 'll make 't my comfort He is a man ". Besides, if *groom* means 'servant', there is no force in " were you a woman "; he might be his groom, if Imogen were a man. *Honesty* frequently means both ' honourable-ness ' and 'chastity'; " in the way of honesty " in this sense is found both in *Merry Wives* and in *Antony and Cleopatra*. The Globe and Cambridge editions read:

> " I should woo hard but be your groom.   In honesty,
>   I bid for you as I 'ld buy ",

which may be paraphrased thus: ' If you were a woman, I would woo you in marriage. You are not, but I speak with perfect sincerity all the same, offering only what I would readily give if circumstances allowed.' *In honesty*, = in truth, occurs nowhere else.

73. to him, to my brother.

76–78. If they had been my father's sons, I should not have been the heir, and thus less of a prize. The metaphor is nautical. Cf. the use of *price* in i. 1. 51.

79. wrings, is visibly pained.

80. free 't, put an end to the distress; as it were, set it free that it might fly away.

85, 86. laying by...multitudes, putting on one side the worth-less praise and false honour of " the still-discordant wavering multi-tude ".

87. out-peer, surpass.

88, 89. It is only with a change of sex that Imogen can even now contemplate the desertion of Posthumus.

92. of, concerning, about.   Cf. iv. 4. 48.

Scene 7.

We learn that Lucius is appointed general of the army to be employed in the war in Britain. This army *is to* consist of the forces " remaining now in Gallia ", supplemented with a levy of the gentry of Rome. This scene is evidently out of place. In any time-scheme it must come much earlier in the drama.—*P. A. Daniel.*

9.⁻ commends, delivers. This is Warburton's conjecture, the Ff. having *commands*. But *commend* was the usual formula, as in *Lear* ii. 4. 28:

"I did commend your highness' letters to them".

14. supplyant, Capell; *suppliant*, Ff. The emendation is convenient for preventing confusion.

Act IV.—Scene I.

Much of this soliloquy is a repetition of one near the close of iii. 5.

8. the lines of my body, &c. Cloten has this much justification, that Imogen mistakes his headless trunk, in the garments of Posthumus, for Posthumus himself. See iv. 2. 308 ff.

11, 12. alike conversant...oppositions, equally experienced in military service, and more distinguished in single combats.

12. imperceiverant, Dyce; *imperseverant*, Ff. The meaning is the same, 'undiscerning'; both spellings were in vogue. *Perseverance*, discernment, and *perseverant*, discerning, both occur not infrequently in authors of the time.

13. What mortality is! What a thing mortality is!

16. thy face. Warburton suggested *her*, which is certainly the meaning. But Clarke defends *thy* on the ground that the confusion of pronouns is "in Cloten's usual blundering, headlong manner".

17. haply. The Ff. have *happily*, as often. In iii. 3. 29 they have *hap'ly*. *Haply* and *happily* are from the same root, one direct, the other *via* 'happy'.

18. power of, control over.

21, 22. This is...meeting-place. [Paraphrase.]

Scene 2.

4, 5. Cf. ll. 246-249.

8. citizen, town-bred, effeminate.

wanton, a person of luxurious habits.

9. so please you = Fr. *s'il vous plaît*.

10. journal, diurnal (from the same root), daily.

10, 11. the breach of custom Is breach of all. [Paraphrase.]

17, 18. The construction of the sentence is irregular, but the sense is quite plain.
Cf. this "instinct of birth" in the brothers with Cymbeline's "instinct of affinity" in v. 5. 109.

(M 332)   L

29. Doth miracle itself, becomes a miracle, is marvellous. With *miracle* used as a verb cf. " That monsters it ", *Lear*, i. 1. 223.

31. So please you, sir. When Belarius says, " 'T is the ninth hour o' the morn ", he turns to a part of the cave, and takes down some of their hunting instruments, reaching one to Arviragus; which is the occasion of the words, "So please you, sir", the reaching being linked with a call (*Capell*). During Imogen's *Aside* the three men are equipping themselves for the hunt.

35. imperious, imperial; so, often.

38. The stage-direction *Swallows some*, inserted here by Dyce, who is followed by the Globe and most modern editions, is not in the Ff., and is probably misleading. The drug is contained in a box, which Imogen would not be likely to produce before the cave in the presence of the three men. She carries out her intention after her *exit* in l. 46.

stir him, persuade him to tell his story.

46. bound, indebted. Belarius may purposely take the word in the sense of ' tied ', or he may mean: "We will never let you repay us ".

47. appears he hath had: a confusion of two constructions, ' appears to have had ', and ' it appears, hath had '.

49. In characters, in the shape of letters. Capell continued this speech, after *cookery*, to Guiderius; Ff. give two following speeches to Arviragus, " He cut our roots ", and " Nobly he yokes ",—an obvious error.

Even in cooking, Imogen's dainty and elegant ways, not unworthy of Juno's attendants, do not desert her. Be intolerant of criticism which suggests that this accomplishment was inconsistent with Imogen's rank. Shakespeare at any rate did not think so.

57. him, Pope; *them*, Ff.

58. spurs, the largest roots of trees, which appear partly above the ground.

patience, Theobald; *patient*, Ff.

59, 60. The vine is of course patience. [Even a usually sane editor like Ingleby says it " is Fidele, or perhaps Fidele's heart ".] ' Let the root of the evil-smelling elder, grief, perish and untwine from the vine, patience, which will then grow all the more freely.' *From* has been proposed for *with*, but there is no reason to doubt that Shakespeare used the same construction with *untwine* as with *twine*. *Perishing* and *unceasing* are used proleptically, *i.e.* by anticipation. Biron in *Love's Labour's Lost* (v. 2. 610) says: " Judas was hanged on an elder ". To this tradition, aided no doubt by its sickly smell, the bad reputation of the tree was due.

61. great morning: possibly imitated from the Fr. *grand jour=* broad day. Fr. *de grand matin=*very early.

63. Belarius' conscience, guilty or not, at once suspects pursuit of himself instigated by the king.

66. saw him not. For the tense, past indefinite = present perfect, cf. l. 191 and iv. 3. 36. This is in accordance with the Greek use of the aorist (cf. the Revised with the Authorized Version of the New Testament), and it is as logical as our more modern use. The difference depends upon a difference of thought, the action being regarded *simply* as *past* without reference to the present or to *completion.* It will be noticed that both the above samples contain a negative. The *indefinite* tense seems to have peculiar propriety when we are denying that an action was performed at *any time whatever* (*Abbott*, § 347).

69. companies: probably here and in l. 101 not in the military sense, but simply 'people' or 'companions', as in *Henry V.*, i. 1. 55:
> "Since his addiction was to courses vain,
> His companies unletter'd ".

The singular is similarly used in l. 129.

71. mountaineers were supposed to be savage and barbarous. Cf. ll. 100, 120, 370, where the spelling of F 1 is *mountaineer*; here it is *mountainer*, just as we also find *enginer*, *mutiner* (as well as *mutineer*).

74. A slave: usually taken to mean 'the epithet *slave*', on the false analogy of *Romeo and Juliet*, iii. 1. 130:
> "Now, Tybalt, take the 'villain' back again ".

It is evident that the use of the indefinite article here makes all the difference, and that Guiderius is hurling Cloten's abusive epithet back, just as he does in l. 89 below.

81. Does Cloten in his anger forget for the moment that he is dressed in the garments of Posthumus? or does he expect to be recognized as Posthumus? Cloten's next speech hardly settles the point, because Guiderius' reply may well have made him look down at his clothes and reminded him that he was in borrowed garments; but it precludes the third supposition, that of an oversight on the part of the dramatist.

92. mere confusion, absolute overthrow. Cf. iii. 1. 64.

101. company's, Ff.; *companies*, Globe. Cf. l. 69.

103. long is it since I saw him: "some twenty years" (i. 1. 62).

105, 106. the snatches in his voice, And burst of speaking is a capital realistic touch, equally helpful to the actor on the stage, and to those of us who prefer to act Shakespeare in our easy-chairs.

106. absolute, certain. Cf. *perfect* in l. 118 and iii. 1. 71.

109, 110. made up...to man [meaning?].

111. **the effect,** Theobald; *defect,* Ff.   Theobald's conjecture gives the required sense, 'Cloten had no judgment, and therefore had no fear'.   Mr. Aldis Wright, in the *Cambridge Shakespeare,* returns to the Ff. reading, and appends this note: "Since none of the proposed emendations can be regarded as perfectly satisfactory, we leave this passage as it stands in the Folios.   Possibly, as some editors have suggested, the author may through inadvertence have said the reverse of what he meant.   Or a whole line, ending with the word 'judgement', may have dropped out, and the original sentence may have been to the following purport: 'for defect of judgement supplies the place of courage while true judgement is oft the cause of fear'."

122. **thank,** Steevens; *thanks,* Ff.

129. **For we do fear the law,** because, forsooth, we are afraid of the law.   For *for* = because see *Abbott,* § 151.

131. **safe,** sound, good.   We still say: "You may safely infer".

132. **humour,** Theobald; *honor,* Ff.

136. For the omission of *as,* cf. ll. 126, 127 above, where both *so* and *as* are omitted.   See *Abbott,* § 281.

141. **fetch us in.**   Cf. iii. 2. 9 (and note), and l. 121 above.

141, 142. **yet is 't...alone.**   [Paraphrase.]

145. **ordinance,** that which is ordained.

146. **howsoe'er,** *sc.* it be; in any case.

149. **Did make my way long forth.**   [Paraphrase.]

152. The omission of the verb of motion is frequent.   See ll. 163, 167.

157. **So,** on the condition that: 'I would gladly bear all the 'consequences for the glory of the deed'.

159–161. **I would revenges...answer.**   [Paraphrase.]

167. **to gain his colour,** to restore the hue of health to his cheeks.

168. **Clotens** is not possessive case, but objective.   **Let blood** (= bleed) is a compound verb, construed with the objective (dative?), and even used in the passive, as in *Troilus and Cressida,* ii. 3. 222: "I'll let his humours blood"; and *Richard III.,* iii. 1. 183:
> "His ancient knot of dangerous adversaries
> To-morrow are let blood at Pomfret-castle".

169. The old man, glorious in his humility, imputes to their royal blood the high and heroic thoughts which his own great and childlike spirit has breathed into them (*Hudson*). Cf. iii. 3. 79, and iv. 2. 25.

170. **how,** Pope; *thou,* F 1.

179. **Civility,** good breeding, refinement.   Cf. *civil*, iii. 6. 23.

186. ingenious, Ff., =ingenuous; but the two forms were used indiscriminately.

190. since death.   *The* was frequently omitted before a noun already defined by another noun, especially in prepositional phrases (*Abbott*, § 89).

193, 194. Exultation over nothing is jollity fit for apes, and lamentation for trifles is grief fit only for boys.

Rimed couplets are introduced in strange and unexpected places in this play.   Probably here and in v. 5. 106, 107 the rime is intended to emphasize the contempt expressed.   From here to l. 290 we have perhaps the finest poetry in the play, not easily surpassed in the whole of Shakespeare's works.

198. on is frequently interchangeable with *of.*   Cf. l. 297, v. 2. 3, and *Tempest*, iv. 1. 157:

> "We are such stuff
> As dreams are made on".

200. To.   [Collect other instances of this redundant *to.*]

204–206.   *Who ever yet could sound thy bottom? find*
   The ooze, to shew what coast thy sluggish care
   Might'st easilest harbour in.   Ff.

   The ooze? or shew what coast thou, sluggish care,
   Might'st easil'est harbour in?   Capell.

Crare is Sympson's brilliant emendation (see Glossary).   Melancholy is compared, first to a bottomless sea, then to a sluggish crare seeking safe anchorage therein.   *Sound thy bottom = find the ooze*, not = 'fathom thy hold', which would complicate the metaphors.   Ingleby proposes *Sound the bottom?*, which has the merit of reducing the two comparisons to one.   Or perhaps we should read, with alternative comparisons:

> *Who ever yet could sound thy bottom, find*
> *The ooze? or shew what coast thy sluggish crare*
> *Might easiliest harbour in?*

The general purport of the passage is clear enough: 'Melancholy is an unfathomable sea, in which it is useless to take soundings in the hope of finding any coast for harbouring'.

207. what man.   *A* was sometimes omitted after *what* in the sense of 'what kind of' (*Abbott*, § 86).   Cf. iv. 4. 35.

   but I, *sc.* know.

210, 211. 'Smiling as if he had been tickled in his sleep by a fly, not smitten by death's dart, for he was still laughing.'

Mr. Spedding compares this with Shakespeare's treatment of the face of a beautiful woman just dead in two other instances, showing his wonderful *imagination* in the two later plays as compared with the mere *fancy* of the earlier.

> " Death lies on her, like an untimely frost
> Upon the fairest flower of all the field ".
>   *Romeo and Juliet* (1596–7), iv. 5. 28, 29.
> " But she looks like sleep,
> As she would catch another Antony
> In her strong toil of grace ".
>   *Antony and Cleopatra* (1607), v. 2. 349–51.

214. clouted brogues, heavy shoes patched with leather. *Brogues* (Gaelic *brog*) are (1) coarse shoes, often of half-dressed leather; hence (2) *brogue* = the dialect of people who wear such. *Clouted shoes* now = shoes whose soles are studded with clout-nails (Fr. *clouter*, to stud). But there can be little doubt that in our older authors the hackneyed expression *clouted shoon* (*Comus*, 635) meant 'shoes patched with clouts (O.E. *clūt*, a patch) of leather'. Cf. *Joshua*, ix. 5: "old shoes and clouted upon their feet"; and Latimer's *Sermons*: "he should not have clouting leather to piece his shoes with".

216. a bed, as fresh and pure as if he were asleep on a bed—such "charming" power has he.

217, 218. Female fairies will fall in love with him and, haunting his tomb, save his body from decay. Cf. the fairies' song in *Midsummer Night's Dream*, ii. 2. 9 ff.:

> " Beetles black, approach not near;
> Worm nor snail, do no offence ".

According to tradition such creatures would not approach where fairies were.

222. azured harebell. The harebell of Shakespeare is undoubtedly the wild hyacinth (Ellacombe, *Plant Lore of Shakespeare*), *Scilla nutans*. Cf. ii. 2. 22.

223. whom not to slander, which, not to slander it.

224. ruddock, Hanmer; *raddock*, Ff. The same legend is found in *The Babes in the Wood*. In Thomas Johnson's *Cornucopia* (1516) we read: "The robin redbreast, if he find a man or a woman dead, will cover all his face with moss, and some think that if the body should remain unburied that he would cover the whole body also".

229. winter-ground. To *winter-ground* a plant is to protect it from the inclemency of the winter season by straw, dung, &c., laid over it (*Steevens*). No other instance of the word is known.

232. admiration: very likely combining here its modern sense with that of 'wonder', seen in i. 6. 37 above.

233. shall 's, shall us, shall we; again in v. 5. 228. *Abbott* (§ 215) connects this with the old impersonal use of the verb, of which he gives no example, and of which very few examples indeed are to be found. I think it more likely to be an irregular extension of the familiar usage after transitive verbs, as in ' Let 's.' for ' Let us '.

237. **As once**; *as once to*, Ff.; Pope omitted *to*.

238. It is noteworthy that these names do not occur in the dirge.

248. **That angel of the world**, the 'guardian angel', 'daemon' (cf. *Antony and Cleopatra*, ii. 3. 19), that keeps security and order in the world.

The idea of reverence and respect for ' degree' as of paramount importance in the maintenance of social order, is found elsewhere in Shakespeare, notably in the fine speech of Ulysses (*Troilus and Cressida*, iv. 1. 83 ff.):

> " O, when degree is shaked,
> Which is the ladder to all high designs,
> Then enterprise is sick . . . .
> Take but degree away, untune that string,
> And hark, what discord follows ! . . .
> Force should be right; or rather, right and wrong,
> Between whose endless jar justice resides,
> Should lose their names, and so should justice too."

252. **Ajax**, son of Telamon, second to Achilles in bravery among the Greeks who took part in the Trojan war, and Thersites, "a deformed and scurrilous Grecian", are both characters in Shakespeare's *Troilus and Cressida*.

255, 256. The Christian custom of burial is to lay the head to the *west* and the feet to the east; "so at the second coming of the Son of Man the, dead might rise and face him in the general resurrection" (Lee's *Glossary of Liturgical and Ecclesiastical Terms*, p. 62). In reversing the position, Shakespeare may have had no other intention than to suit the pre-Christian period of his play. But it is at least possible that he was aware of the classical (and Celtic) myth which located the ' Earthly Paradise' in the Fortunate Islands (Avalon) across the western ocean, and which gave rise to the custom of burying the dead with their faces set thitherwards. (See Tylor's *Primitive Culture*, vol. ii. pp. 48, 422, and Baring Gould's *Curious Myths of the Middle Ages*.)

267. [What is the meaning of this line?]

271. **thunder-stone**, thunderbolt (*not* meteorite).

275. **Consign to thee**, sign the same contract with thee, submit to the same terms.

276. **exorciser** (unique instance), *exorcist* (occurs twice), and *exorcism* (once), are always used by Shakespeare in connection with raising spirits, not, as now, with laying them or casting them out.

278. **forbear thee**, let thee alone, forbear to disturb thee. [Assign the exact meaning of this word and of *forbearance* in each of the

following passages: i. 1. 68; ii. 3. 97; iii. 5. 39; and v. 5. 124.   Which
of these meanings do these words still retain?]

280. consummation.   Cf. the closing prayer of the Church of
England Burial Service: "that we, with all those that are departed
in the true faith of thy holy Name, may have our perfect consummation and bliss, both in body and soul, in thy eternal and everlasting glory".

285. Upon their faces, *sc.* strew the flowers.   Possibly Shakespeare for the moment forgot that Cloten's "clotpoll" had gone to
tell the fishes he was the queen's son.   Staunton proposed *Upon
th' earth's face*, without a stop at *face*.

290. is, Pope; *are*, Ff.

293. 'Ods pittikins! a diminutive corruption of 'God's pity';
cf. "God's bodykins" (for *body*), in *Hamlet*, ii. 2. 554.

297–312.   Imogen wakes to semi-consciousness, and only by
degrees shakes off the effects of the drug.   Finding a "bloody man"
by her side she hopes she is dreaming now, and that *so* (observe this
pregnant word in l. 298) her life in the cave was a reality; but,
praying with averted eyes for mercy, she looks again at the man
(l. 306), and concludes that this is the reality and that the dream.
Next she sees that the man is headless.   Then the recognition of the
garments of Posthumus suddenly removes all effects of the trance
together with the memory of all that has immediately preceded, so
that in a second she makes the awful discovery that the face and
head are gone.

300, 301. 'T was but a phantasm of the brain, an arrow made of
nothing and shot at nothing.

310, 311. Mercurial, &c., of Mercury, of Mars, of Jove.

311. brawns, brawny arms.

313. madded Hecuba.   Hecuba, Hector's mother, maddened
at his death.

315. irregulous (L. *regula*), lawless, licentious.   Found nowhere
else.

316. Hast, Pope; *Hath*, Ff.

320. Posthumus; accented everywhere else on the penult.   This
fact has of course been used by the supporters of the double-date
theory (see *Introduction*, p. ix).

325. pregnant, evident; so, frequently.

329. Cloten's, Pope; *Cloten*, Ff.

333. To, in addition to.

337. confiners (unique instance) = either 'borderers' or 'inhabitants'.   *Confines* in Shakespeare usually = district, territory, not
'borders'.

341. Syenna's brother, brother of the ruler of Siena, a town and province in Tuscany. In the middle ages it was the chief of the Ghibelline towns, in the struggle with the Guelphs.

347. fast, fasted. In verbs in which the infinitive ends in *t, ed* is often omitted in the past indicative for euphony (*Abbott,* § 341).

348. wing'd, having flown.

363–365. Who has changed that noble picture to something quite different from what noble nature made it?

373. The commas punctuate Imogen's sobs.

389. pickaxes, her hands.

400. arm him, take him up in your arms.

403. Cf. this sentiment and that of iv. 3. 46 with v. 4. 101, 102.

Scene 3

shows us Cymbeline in a most unfavourable light. In a great emergency he appears utterly incapable and incompetent, "amazed with matter", looking for the counsel of others who cannot give it, and thinking that in his stepson he has lost a great strategist or a great general ("so needful for this present").

6. Upon a desperate bed, so ill that her life is almost despaired of.

8. it strikes me, this succession of blows falls upon me.

17. missing = missed, and thus the statement is literally true (see iii. 5).

21. For the omission of the nominative see *Abbott,* § 400.

troublesome [meaning?].

22. slip, as a greyhound from the leash in coursing.

22, 23. but our jealousy Does yet depend, 'but you are not yet free from our suspicion, which is still hanging over you'.

28. amazed with matter, bewildered with pressing business.

29, 30. can affront no less Than, is equal to meeting as many as. Cf. the noun *affront* in v. 3. 87.

36. I heard no letter = 'I have not had a line', whatever the precise meaning of *letter* may be here.

40. betid, Hanmer; *betide,* Ff. Such contraction in preterites and past participles was particularly common after dentals even from the Old English period. Cf. *bestrid,* iv. 4. 38.

44. Even to the note o' the king, so that even the king should be compelled to notice my valour. Cf. *upon our note* (iv. 4. 20), 'in taking note of us',

Scene 4.

4. This way, if we do so, *i.e.* hide here. [Paraphrase the rest of the sentence.]

6. revolts, revolters; occurs also in *King John*. Cf. *revenges*, iv. 2. 159, and see *Abbott*, § 433.

11. render, account, confession. The verb is used similarly in v. 5. 135.

13. whose answer, the punishment of which.

17. the, Rowe; *their*, Ff.

18. their quarter'd fires, burning in the several quarters of their camp.

19. cloy'd importantly, stopped up (O. Fr. *cloyer*, *cloer*, to stop up, nail), filled with matters of great importance.

27. The certainty, 'which is the certain consequence'.

29. But [destined, doomed] **to be.**

33. thereto so o'ergrown, moreover so covered with hair and beard. Cf. v. 3. 17.

35. thing: almost = reproach.

46. The hazard therefore due. [Explain.]

Act V.—Scene I.

There is nothing corresponding to this scene in any of Shakespeare's possible sources, wherein none of the villains have any thought of guilt or repentance until their wives' innocence is made clear at the close. Thus Shakespeare always transmutes his material into something nobler, more true to life, more deeply significant.

1. wish'd, Pope; *am wisht*, Ff.

The bloody cloth is the "bloody sign" of iii. 4. 125 (see note).

5. wrying, going awry or astray. No other instance of this verb used intransitively is known.

7. bond, obligation. Observe how completely Pisanio's actual course of action is here justified by his master.

9. to put on this, to instigate this vengeance. It was the wager between Posthumus and Iachimo which had led to Imogen's supposed fall.

13-15. Some you snatch from hence for little faults; others you suffer to heap ills on ills, and afterwards make them dread their

having done so, to the eternal welfare of the doers (*Mason*). Cf.
Lucrece, 939-943:

> "Time's glory is   .   .   .
> To wrong the wronger till he render right".

For **thrift** = thriving, welfare, cf. *Merchant of Venice*, i. 1. 175: "I
have a mind presages me such thrift".

each elder worse is one of those daring usages in which Shakespeare would doubtless have delighted still more if he could have
known what a godsend they were destined to be to his ultra-logical
commentators.   The words must mean 'each ill or crime worse
than the one which had preceded it', the crime being termed *elder*
because committed at a more advanced age.   Cf. Bacon's *Advance-
ment of Learning*, i. 5: "These times are the ancient times when
the world is ancient".

16. The connection is best seen by regarding the last sentence as
parenthetical; the line of thought interrupted at "vengeance" in
l. 11 is here resumed.

21. **thee, Britain**, not 'peace'.

23. **suit** [meaning?].

30. **habits**, clothes (Fr. *habits*).

32, 33. The guise or fashion of the world being then as now
'more without and less within'.

Scene 2.

Iachimo's sense of guilt is again entirely an addition of Shakespeare's own, and prepares the way for his repentant confession in
Sc. 5.   Posthumus here consummates his own repentance by his
magnanimous sparing of the life of him who had wrought all his
woe.   That he recognized Iachimo is proved by v. 5. 136, 410-412.

15. See Appendix B (5).

Scene 3.

Observe how modestly Posthumus omits all mention of his own
distinguished share in the Romans' defeat.   He is at first (l. 3)
politely sympathetic with the noble Lord; but when the bearing of
the latter, and his evident lack of patriotism, convince Posthumus
that he is a coward at heart, he cannot refrain from contemptuous
sarcasms.   The scene serves the double purpose of describing the
battle and showing how completely the victory was due to the valour
of Belarius, Guiderius, Arviragus, and Posthumus.

4. See Appendix B (5).

14. **wall'd with turf**, with banks of turf outside the ditches.

16-18. **who deserved...for's country**, who, by doing this for his country, earned the support it had given him during the long life indicated by his white beard.

20. **The country base,** the country game of prisoner's base; also called *chivy* (from Chevy Chase).

21, 22. Masks were worn by ladies for two purposes, to preserve their complexions, and for concealment. Hence the meaning is: 'With faces fair enough for masks, or rather even fairer than faces that are masked for preservation or to guard against impertinent curiosity'. shame = the desire not to be recognized.

23. **Made good the passage.** [Explain.]

24. **harts,** Theobald; *hearts,* Ff.

24-51. [Paraphrase this passage.]

32. 'Aided by the advantage of the place, and influencing others as if by magic.' *Or,* "more charming" may mean that they infected [others] with their nobleness even *more* than they were aided by position. In l. 68 *charm'd* = protected as if by magic spells. See also i. 3. 35, and note.

34. **gilded pale looks,** brought the colour back to faces blanched through fear. *Gilded* is the principal verb to *These three* (l. 28). Cf. *Macbeth*, ii. 2. 56: "I'll gild the faces of the grooms"; and *Tempest*, v. 280: "This grand liquor that hath gilded them".

35. **Part ... renewed,** partly revived their sense of shame, partly their courage.

40. **A stop i' the chaser,** a halt by the pursuer.

42. **stoop'd,** Rowe; *stopt,* Ff. *Stoop'd* = swooped; it is a technical term for the pouncing of birds of prey. Cf. v. 4. 126.

43. **they,** Theobald; *the,* Ff. The construction is exactly parallel to that of the preceding lines. Observe the appropriateness of *strides* for *victors.*

45. **need,** extremity, emergency.

47. The punctuation in the text is my own. It is impossible that the three **somes** are nominatives, because **Some slain before** cannot possibly = some wound those slain before. The first two, therefore, are accusatives; the third makes equally good sense as accusative or nominative, *i.e.* according as we supply 'who were' or 'wound' after it; but it is more probably accusative like the first two.

51. **mortal bugs,** objects of deadly terror (Welsh *bwg,* a spectre). *Mortal* in this sense occurs repeatedly in this play.

51, 52. The well-bred irony of unpatriotic indifference and unconcern arouse Posthumus' anger.

53-55. Posthumus first bids him not wonder, then tells him in another mode of reproach that wonder is all that he was made for (*Johnson*).

61. as he is made to do, what he is naturally qualified to do, *i.e.* fly.

64. Still going? *i.e.* you run away from me as you did from the enemy.

64, 65. O noble misery, &c. What miserable nobility, to be present on the battle-field and yet, so far from fighting (see l. 2), have to ask a poor peasant-soldier what took place.

74–76. The probable meaning is: 'I have returned to the side on which I came hither (cf. v. 1. 25), being now an Italian again, though at heart favouring the Britons'. Capell suggested that l. 74 referred to Death: 'Death being now a favourer to the Briton, I am more likely to meet with him by rejoining the Romans'. I reject this interpretation as not being the natural meaning of the passage (the colon at the close of l. 73 is in the earliest text). It seems to me obvious that "a favourer to the Briton" and "no more a Briton" refer to the same person, the "I" of l. 75. Moreover, added point is given to this explanation if we suppose that Post-humus has now resumed his "Italian weeds". At the beginning of the scene, in his conversation with the British Lord, he is evidently a British soldier; at its close he is taken prisoner as an *Italian*. Why may we not suppose the change to have been effected at this point and to be glanced at in these lines?—'Though still at heart favouring the Britons, I have joined the Romans again, for among them, the vanquished, I shall meet with death'.

78. touch my shoulder, the usual way of arresting a prisoner. Cf. *As You Like It*, iv. 1. 48: "Cupid hath clapped him o' the shoulder".

81. 'On one side or the other (*i.e.* for or against the Britons) I am come to end my life.'

90, 91. if seconds Had answer'd him, if he had been seconded with valour equal to his own.

92. leg. Cf. *Richard II.*, ii. 3. 90:
"Why have those banish'd and forbidden legs
    Dared once to touch a dust of England's ground?"

Scene 4.

It is somewhat difficult to be altogether patient with any part of this scene but the opening soliloquy of Posthumus, except as a foil to the intense interest of that which follows it. The genuineness of ll. 30–122 (not of the dumb-show) has been questioned. See Appendix E.

1, 2. The reference is to the custom of putting a lock on a horse's leg when he is turned out to pasture.

8. unbar these locks. Cf. *pick that bolt* (l. 10). We now speak of 'picking a lock' and 'unbarring a door', &c.

8–28. [Paraphrase this passage.]

10. The penitent instrument to pick that bolt, the means of showing his repentance, by which he may free his conscience. Ingleby explains *the penitent instrument* in the following note: "In this speech Posthumus is made to employ the language of the early divines, in distinguishing the three parts (primary, secondary, and 'main') of Repentance, as the condition of Remission of Sins. 1. Attrition, or sorrow for sin: 'Is't enough I am sorry?' 2. Penance; which was held to convert attrition into contrition, or godly sorrow: 'Must I repent?' 3. Satisfaction: 'to satisfy'. And he contends that as he has fulfilled the former requirements, he is willing to fulfil the last—to pay his debt, for having taken Imogen's life, by giving up his own."

16. If...part, if satisfaction is the main condition of my freedom of conscience.

17. stricter. It is contended that *stricter* (L. *strictus*, tightened) here = 'more restricted', 'less severe', because the gods could not demand a *more* severe "render" than his all. The word occurs in Hooker in that sense, but nowhere else in Shakespeare. But the whole point of the speech is that the gods show mercy in proportion as they inflict penance. Therefore, when Posthumus bids them take no "stricter" render than his all, he means no *less* a penance than his life. The student will find that the speech repays careful thought, without which, indeed, its full meaning cannot be appreciated.

18–21. I ask not to be allowed to compound with my creditors, which would be no clemency to me.

24, 25. Stamped coins, though light, are accepted for the sake of the figure stamped upon them.

26. You...yours, you should the rather take mine because "you coin'd it" (l. 23).

27. take this audit, accept the statement of account I offer. Posthumus has made out the account against himself, and offers *per contra* the life he has to give as the "main part" of his Repentance. He now asks the gods to accept his audit, and in discharge to take his life (*Ingleby*).

28. cancel these cold bonds, free me from these cold (iron) gyves by death.

43. Lucina, the goddess who presides over child-birth: Juno or Diana.

60. Leonati. Abbott, § 22, attributes this quasi-adjectival use of *Leonati* to an increasing dislike and disuse of the inflection in 's.

97. Elysium, the abode of the shades of the blest in the lower world.

102. delighted, delighting, delightful; passive for active.

114–117. 'He came down in thunder and sulphurous smoke; he ascends with an odour sweeter than the scents of the "beatific Asphodel meadows" of Elysium'.

116. foot, strike with his claws.

118. cloys, cleys, clees, claws (*Farmer*), as hawks and eagles are fond of doing; no other instance of the word is known.

120. is enter'd: cf. Fr. *est entré*, and see *Abbott*, § 295. But "are born" (v. 5. 17)=Fr. *nous sommes nés*=we *were* born.

129. I swerve [meaning ?].

135–137. let thy effects...promise. [Paraphrase.]

149. The action of my life is like it, the course of my life is an equally hopeless enigma.

159, 160. which are often...mirth. [Paraphrase.]

164. heaviness: of, Globe. F1 has *heaviness. Oh, of,* by anticipation of *Oh* in the next line.

167. debitor and creditor, account-book or ledger.

169. counters, round pieces of base metal used in making calculations.

172. that were to sleep, who was destined to sleep.

179. to take. This redundant *to* is frequently found before the second of two parallel infinitives. See *Abbott*, § 350.

180. jump, risk, hazard. Cf. *Macbeth*, i. 7. 7:
> "We 'ld jump the life to come".

198, 199. for all he be, despite his being.

203. my wish hath a preferment in 't, if my wish were fulfilled I should hope for preferment to a better office.

Scene 5.

For a proper appreciation of the wonderful *dénouement* of this scene it must be remembered how much there is to be unravelled, not for the spectators only, but still more for the actors themselves. For, it may be borne in mind, we, as readers or spectators, know a great deal more about the several *personæ* than they know about one another, and our own interest is greatly enhanced by a sympathetic interest in the disentanglement of the intricate knots of the play from the personal stand-point of each of the principal characters. To take one illustration: *we* know that Imogen's virtue has remained unspotted throughout; Posthumus does not know it; *we* recognize his wife in the page of Lucius; *he* does not. We look with *personal* interest to see how the revelation and the recognition will be brought about; we look with something of *sympathetic* interest to see how Posthumus and Imogen will be affected by the revelation and the recognition.

5. **targes of proof**, shields of proof; *of proof* is a technical expression, frequently applied to armour that had been satisfactorily tested after manufacture. *Targes* is here a monosyllable.

9, 10. **Such precious...poor looks.** [Paraphrase.]

14. **liver, heart and brain:** standing for all the vital forces of the body.

16. **of whence** = of from where, *i.e.* of where, *or* whence.

22. **estates,** rank, dignity. Cf. with i. 4. 95, 108. In l. 74, *estate* = state, condition.

31. **like her life,** which had been a mad horror of wickedness and unrest.

36. **finish'd,** died; see l. 412.

38. **Affected,** loved.

43. **bore in hand,** made believe, pretended; not uncommon.

54–56. Win your heart by her show of affection, and in time, when she had thus got you into a fit frame of mind to accept her proposal, to secure the adoption of her son as heir to the crown.

62–66. Cymbeline here confesses his own lack of insight and weakness of character.

68. **And prove it in thy feeling.** [Explain.]

83. **peculiar,** personal, of myself.

86 ff. This recalls Boccaccio's description of Bernabo Lomellin's wife, the Imogen of the tale: "She was goodly of person, and yet very young, quick, quaint, mild, and courteous, and not wanting anything appertaining to the office of a wife, either for domestic affairs, or any other employment whatsoever".

87. **So tender over his occasions,** so nicely sensible of his wants (*Schmidt*).

95. **nor,** Rowe; Ff. omit.

96. **To say,** I should say.

103. **a thing,** *i.e.* the ring she had given Posthumus on the finger of her tempter Iachimo, whom she recognizes among the prisoners. What wild possibilities this sight must send thronging through her brain!

120–122. One sand does not resemble another more closely [than he resembles] that sweet rosy lad who died, and was Fidele. There is no reason to doubt the correctness of the Folio reading. These latest plays are full of "rapid and abrupt turnings of thought, so quick that language can hardly follow fast enough; impatient activity of intellect and fancy, which, having once disclosed an idea, cannot wait to work it orderly out".

126. saw, Rowe; *see*, Ff.

127. It is not to be wondered at that Pisanio is the first to identify his mistress, for he alone was privy to her disguise. Bear in mind that Imogen has not revealed herself to Cymbeline in their private conference. It is worth while at this point to run over in your mind how much of the exact state of affairs is known to each of the principal characters, *e.g.* Iachimo knows that he obtained the ring by wronging Cymbeline's daughter and her husband, but does not recognize either of the latter; on the other hand, Posthumus knows him (see l. 136).

139, 140. Since what I have to say will torture you, you will [if wise] torture me to leave it unsaid. See l. 133.

155 ff. Iachimo's narration differs so widely from the facts as given in i. 4., that it is evident Shakespeare was thinking, not of what he had previously written, but of the "Italian merchants who accidentally met in Paris at supper, and talked freely of their wives at home" (in Boccaccio). In i. 4 there is no "feast", no Posthumus "sitting sadly", no gallants praising their "loves of Italy", &c.

163-165. for feature...nature, for grace and dignity of form, surpassing those antique statues of Venus and Minerva whose attitudes are unattainable by nature (*Staunton*).

165. brief, transient. Art idealizes and makes permanent the changing, fleeting forms of nature.

condition, disposition, character.

167, 168. besides that hook of wiving, Fairness, besides that hook which catches a husband, beauty.

176-178. Either our boasted loves were actually mere kitchen-trulls (see Glossary) as compared with his, or we in describing them were as dumb fools compared with him.

182. Made scruple of, expressed doubt with regard to.

185. In suit, by making suit to her.

186. hers and mine adultery. We should now say 'my adultery and hers'. "It is felt that the ear cannot wait till the end of the sentence while so slight a word as *her* remains with nothing to depend on" (*Abbott*, § 238). Cf. l. 230.

190. Phœbus' wheel, a wheel of the fabled chariot of the sun.

194, 195. 'Between the pure passion of a pure woman and passion adulterate with lust.'

196. mine Italian brain. Shakespeare intended Iachimo as a foil to Posthumus, not only as regards purity of morals, but also as regards open directness of conduct. Here there is not improbably a reference to the Machiavelism of his day. Machiavel, who died 1530, taught that in government right should be subordinated to expediency. Cf. iii. 4. 15.

199. practice, plot, stratagem.

206, 207. he could not But think. It is essential to remember this opinion of Iachimo in order to the formation of a correct judgment as to the blameworthiness or otherwise of Posthumus' conduct. See "Critical Comments", and i. 4 and ii. 4.

209 ff. What a magnificent dramatic moment! Observe that all these opprobrious epithets are intended for himself, not for Iachimo. Fletcher well says: "Nothing can exceed the dramatic beauty of this electric burst of agonizing shame and remorse from the husband's heart, thus taking the place of Iachimo's intended account of the transport of vindictive rage into which he had fallen when first persuaded of his wife's infidelity. The atonement to the injured name of Imogen is now complete, and the catastrophe of the drama fully prepared."

216, 217. That all...than they. [Paraphrase.] Cf. l. 225.

221. she herself, virtue herself.

227. Here for the first and only time Imogen seems to forget that she is in male disguise, and thus brings on herself that blow from her husband which still further heightens the interest of this pathetic climax.

228, 229. If we're going to make a play of it, act your part by lying there.

233. come, Rowe; *comes*, Ff.

238. The tune of Imogen: 'Imogen's musical voice' is surely implied. Cf. iii. 4. 174, 175.

240. stones of sulphur, thunderbolts.

250. temper, mix, compound.

261. from. Here and in one other place (not in this play) the Ff. have *fro*.

262, 263. Think...again. Imogen seems to be carrying out the image suggested by her own question. 'Imagine yourself upon a rock, where you may easily throw me from you again, and now [as she embraces Posthumus] see if you can do so!' What a world of meaning is conveyed by this simple challenge!

275. missing, being absent (and missed).

277. discover'd, revealed, disclosed; so in i. 6. 97 and iii. 5. 95.

284. But Pisanio was not present when Cloten announced this purpose in iii. 5. 134 ff.

286. It is not altogether satisfactory to me that Pisanio here drops out of the play without any recognition from Posthumus and Imogen of his sterling fidelity.

297. of mine : *i.e.* of my head being cut off.

298, 299. Cymbeline refuses to redeem his character up to the last. Nothing could possibly show him in a worse light than this speech to the slayer of the villain who, as he had just heard, was bent upon treating his daughter in a way worse than death.

303–305. He has deserved better of you than a whole band of Clotens ever did by any service in which they received scars.

307, 308. Will you undo the worthy service for which you are not yet rewarded by doing that for which you must experience our wrath?

311. But I will prove, if I do not prove.

319. Assumed this age, taken on this appearance of age (since last you saw him).

334, 335. 'My entire (*or* only) offence, my very punishment, and my treason, were the creation and outcome solely of your caprice.'

334. mere, Tyrwhitt; *near*, Ff.

338. For *as* (instead of *which*), correlative with *that*, see *Abbott*, § 280.

346, 347. the more it shaped Unto my end of stealing them, the better it fulfilled the purpose for which I stole them.

351. worthy, *sc.* to be used.

352–354. Thy tears give testimony to the sincerity of thy relation; and I have the less reason to be incredulous, because the actions which you have done within my knowledge are more incredible than the story which you relate (*Johnson*).

371. orbs, orbits, or the revolving spheres to which the planets were fastened in the Ptolemaic astronomy.

378. ye, Rowe; *we*, Ff.

e'er, Rowe; *ere*, Ff.

383, 384. which Distinction should be rich in, which the discrimination and following out of the different parts of the narrative will be sure to reveal fully.

385. you (emphatic), Imogen.

386. brothers, Rowe; *brother*, Ff.

388. your three motives, the motives of you three (Belarius and the two brothers).

395. her master, Lucius. Here, at the close of the drama,

Imogen is in her rightful place: though she has lost a kingdom, she is queen of every heart.

396, 397. the counterchange...all. [Paraphrase.]

409. beseeming, seeming, appearance; unique instance.

fitment, suitable attire.

421. freeness, generosity; unique instance.

428. spritely shows, ghostly apparitions.

430–432. whose containing ... collection of it, the contents of which are so hard to make sense of that I can draw no inference from it. *From* is often a pregnant word in Shakespeare; see *Abbott*, § 158.

446, 447. Mr. Aldis Wright cites this identical derivation, worthy to rank with that of *rat* from *mouse*, from Henry Stephen's *World of Wonders*, 1607: "If any should reply and say, that it is not to be wondered at that the ancient Latinists never mentioned these Etymologies, considering the names were not then in use; I answer, that they had no good dexterity in giving Etymologies of Ancient latin words; witness the notation of *Mulier, quasi mollis aer*".

448–450. There is something of confusion here, which Capell proposed to remove by reading *thy* for *this*. If *who* (l. 448) be addressed to Posthumus, the sense is clear; but it apparently means Imogen, and in that case it is possible that the *you* in l. 450 stepped into the place of the real subject and thus led to a change in the voice of the verb.

458 My, Ff.; Hanmer proposed *By*.

459. Cymbeline was personally indebted to Cæsar; see iii. 1. 68, 69.

464. The sense is clear, and the construction may be rectified by supplying *upon* at the close of this line.

APPENDIX A

PROSODY

Cymbeline is the longest but three of all Shakespeare's plays: *Antony and Cleopatra* has 3964 lines, *Hamlet* 3924, *Richard III.* 3599, *Cymbeline* 3448. Mr. F. G. Fleay, to whom the above numbers are due, also gives the following totals in *Cymbeline*: Prose, 638 lines; blank verse, 2585 lines; decasyllabic rhyming lines, 107. I make the number of lines in rhyming couplets somewhat different; but the essential thing to note is, that, for so late a play, decasyllabic rhyming couplets are unusually frequent, especially the rhymed tags at the close of scenes and important passages. Mr. Fleay gives the following numbers:

			No. of scenes in play.	No. of scenes with tags.	No. of tag rhymes.
Cymbeline,	...	...	27	11	16
Tempest, ...	...	...	9	1	1
Winter's Tale, ...	...	15	0	0

The study of the prosody of a play of Shakespeare's is of use for two important practical purposes: First, the characteristics of the versification vary greatly at different periods of the dramatist's career, and a careful study of these characteristics has proved a great aid in determining the approximate order of composition of the plays. And the knowledge of this order enables us to read the plays in chronological sequence—by far the best order in which to read them—and thus to trace the gradual growth of Shakespeare's marvellous powers. See "Date, History, &c., of the Play", Introduction, § 1. Secondly, some knowledge of scansion is necessary for the intelligent reading of a play aloud: for the avoidance at the one extreme of reading poetry exactly as if it were prose (sometimes not even prose cut up into lengths), and at the other of reading it in a monotonous singsong way, every line on one pattern, thus—

"As *to* seek *through* the *re*-gions *of* the *earth*",

without regard to the comparative importance and emphasis, or unimportance and lack of emphasis, of each word. Now, inasmuch as the knowledge of scansion necessary for this purpose is not great, and because the subject is not of thrilling interest in itself, being moreover utterly inadequate and useless unless backed by an enthusiastic desire to derive the fullest meaning and pleasure from what is read, I shall say what I have to say as simply and briefly as possible.

Feet.—English prosody has adopted most of its terminology from classical prosody; it is therefore the more necessary to bear in mind this essential difference between the two systems: classical scansion divided syllables into long and short, English divides them into accented or stressed and unaccented or unstressed. If we represent an accented syllable by *a* and an unaccented syllable by *x*, we can easily exemplify the commonest kinds of metrical feet:

Symbol.	Name.	Example.
x a	Iambic	machine.
a x	Trochaic	father.
x x a	Anapæstic	interfere.
a x x	Dactylic	carpenter.

Lines.—When a line consists of five feet it is called a pentameter, if of six feet a hexameter. When a pentametric line or pentameter is made up of five (mostly) iambic feet, it is called an iambic penta-meter. The great majority of the lines in this play are iambic penta-meters; but if they are unrhymed, they are conveniently and shortly called *blank verse* (lines). Here is an example of such a line:

"As he | was born. | The king | he takes | the babe" (i. 1. 40).
  x a   *x a*   *x a*   *x a*   *x a*

Variations.—I purposely selected the above line because each foot is a very fair iambic. But it happens only rarely, perhaps not oftener than once in every twelve to twenty lines, that a line consists of five normal iambic feet. Were it otherwise, blank verse would become as intolerably monotonous as Pope's couplets. The highest technical art is shown in the way great poets vary the music of their verse by varying the feet they employ.

For my present purpose I leave *degrees of stress* out of account. It is obvious that a syllable may have any degree of strength or weak-ness, *i.e.* of stress or lack of stress. And it would be possible to indicate these variations by a more or less complicated system of symbols. But there is this serious objection to any such system, that, whereas different persons usually agree as to whether a syllable is stressed or unstressed, they as frequently differ as to the amount of stress to be laid on any particular syllable. I divide all syllables, therefore, simply into stressed and unstressed (denoted respectively by *a* and *x*). This enables me to arrange all variations in three classes: (I.) dissyllabic, (II.) trisyllabic, (III.) monosyllabic.

I. *Dissyllabic variations.*—There are four kinds of dissyllabic feet: (1) *x a*, iambus; (2) *a x*, trochee; (3) *a a*, spondee; (4) *x x*, pyrrhic. Of these the iambic, as we have seen, is the normal foot in dramatic blank verse; the trochaic foot is the commonest dissyllabic variation; and examples of *a a* and *x x* are not uncommon. Mr. J. C. Smith (in the Arden *As You Like It*) lays down the following limitations to the occurrence of the trochaic variation *a x*:

(*a*) It is commonest after a pause; *i.e.* either in the first foot (after the pause at the end of the previous line) or after the pause so often found in the middle of a line (usually in the third or fourth foot), called the *cæsura* or cæsural pause. It is not often found in the second foot.

(*b*) It is very rare in the last foot, because a change of rhythm in that place produces a halting effect. There is one example in iv. 3. 9:

"The hope | of com | fort. But | for thee, | fellow".
 x   a   x   a   x   a   x   a   a x

(*c*) There are never more than two trochaic feet in a line—a majority of trochaics would alter the character of the rhythm of the line.

(*d*) Two trochaic feet rarely come together.

II. *Trisyllabic variations* are less common. There are the following possible varieties: *a x x* (dactyl), *x x a* (anapæst), *x a x* (amphibrach)—all pretty common; *x x x* (tribrach), and those containing two or three accented syllables, *x a a, a x a, a a x, a a a*—all rare.

III. *Monosyllabic variation.*—Occasionally we find a foot consisting of a single accented syllable. This is especially the case when the preceding syllable (often a monosyllable) is unusually emphatic, so that, through the voice dwelling heavily or long upon it, the absence of the unstressed syllable in the next foot is rendered much less conspicuous. An extreme instance is seen in v. 5. 54:

"O'ercome | you with | her show, | and | in time".
 x   a   x   x   x   a   a   x   a

Here the effect is displeasing, because "and" is inadequate to bear the stress of a whole foot, however emphatic the preceding syllable may be.

IV. *Hypermetrical lines.*—In addition to the above variations, any line may have one, or even two, supernumerary final syllables. A few figures will show that eleven-syllabled lines, or lines with one extra unaccented syllable after the fifth foot, are very much more frequent in the late than in the early plays of Shakespeare. The number opposite each play is the percentage of eleven-syllabled lines to all the other lines in the play.

					per cent.
Love's Labour's Lost	...	...	...		4
Richard II.	...	...	...	...	11˙39
Merchant of Venice	...	...	...		15
As You Like It	...	...	...	...	18
Othello	...	...	...	...	26
Winter's Tale	...	...	...	...	31˙09
Cymbeline	...	...	...	...	32
Tempest	...	...	...	...	33

Two things remain: (1) to scan several consecutive lines in illustration of the foregoing remarks; (2) to scan some of the most irregular and difficult lines in the play. In both cases, it may be well to state, there can often be no absolute certainty as to the right scansion of a line; much depends, for one thing, on the feeling of the reader.

(1) I select one of the most finely poetical passages in the poem for consecutive scansion—ii. 2. 11–30:

"The cric | kets sing, | and man's | o'er-la | bour'd sense
x   a   x   a   x   a   a a   x   a
Repairs | itself | by rest. | Our Tar | quin thus
x a   x a   x a   a a   x   a
. Did soft | ly press | the rush | es, ere | he wa | ken'd
x   a   x a   x   a   x   a   x   a   x
The chas | tity | he woun | ded. Cy | there | a,
x   a   x x   x a   x   a   x a x
How brave | ly thou | becomest | thy bed, | fresh li | ly,
a   a   x a   x a x   x a   a a x
And whi | ter than | the sheets! | That I | might touch!
x   a   x a   x a   x a   x   a
But. kiss; | one kiss! | Rubies | unpa | ragon'd,
a   a   a a   a x   x a   x a
How dear | ly they do't! | 'T is | her brea | thing that
x   a   x x   a   x a   x   a
Perfumes | the cham | ber thus: | the flame | o' the ta | per
x   a   x   a   x   a   x   a   x x   a   x
Bows to | ward her, | and would un | der-peep | her lids,
a   x   x   a   x   x   a   x   a   x   a
To see | the enclo | sed lights, | now ca | nopied
x a   x   a   x   a   x a   x a
Under | these win | dows, white | and a | zure, laced
a x   x   a   x   a   x a   x   a
With blue | of heaven's | own tinct. | But my | design,
x   a   x   a   x   a   a x   x a
To note | the cham | ber: I | will write | all down:
x a   x   a   x   a   x   a   a   a
Such and | such pic | tures; there | the win | dow; such
a   x   a a   x   a   x a   x   a
The adorn | ment of | her bed; | the ar | ras; fi | gures,
x   a   x x   x a   x a   x   a   x
Why, such | and such; | and the | contents | o' the sto | ry.
a   a   x a   x x   x a   x x a   x
Ah, but | some na | tural notes | about | her bo | dy
a x   x a   x   a   x a   x a   x
Above | ten thou | sand mea | ner mo | vables
x a   x   a   x   a   x a   x x
Would tes | tify, | to enrich | mine inven | tory".
x   a   x x   x   a   x   x a   x x

(2) The following lines afford samples of **special irregularities,** some of which are of frequent occurrence.

"A sample | to the youn | gest, to | the more | mature" (i. 1. 48).
x   a   x x   a   x   a   x   a   x a

This and the next two examples illustrate the taking up into the previous syllable or else the slurring of final unstressed *-le*, *-er*, especially before a vowel or quasi-mute *h*, a pause, or an unstressed syllable.

> " Myself | by with | a needle, | that I | might prick " (i. 1. 168).
>   *x a   a   x   x   a   x a   x   a*
> " Report | should ren | der him hour | ly to | your ear" (iii. 4. 150).
>   *x a   x   a   x x   a   x x   x   a*

The next examples show the compressing almost into monosyllables of such words as *having* and *evil*:

> " The life | o' the need: | having found | the back- | door open " (v. 3. 45).
>   *x   a   x   x   a   x   a   x   a   x   a*

> "The evils | she hatch'd | were not | effec | ted; so " (v. 5. 60).
>   *x   a   x   a   x   a   x a   x   a*

But in i. 1. 72 I prefer this scansion:

> " Evil- | eyed un | to you : you 're | my pri | soner, but ".
>   *a x   a   a   x   x   a   x   a   x   a*

The next five lines show the elision of a whole foot after a well-marked pause; they are, in fact, tetrametric lines:

> "That shouldst | repair | my youth, | thou heap'st " (i. 1. 132).
>   *x   a   x a   x   a   a   a*
> " Will I | first work: | he 's for | his mas | ter " (i. 5. 28).
>   *x   a   a   a   a   x   x   a   x*
> "Last night | 't was on | mine arm ; | I kiss'd | it " (ii. 3. 145).
>   *x   a   x   a   x   a   x   a   x*
> "And leave | eighteen. | Alas, | poor prin | cess " (ii. 1. 53).
>   *x   a   x   a   x a   a   a   x*
> "A prin | ce's courage. | Away, | I pri | thee " (iii. 4. 184).
>   *x a   x   a   x   x a   x a   x*

And so is

> "With that | harsh, no | ble, sim | ple no | thing " (iii. 4. 132).
>   *x   a   a   a   x   a   x   a   x*

I. 3. 7 is difficult.   To avoid three successive trochees (see p. 153 above), we must make the first foot monosyllabic:

> "Sense | less li | nen! hap | pier therein | than I !"
>   *a   x   a   x   a   x   x a   x a*

Some of the following lines require no special comment; in some the scansion is tentative:

> " But, | though slow, | deadly. |
> *Queen.*   I won | der, doc | tor" (i. 5. 10).
>   *a   x   a   a x   x a   x   a   x*

Lines divided between two speakers are specially liable to irregularities. Cf.:

> "The than | kings of | a king. |
> *Post.*   I | am, sir" (v. 5. 407).
>   x   a   x   x   x   a   a   x   a
> "Try ma | ny, a | ll good, | serve tru | ly, ne | ver" (iv. 2. 373).
>   x   a   x   a x   a   a   a   x   a   x

If, as I believe, Imogen is sobbing in this line, *all* would easily become dissyllabic.

> "That sa | tiate yet | unsa | tisfied | desire, | that tub" (i. 6. 47)
>   x   a   x   a   x a   x   a   x   a   x   a

is a hexameter or alexandrine.

> "With gol | den che | rubins | is fretted: | her and | irons" (ii. 4. 88)
>   x   a   x   a   x a   x   a x   x   a   x x

has two supernumerary final syllables.

Unless we are to make iv. 2. 26 into a half-trochaic, half-iambic line, it is best taken thus:

> "Cowards fa | ther cowards | and base | things si | re base".
>   a   a   x   a   x   x   a   x   a   x   a

There is no need to compress the second *cowards* before the cæsural pause.

> "I hum | bly set it | at your will; | but, for | my mis | tress" (iv. 3. 13).
>   x a   x   a x x x   a   a   x   x   a   x
> "Nor when | she purposes | return. | Beseech | your high | ness" (iv. 3. 15).
>   x   a   x   a x   x   a   x   a   x   a   x

APPENDIX B

HISTORY AND HOLINSHED

History.—The various sources whence Shakespeare drew his materials for *Cymbeline* and *King Lear* are largely mythical; and very little is actually known of the history of Britain at the beginning of our era. Cæsar and Tacitus tell us the bulk of what we know about the manners and customs of its then inhabitants: the facts, names and events that these chance observers report have been verified or disproved, rarely supplemented, by the researches of the philologist and the numismatologist. Putting these old and new authorities together we learn that the island was inhabited by various tribes mainly of Keltic stock; that these differed widely in race, religion, and polity; that the civilization of these tribes varied inversely with their distance from Gaul; that by Cymbeline's time a

considerable trade had sprung up across the Channel, the exports
being tin, iron, and grain, the imports being bronze and kickshaws;
and that, in the interval between the invasion of Julius Cæsar
(55 and 54 B.C.) and that under the auspices of the emperor
Claudius, in 43 A.D., Roman influences were quietly making themselves felt among the southern peoples, who had hitherto owed their
civility to the Greek merchants from Massalia (Marseilles).

Cymbeline belonged, in all probability, to the only Briton family
of the day that has left its footprints on the sands of time. His
father, Tasciovant, was most likely the grandson of the Caswallon
or Cassibelaunos who resisted Julius Cæsar; one of his sons was the
Caradoc or Caractacus who headed first his own people, afterwards
the Silures (of the Wye valley) against the later and more permanent
Roman invasions, and who, in 50 A.D., was carried off to grace an
imperial triumph in Rome. Cunobelin—as he calls himself on his
coins—lived, it would appear, till the eve of the Claudian invasion,
and exercised a kind of suzerainty over the south-east of the island.
The Catuvelauni, of whose hereditary dynasty he was a member,
had their head-quarters at Verulam, near S. Albans; but Cunobelin
moved his residence to Camalodun (Colchester), the chief town of
the Trinobantes. The greater part of the Midlands and a considerable region between the Thames and the south coast seem to have
owned his sway: hence the Roman biographer Suetonius speaks of
him—somewhat loosely—as "*Rex Britannorum*". But his over-
lordship was precarious, and his military power melted like wax at
the presence of the Roman legions: even so, seventeen centuries
later, did the empire of the Great Múghal collapse at the presence
of the British.

Holinshed.—It was from Holinshed's *Chronicles*, the first edition
of which appeared in 1577, that Shakespeare derived the materials
for nearly all his historical plays, as well as the historical material for
Macbeth, Lear, and Cymbeline. The following quotations from the
edition of 1807–8, but with modernized spelling, show the extent of
his indebtedness to Holinshed in this play :—

(1) The heading of the first chapter of "The Third Book of the
History of England" is: "Of Mulmutius, the first king of Britain,
who was crowned with a golden crown, his laws, his foundations,
with other his acts and deeds". In this chapter we read: "Mulmucius Dunwallo...the son of Cloton (as testifieth...Geffrey of Mon-
mouth) got the upper hand of the other dukes or rulers: and after
his father's decease began his reign over the whole monarchy of Britain in the year of the world 3529, after the building of Rome 314,
and after the deliverance of the Israelites out of captivity 97, and
about the 26 year of Darius Artaxerxes Longimanus, the fifth king
of the Persians. ... He also made many good laws, which were long
after used, called Mulmucius' laws, turned out of the British speech
into the Latin by Gildas Priscus, and long time after translated out
of Latin into English by Alfred, king of England, and mingled in
his statutes....After he had established his land, and set his Britons

['Britains'] in good and convenient order, he ordained him by the advice of his lords a crown of gold, and caused himself with great solemnity to be crowned, according to the custom of the pagan laws then in use: and because he was the first that bare a crown here in Britain, after the opinion of some writers, he is named the first king of Britain, and all the other before rehearsed are named rulers, dukes, or governors."

(2) [From Book III., chap. 13.]   The same history also maketh mention of one Belinus that was general of Cassibelan's army, and likewise of Nenius brother to Cassibelan, who in fight happened to get Cæsar's sword fastened in his shield by a blow which Cæsar struck ["stroke", like the Folios] at him.

(3) [From Book III., chap. 16.]   Thus, according to that which Cæsar himself and other authentic authors have written, was Britain made tributary to the Romans by the conduct of the same Cæsar. But our histories far differ from this, affirming that Cæsar coming the second time, was by the Britons with valiancy and martial prowess beaten and repelled, as he was at the first, and specially by means that Cassibelan had pight in the Thames great piles of trees piked with iron, through which his ships being entered the river, were perished and lost.   And after his coming aland, he was vanquished in battle, and constrained to flee into Gallia with those ships that remained.   For joy of this second victory (saith Galfrid) Cassibelan made a great feast at London, and there did sacrifice to the gods.

(4) [From Book III., chap. 18.]   After the death of Cassibelan, Theomantius or Tenantius, the youngest son of Lud, was made king of Britain in the year of the world 3921, after the building of Rome 706, and before the coming of Christ 45. ... Theomantius ruled the land in good quiet, and paid the tribute to the Romans which Cassibelan had granted, and finally departed this life after he had reigned 22 years, and was buried at London.

Kymbeline or Cimbeline the son of Theomantius was of the Britons made king after the decease of his father, in the year of the world 3944, after the building of Rome 728, and before the birth of our Saviour 23.   This man (as some write) was brought up at Rome, and there made knight by Augustus Cæsar, under whom he served in the wars, and was in such favour with him, that he was at liberty to pay his tribute or not.   Little other mention is made of his doings, except that during his reign, the Saviour of the world our Lord Jesus Christ the only son of God was born of a virgin, about the 23 year of the reign of this Kymbeline, and in the 42 year of the emperor Octavius Augustus, that is to wit, in the year of the world 3966, in the second year of the 194 Olympiad, after the building of the city of Rome 750 nigh at an end, after the universal flood 2311, from the birth of Abraham 2019, after the departure of the Israelites out of Egypt 1513, after the captivity of Babylon 535, from the building of the temple by Solomon 1034, and from the arrival of Brute 1116, complete.   Touching the continuance of the years of

Kymbeline's reign, some writers do vary, but the best approved
affirm, that he reigned 35 years and then died, and was buried at
London, leaving behind him two sons, Guiderius and Arviragus.
But here is to be noted, that although our histories do affirm, that
as well this Kymbeline as also his father Theomantius lived in quiet
with the Romans and continually to them paid the tributes which
the Britons had covenanted with Julius Cæsar to pay, yet we find in
the Roman writers that after Julius Cæsar's death, when Augustus
had taken upon him the rule of the empire, the Britons refused to
pay that tribute: whereat as Cornelius Tacitus reporteth, Augustus
(being otherwise occupied) was contented to wink; howbeit, through
earnest calling upon to recover his right by such as were desirous to see
the uttermost of the British kingdom; at length, to wit, in the tenth
year after the death of Julius Cæsar, which was about the thirteenth
year of the said Theomantius, Augustus made provision to pass with
an army over into Britain, and was come forward upon his journey
into Gallia Celtica: or as we may say, into these hither parts of
France.

But receiving advertisements that the Pannonians, which inhabited
the country now called Hungary, and the Dalmatians whom now we
call Slavons had rebelled, he thought it best first to subdue those
rebels near home, rather than to seek new countries, and leave such
in hazard whereof he had present possession, and so turning his
power against the Pannonians and Dalmatians, he left off for a time
the wars of Britain, whereby the land remained without fear of any
invasion to be made by the Romans, till the year after the building
of the city of Rome 725, and about the 19 year of king Theomantius'
reign, that Augustus with an army departed once again from Rome
to pass over into Britain, there to make war.   But after his coming
into Gallia, when the Britons sent to him certain ambassadors to
treat with him of peace, he stayed there to settle the state of things
among the Gauls, for that they were not in very good order.   And
having finished there, he went into Spain, and so his journey into
Britain was put off till the next year, that is the 726 after the building of Rome, which fell before the birth of our Saviour 25, about
which time Augustus eftsoons meant the third time to have made a
voyage into Britain, because they could not agree upon covenants.
But as the Pannonians and Dalmatians had aforetime stayed him,
when (as before is said) he meant to have gone against the Britons:
so even now the Salassians (a people inhabiting about Italy and
Switzerland), the Cantabrians and Asturians by such rebellious stirs
as they raised, withdrew him from his purposed journey.   But
whether this controversy which appeareth to fall forth betwixt the
Britons and Augustus was occasioned by Kymbeline, or some other
prince of the Britons, I have not to avouch: for that by our writers
it is reported, that Kymbeline being brought up in Rome, and
knighted in the court of Augustus, ever showed himself a friend to
the Romans, and chiefly was loth to break with them, because the
youth of the Briton nation should not be deprived of the benefit to

be trained and brought up among the Romans, whereby they might learn both to behave themselves like civil men, and to attain to the knowledge of feats of war.

(5) [*The History of Scotland*, reign of Kenneth; Holinshed's *Chronicles*, 1807–8, vol. v., pp. 243, 244.] For as it chanced, there was in the next field at the same time an husbandman, with two of his sons busy about his work, named Hay, a man strong and stiff in making and shape of body, but indued with a valiant courage. This Hay beholding the king with the most part of the nobles, fighting with great valiancy in the middle ward, now destitute of the wings, and in great danger to be oppressed by the great violence of his enemies, caught a plough-beam in his hand, and with the same, exhorting his sons to do the like, hasted towards the battle, there to die rather amongst other in defence of his country, than to remain alive after the discomfiture in miserable thraldom and bondage of the cruel and most unmerciful enemies. There was near to the place of the battle, a long lane fenced on the sides with ditches and walls made of turf, through the which the Scots which fled were beaten down by the enemies on heaps.

Here Hay with his sons, supposing they might best stay the flight, placed themselves overthwart the lane, beat them back whom they met fleeing, and spared neither friend nor foe : but down they went all such as came within their reach, wherewith divers hardy person-ages cried unto their fellows to return back unto the battle, for there was a new power of Scottishmen come to their succours, by whose aid the victory might be easily obtained of their most cruel adversaries the Danes: therefore might they choose whether they would be slain of their own fellows coming to their aid, or to return again to fight with the enemies. The Danes being here stayed in the lane by the great valiancy of the father and the sons, thought verily there had been some great succours of Scots come to the aid of their king, and thereupon ceasing from further pursuit, fled back in great dis-order unto the other of their fellows fighting with the middle ward of the Scots. . . .

Thus Hay being honoured of all estates, within certain days after, at a council holden at Scone, it was ordained, that both he and his posterity should be accepted amongst the number of the chiefest nobles and peers of the realm, being rewarded (besides many and other great gifts) with islands and revenues, such as he should choose sufficient for the maintenance of their estates.

APPENDIX C

A short sketch of the Tale told by the Fishwife of Stand on the Green, in " Westward for Smelts, or the Waterman's Fare of mad Merry Western Wenches, whose Tongues albeit, like Bell-clappers, they never leave ringing, yet their Tales are sweet, and will much content you: Written by kind Kitt of Kingstone".[1]

In the reign of Henry VI. there dwelt in Waltham, near London, a gentleman with a beautiful wife, who was as rare and unparalleled in body as in her gifts of mind. Her husband "having business one day to London, took up his inn" there, and supped with other gentlemen. A discussion arising about woman's constancy, he said that another speaker should not be so bitter—all were not faulty, instancing his own wife, who was "as free from disloyalty as the sun from darkness or the fire from cold". The first speaker replied that if he knew that same saint, he would obtain some manifest token of her disloyalty, taunting him that his youth and inexperience made him credulous. The husband, saying that for his wife's sake he spoke on behalf of all women, now laid a wager of £100 to the other's £50, that he could not within a month's space bring a token of his wife's falseness, and bound himself not to forewarn her. This was accepted, and the money delivered into the "oast of the house his hands".

The next day, having knowledge of the place, this man rode thither, vowing " by force, policy, or free will to get some jewel or other toy from her", that would win the wager. The villain lay at Waltham a whole day, when seeing the gentlewoman in the fields he went and kissed her, giving a message from her husband. She very modestly bade him welcome, and gave him such entertainment as was fit. He lay two nights at her house; on the third he feigned to be ill and went to bed "timelier than was his wont". Going thence to her chamber he placed himself under the bed, and soon came in the gentlewoman and her maiden. "She, preparing herself to bedward", lay her jewels on a table thereby—he specially noting the gold crucifix worn next her heart. Being "untyred" she went to bed, and the maid bolting the door withdrew to sleep behind the arras. When the cunning villain heard her "draw her breath long", he rose without noise, took the crucifix, and unbolted the door. In the early morning he started for London, where he found the husband still asleep. The latter quickly rose, and was told that his wife was untrue to him, the crucifix being shown as proof. At sight of this "his blood left his face, running to comfort his faint heart". He was minded to fall upon his sword, and so end all his miseries at once, but he decided to punish her with death, and himself to follow the fortunes of Henry VI.

[1] Given in full in J. Payne Collier's *Shakespeare's Library*, vol. ii. p. 35.

Calling his servant George to him, he sent him home to tell his mistress to meet him half-way to London; then, having her by the way, in some private place, he was to kill her: "I mean as I speak; kill her, I say; this is my command". He gave him his ring and told him to govern his estate till his return. The wife surprised to see the servant rather than her husband, was told she was to meet the latter at Enfield. Starting at once and having come to a bye-way, George asked her what the woman deserved who through her behaviour "has made her husband to neglect his estate and means of life, seeking by all means to die".

"Why, George," quoth she, "hast thou met with some such creature?—I should think her worthy of death." "Faith, mistress, I think so too. Mistress, you are this woman." On hearing this she looked as one dead, but denied the charge, and sent a message to her husband entreating he would not speak aught ill of her when dead, for in good troth she had deserved none. George, finding it impossible to kill her, being persuaded of her innocence, advised her to "live in some disguise till time have opened the cause of his mistrust". She agreed; and parting with tears in their eyes, George went to govern the house, and she in boy's attire to wander about until she fell in with King Edward [the Fourth] and two or three noblemen.

She followed the king's fortunes until "the battle at Barnet", when seeing her late guest lying for dead she opened his breast to dress his wounds, and saw there her crucifix. She had him taken to London, where he told her that he obtained it wrongfully: words which she caused the owner of the house to remember. Begging the king to right her she had her husband, who was taken prisoner at Barnet, and her traducer brought before him. Discrepancies in the account of how the jewel was obtained, led finally to the villain's confession. The king speaking to the husband, "Your wife shall be your judge", Mistress Dorrill went to her husband, saying: "All my anger I lay down with this kiss". The king gave judgment that the villain "should restore the money treble which he had wrongfully got from him: and so was to have a year's imprisonment. So, this gentleman and his wife went lovingly home, where they were kindly welcomed by George, to whom for recompense he gave the money which he received. So lived they ever after in great content."

APPENDIX D

SUSPECTED PASSAGES

Two parts of this play have been suspected of not being wholly Shakespeare's work: (a) the dirge in iv. 2. 258–281; (b) the masque, vision, and tablet in v. 4 and 5.

(*a*) iv. 2. 258-281.

Staunton, quoted by Aldis Wright, says: " There is something so strikingly inferior, both in the thoughts and expression of the concluding couplet to each stanza in this song, that we may fairly set them down as additions from the same hand which furnished the contemptible *Masque* or *Vision* that deforms the last act".

It had been arranged (ll. 237, 238), that they were to "use like note and words, Save that 'Euriphile' must be 'Fidele'". Since no name is found in the dirge as it stands, either Shakespeare must have forgotten the arrangement, or some colour is given to Staunton's suggestion above.

(*b*) But the chief controversy has raged around the **Masque, vision and tablet** in Act v., scs. 4 and 5.

I. And first, let us hear the attacking critics:

(1) Pope is sweeping: " Here follow a *vision*, a *masque*, and a *prophecy*, which interrupt the fable [plot] without the least necessity, and immeasurably lengthen this act. I think it plainly foisted in afterwards for mere show, and apparently not of Shakespeare."

(2) Coleridge is impatient merely with the tablet (v. 4. 138-144): "It is not easy to conjecture why Shakespeare should have introduced this ludicrous scroll, which answers no one purpose, either propulsive or explicatory, unless as a joke on etymology".[1]

(3) Staunton. See (*a*) above.

(4) Prof. Hudson: " The play has one very serious and decided blemish. I refer to the piece of dull impertinence in the fifth act, including the vision of Posthumus while asleep in the prison, the absurd 'label' found on his bosom when he awakes, and the Soothsayer's still more absurd interpretation of the label at the close. For nothing can well be plainer than that the whole thing is strictly irrelevant: it does not throw the least particle of light on the character or motive of any person; has indeed no business whatever with the action of the drama, except to hinder and embarrass it. This matter apart, the *dénouement* is perfect, and the preparation for it made with consummate judgment and skill. And it is a noteworthy fact that, if the apparition, the dialogue that follows with the Jailer, the tablet, and all that relates to it, be omitted, there will appear no rent, no loose stitch, nor anything wanting to the completeness of the work.[2]

" It is difficult to believe that Shakespeare wrote the passages in question at any time; impossible, that he did so at or near the time when the rest of the play was written. For I think every discerning student will perceive at once that the style of this matter is totally different from that of all the other parts. How, then, came it there?

---

[1] See note on v. 5. 446, 447.

[2] But elsewhere (*Critical Notes*) Prof. Hudson partly contradicts himself: "The 'label' is perhaps the absurdest and most unShakespearian part of the whole; yet the contents of it are, by the still more absurd interpretation of them at the close, so wrought into the dialogue as to make the 'label' itself an inseparable item of the drama".

Some consider it a relic of an older drama, perhaps one written by Shakespeare in his youth. But the more common opinion is, that it was foisted in by the players, the poet himself having nothing to do with it. There is no doubt that such things were sometimes done."

(5) Fleay makes an important distinction between the masque and the vision, or rather between the dumb-show and the verse of the masque: "The verse of the vision, v. 4. 30–122, is palpably by an inferior hand, and was probably inserted for some court performance after Shakespeare had left the stage. Of course the stage-directions for the dumb-show are genuine. This would not have been worth mentioning but for the silly arguments of some who defend the Shakespearian authorship of these lines, and maintain that the play would be maimed without them."

(6) Ingleby: "The dream-interlude that follows is too poor a composition to be imputed to Shakespeare at any period of his career, or on any dramatic ground. It is at least open to argument whether Posthumus's speech on awaking bears signs of Shakespeare's hand. Certainly from l. 123 to l. 137 it is a very poor production. The remaining half-dozen lines are not unlike Shakespeare."

II. I now call on the counsel for the defence:

(1) Gervinus ably defends the least assailable part, the dumb-show, but it will be seen that the main purport of his argument would not be affected by the excision of ll. 30–122: "Shakespeare here allows the rulers of the world to mix personally in the drama, as is usual in the epos, where the actors are in harmony with the divinity and his laws. This epic character and the happy termination of the epos were necessarily given to this drama also. For the personages who here act and err are friends and favourites of the gods, because even that which in calm certainty or uncertain passion they do contrary to the maxims of morality, is done from moral motives or in moral indignation; so that the drama with a tragic ending would have been an impeachment of the world's government. Hence I do not think that Shakespeare would have admitted the introduction of Jupiter to be a blunder, as Ulrici calls it, or that he needs Tieck's apology, that this scene was a fragment of a youthful attempt at this play. Far rather does it appear to me that the introduction of the divinity in this dramatised epos testifies to the same deep and remarkable instinct with which Shakespeare entered into the nature of poetry and its various styles and requirements."

(2) Schlegel is more uncompromising: "Steevens accedes to the opinion of Pope respecting the apparition of the ghosts and of Jupiter in *Cymbeline*, while Posthumus is sleeping in the dungeon. But Posthumus finds, on waking, a tablet on his breast, with a prophecy on which the *dénouement* of the piece depends. Is it to be imagined that Shakespeare would require of his spectators the belief in a wonder without a visible cause? Is Posthumus to dream this tablet with the prophecy? But these gentlemen do not descend to this

objection. The verses which the apparitions deliver do not appear to them good enough to be Shakespeare's. I imagine I can discover why the poet has not given them more of the splendour of diction. They are the aged parents and brothers of Posthumus, who, from concern for his fate, return from the world below. They ought, consequently, to speak the language of a more simple olden time, and their voices ought also to appear as a feeble sound of wailing, when contrasted with the thundering oracular language of Jupiter. For this reason Shakespeare chose a syllabic measure, which was very common before his time, but which was then getting out of fashion, though it still continued to be frequently used, especially in translations of classical poets. In some such manner might the shades express themselves in the then existing translations of Homer and Virgil. The speech of Jupiter is on the other hand majestic, and in form and style bears a complete resemblance to the sonnets of Shakespeare."

(3) Fletcher is almost uncritically enthusiastic on the same side: "The total omission of these prison scenes in acting is another great injury done to the dramatic interest as conducted by the poet. There may, indeed, be valid theatrical reasons for suppressing the vision of Posthumus during the slumber which is supposed to terminate his soliloquy; but the suppression deprives us of the solemnly pathetic effect of the simple chorus, which is plainly introduced in order, by recalling the whole tenour of the story, to remind the auditor that the hero is much more unfortunate than criminal, and to relieve our feelings by announcing an approaching deliverance from adversity,—at the same time that curiosity is kept alive by the mysterious terms in which the prediction is made. The attendant music adds to the soothing solemnity of the scene. How beautiful, too, is the plaintive simplicity of the ballad verses reciting his fortune, chanted by the apparitions of his deceased relatives, not one of whom has he seen in life." And so on. Fletcher, in fact, has nothing but praise for the whole scene.

(4) Watkiss Lloyd: "The vision and the oracular tablet are so utterly unnecessary to the disknotting of the main intrigue of the play, that they must have been recommended by some special purpose and propriety, if we are only wise enough to see it. It will be found that they only contribute to the arrangement of the terms of peace at last, and thus Jupiter with his thunderbolts from the machine is rendered available for what the poet thought a worthy service,—an apology for a submission that made Britain tributary."

(5) Prof. A. W. Ward: "The episode in rhymed verse inserted in V. iv. was doubtless, like the Mask introduced into the *Tempest*, in accordance with the taste of the period; there is no reason, on account of its style, which reminds one of the prefatory lines to the Cantos of the *Faerie Queene*, to impugn Shakespeare's authorship of it".

III. I have given the defendants more ample space because my brief summing up will not be wholly in their favour. The "tablet" or label is, unfortunately, very hard to be rid of, however much one may wish it away, for it is involved, not only in the vision, but in the remainder of the scene, and in the close of the play. Perhaps, on the whole, we may hold it justified by the consideration urged by Watkiss Lloyd above. The political conclusion which it gives to the play resembles that given by the arrival of Fortinbras in *Hamlet*, and the very similarity of the circumstances and of the lessening hold upon the spectator's interest in each case,—coming too near the close to be dramatically serious,—may be regarded as an additional justification here.

For the rest, I hold with Fleay that the dumb-show and the verses of the masque must be separated. None of the objections urged against the latter apply to the former, or not with equal force; in fact, no weighty objection has been urged against it. On the other hand, I read ll. 30–122 with an impatience begotten of the belief that they are not Shakespeare's. I cannot see Shakespeare's touch or hear his music in any part of them. I recommend any one who is sceptical on the point to test Jupiter's opening quatrain by comparison with any serious passage of Shakespeare's undoubted work. Prof. Ward is reminded of the prefatory lines to the Cantos of the *Faerie Queene*. Exactly; but did Shakespeare ever seriously compose such doggerel as this?—

> "The maske of Cupid, and th' enchant-
>   ed Chamber are displayd;
> Whence Britomart redeemes fair A-
>   moret through charmes decayd". (*F. Q.* iii. **12**.)

Almost in the same breath Prof. Ward seems to imply that this masque resembles that in the *Tempest*. No other touchstone is needed. Let any one read Act iv. of the *Tempest* and then decide if the masque in this play can be by the same hand.

APPENDIX E

THE TITLE OF THE PLAY

Prof. Dowden: "'Posthumus and Imogen' would be a fitter name for the play than *Cymbeline*".

Prof. Hudson: "It is not very apparent why this play should be named as it is. For Cymbeline himself is but a cypher, having no value of his own, and all his value depending on what stands before him; that is, he has no force but to augment the force of somebody else. But his very impotence personally renders him important dramatically; that he has no spring in himself makes him in some sort the mainspring of the play. It was because he was weak that he drove Belarius into exile, and thus prepared one great source of wealth to the drama. It is for the same cause that he prefers the Queen's rickety, spluttering, blustering lump of flesh for his son-in-law, and banishes Posthumus, and withholds the Roman tribute. Therefore it is, too, that the Queen is able to hoodwink him so completely, that she feels safe in scheming against Imogen's life, and to that end gets the cordial which afterwards produces upon her the semblance of death. Hence also Cloten, with his empty head and savage heart, is encouraged to that pitch of insolence which prompts the flight and disguise of Imogen, that she may have 'no more ado with that harsh, noble, simple nothing, whose love-suit hath been to her as fearful as a siege'.[1] Thus the king's weakness proves the seed-plot of the entire action. So that I suspect the play is rightly named, though some have thought otherwise."

A good name, a *taking* title, is as essential for the playbill of a drama as for the announcement of a book. From this point of view, "Cymbeline" is a much better name than any alternative I have seen suggested, and I have a suspicion that Shakespeare may have known his own business best.

[1] iii. 4. 134; but Prof. Hudson is evidently here not speaking by the book.

GLOSSARY

affiance (i. 6. 155), trust, confidence. O. Fr. *afiance = a* (Lat. *ad*) + *fiance*, ultimately from Lat. *fidere*, to trust. Cf. Prayer-Book: "that she may evermore have *affiance* in thee".

an (iv. 2. 387), if. The same word as *and*, though it is not certain how *and* came to have this meaning, which is, however, found also in cognate languages. Shakespeare and his contemporaries usually employed the full form *and*, and the intensified *and if*. Except in *an't*, *an* occurs only once in the First Folio.

andirons (ii. 4. 88), fire-dogs. O. Fr. *andier*. In English the termination was at an early date identified with the word *yren*, iron, whence the later illusive spellings.

arras (ii. 2. 26), a hanging screen, made of a rich tapestry fabric, in which figures and scenes are woven in colours; formerly placed round the walls of household apartments. From *Arras*, the name of a town in France famed for its manufacture.

arrearages (ii. 4. 13), arrears, tribute overdue. O. Fr. *arerage*, from *arere*, behind.

bauble (iii. 2. 20), toy; a mere toy (iii. 1. 27), and thus too small or weak for the work in hand. O. Fr. *babel*, also *baubel*, child's toy.

boot (i. 5. 69), original meaning 'good, advantage, profit'. Hence **to boot**, 'to the good', into the bargain, in addition, moreover. O. E. *bōt*, remedy.

carl (v. 2. 4), churl (iii. 6. 65), "a very drudge of nature's"; originally 'a man of the common people, a countryman'. O. Norse *karl*, cognate with *churl*, O. E. *ceorl*.

clotpoll (iv. 2. 184), thick or 'wooden' head. Also 'blockhead'. Cf. *clodpoll*, *clodpate*.

crare (iv. 2. 205), **crayer**, a small trading vessel. O. Fr. *crayer*, *craier*; medieval Lat. *craiera*.

curious (i. 6. 183), anxious, concerned, solicitous. O. Fr. *curius*, Lat. *curiosus*.

eglantine (iv. 2. 223), sweet briar (*Rosa rubiginosa*). Fr. *églantine*, O. Fr. *aiglent*, probably from Lat. **aculentus*, prickly.

fangled (v. 4. 134), characterized by crotchets or fopperies. Apparently from a mistaken analysis of *new-fangled*, later form of *new-fangle*, eager for novelty, from *fangel*, ready to catch, from O. E. *fangen*, p.p. of *fōn*, to catch.

fatherly, *adv.* (ii. 3. 34), in a fatherly manner. In O. E. adjectives were formed by means of the suffix *līc*, like, e.g. *fæderlīc*, fatherly, *frēondlīc*, friendly; and from these adjectives adverbs were formed by the adverbial termination *-e*, *fæderlīce*, *frēondlīce*. Subsequently, both these terminations were represented by *-ly*, so that etymologically *fatherly, friendly, ungodly*, &c., are equally correct as adverbs and as adjectives.

feat, *v.* (i. 1. 49), to constrain to propriety (? *New Eng. Dict.*): unique instance in this meaning of a rare verb; from

feat, *adj.* (v. 5. 87), apt, adroit, dexterous, graceful. From O.Fr. *fait*, made, Lat. *factus*.

feodary (iii. 2. 21), better spelt **fedary**, confederate, accomplice (Lat. *fœdus*). In *Winter's Tale*, ii. 1. 90, we find the form *federary*.

fleet (v. 3. 25), move swiftly. O.E. *flēotan*, float.

fraught (i. 1. 126), to freight a ship, hence 'to burden': M.Du. *vrachten*. Commonly used only in the p.p. *fraught*. *Freight* is probably a later form of the same word.

fretted (ii. 4. 88), ornamented, adorned; O.E. *frætwan*. Ingleby explains: "The fretwork of Imogen's ceiling had golden ornaments, like cherubim, at the intersection of the bands". But this explanation is unnecessarily complicated by the supposed reference to interlacing *fretwork* (a word of quite different origin), a reference which is not supported by the quotation from *Hamlet* (ii. 3. 313) which Ingleby appends to his note: "This majestical roof fretted with golden fire".

garbage (i. 6. 49), rubbish, offal. Probably from *garble-age* (Skeat), and hence 'the coarse or refuse parts from which all that is good has been sifted and removed'.

geck (v. 4. 67), object of derision or contempt, dupe; Du. *gek*, fool.

gentle (iv. 2. 39), of gentle birth (cf. *gentleman*), high-born. Etymologically the same word as *genteel* and *gentile*; O.Fr. *gentil*, Lat. *gentilis*.

giglot (iii. 1. 31), **giglet**, fickle,

inconstant; diminutive of *gigle*, a flirt (Cotgrave). Probably allied to *jig*.

gripe, *n.* (i. 6. 105), grip, clasp of the hand. From

gripe, *v.* (iii. 1. 39), grip, clutch with the hand; O.E. *grīpan*, to seize.

gyves (v. 4. 14), fetters; of Keltic origin.

hardiment (v. 4. 75), hardihood (a hybrid), bravery. Fr. *hardi*, brave, bold, + suffix *ment*, Lat. *mens, mentis*.

haviour (iii. 4. 9), shortened form of *behaviour*, formed abnormally from the verb *behave*.

hilding (ii. 3. 122), a mean base fellow. Short for provincial E. *hilderling* or *hinderling*, a wretch; from O.E. *hinderling*, a mean wretch; from *hinder*, backwards, + suffix *ling*.

hind (v. 3. 77), peasant, rustic. The final *d* is epithetic. M.E. *hine*, a domestic; O.E. *hīna*, gen. of *hīwan*, pl., members of a family.

holp (v. 5. 422), helped. In O.E. *helpan* is a strong verb, pret. *healp*, but in Anglian dialects *hālp*, whence *holp* is regularly descended.

jackanapes (ii. 1. 3), coxcomb, upstart: = *Jack o' apes* (with epenthetic *n* to prevent *hiatus*), a man who exhibited performing apes (Skeat). Cf. *Jack-slave* (ii. 1. 22).

jet (iii. 3. 5), stalk, strut. Cf. *Twelfth Night*, ii. 5. 36:

"how he jets under his advanced plumes!",

and *Ralph Roister Doister*, iii. 3. 121:

"Then must ye stately goe, jetting up and downe".

Fr. *jeter*, to throw.

ken (iii. 6. 6), sight, distance within which recognition is possible. Coined from *ken*, to know, M.E. *kennen*, Icel. *kenna*, to know.

kitchen-trulls (v. 5. 177), kitchen-wenches, drabs. Ger. *trulle, trolle*, a trull.

lapp'd (v. 5. 360), wrapped: M.Du. *lappen*. Skeat gives "M.E. *lappen*, also *wlappen*, another form of *wrappen*", apparently on the basis of a pret. *wlappide* in Wyclif.

learn'd (i. 5. 12), taught; O.E. *leornian*, learn. The confusion with M.E. *leren*, O.E. *lǣran*, teach, as exemplified here and in *Ps.* xxv. 4 (Prayer-Book), is late.

lesser (v. 5. 187), *compar. adv.*, less (O.E. *lǣs*). The comparative suffix *-er* is here redundant and irregular, but is not incorrect in the adjective lesser (O.E. *lǣssa* < *lǣsra*).

lieger (i. 5. 80), **leiger, leger**, ambassador; properly *leger ambassador*, one that *remained* some time at a foreign court. The same word as *ledger*; Du. *legger*, one that lies down. Cf. O.E. *licgan*, to lie, p.p. *legen*.

like (ii. 3. 53), *impers. v. with dat.*, please. Thus "so like you" is almost the exact equivalent of Fr. *s'il vous plaît*. From O.E. *gelician*, used in precisely the same way: "gif hit ðām pāpan swā gelīcode", if it so pleased the pope.

limb-meal (ii. 4. 143), limb from limb. *Meal*, here and in *piecemeal*, &c., is from O.E. *mǣlum*, which was used as an adverbial suffix, dat. pl. of *mǣl*, measure.

long of (v. 5. 271), on account of, due to; still common in provincial English. O.E. *gelang æt*: in the O.E. poem *Beowulf*, Hrothgar says to the hero: "Nū is se rǣd *gelang* eft æt ðē ānum", Now is help again *long of*, dependent on, thee alone.

minion (ii. 3. 40), favourite, darling: Fr. *mignon*.

moe (iii. 1. 36), more. In O.E. *mā* is the comparative adverb, *māra* the comparative adjective. Later, *moe* was used as the comparative of *many*, while *more* remained the comparative of *much*. In Shakespeare's day *moe* was obsolescent.

mows (i. 6. 40), grimaces. Fr. *moue*, 'a moe or mouth' (Cotgrave); from O.Du. *mouwe*, the protruded underlip, in making a grimace (Skeat).

or (ii. 4. 14), ere. The spelling *or* partly represents O.Norse *ār*, and partly arises from O.E. *ǣr* through loss of stress.

or ere (iii. 2. 64, v. 3. 50. In i. 3. 33 each word has its own independent force, and the following note does not apply), a strengthened form of *or*=ere, before (see *or* above), with a tinge of the meaning of *ever*. The form *or ere* (= O.E. *ǣr + ǣr*), *i.e.* merely a strengthened form of *ere*, had long been familiar. But in Shakespeare's day *ere* was also current as a poetic and colloquial variant of *ever*. Hence *or ere* would have originated from *or ever* even if no phrase of similar form had previously existed. It is impossible, then, to distinguish *or ere* and *or ever*. But it must be understood that the notion of *ever* was probably not very distinctly felt in *or ere*; rather, that the older pleonastic expression was the more strongly felt element. In any case, it is unlikely that Shakespeare or his contemporaries had any consciousness that there were two coincident phrases *or ere* of distinct origin.[1]

owe (iii. 1. 37), possess, own: O.E. *āgan*, to possess, while *own* is from the derivative O.E. *āgnian*, to own.

paled in (iii. 1. 19), enclosed or

---

[1] I am indebted for full information on this interesting point to Mr. Henry Bradley.

fenced in (with paling). From Fr. *pal*, Lat. *palus*, a stake.

partisan (iv. 2. 399), halberd; a staff headed by a blade having lateral projections; now only used in ceremonial observances. O. Fr. *pourtisaine*, probably from O. H.G. *partá*, a battle-axe, but with a romance suffix.

prone (v. 4. 197), inclined, eager, *sc.* for the gallows: Lat. *ðronus*, inclined forwards.

proper (iv. 2. 97), own; Lat. *proprius*.

puttock (i. 1. 140), the common kite. "Just as a *sparrow-hawk* is named from *sparrows*, I suppose that the *puttock* is named from the *poots* or *pouts*, *i.e.* small birds on which it preys. *Pout* stands for *poult=pullet*. The suffix -*ock* may be the usual E. dimin. suffix -*ock*, used adjectivally; or, if we should suppose *puttock* to be a corruption of *poot-hawk*, this is not a violent nor unlikely change" (Skeat).

quire (iii. 3. 43), choir, a place for singers; M.E. *que(i)r*, O.Fr. *choeur*, 'the quire of a church, a troop of singers' (Cotgrave); Lat. *chorus*. Quire ("In quires and places where they sing", *Prayer-Book*) and *choir* are merely different spellings of the same word.

raps (i. 6. 50), affects with ecstasy, transports; elsewhere used by Shakespeare with this meaning only in the p.p. From *rap*, to snatch, seize hastily; Swedish *rappa*, to seize.

resty (iii. 6. 34), unwilling to go forward, obstinate, stubborn, a shortened form of *restive*. O. Fr. *restif*, 'restie, stubborn, drawing backward, that will not go forward' (Cotgrave); from the same root as Fr. *rester*, to remain. I suspect that its use here and elsewhere was influenced by popular etymology connecting the word

with E. *rest*, from O.E. *rest*, rest, quiet.

rowel (iv. 4. 39), a little wheel with sharp points at the end of a spur: Fr. *rouelle*, Low Lat. *rotella*, a little wheel, diminutive of *rota*, a wheel.

sear (i. 1. 116), cere, cover with wax; chiefly used of dipping linen cloth in melted wax, to be used as a shroud. The shroud was called a *cerecloth* or *cerement* (here "bonds of death"). The former was often written *searcloth*, wrongly (Skeat). Lat. *cerare*, to wax, from *cera*, wax. This explanation suits the passage so well, that I doubt very much if there is, as has been suggested, any reference to the proper sense of *sear*, to dry up, burn up.

shanks (v. 4. 9), legs from knee to ankle; O.E. *scanca*, shank, shin.

shot (v. 4. 156), reckoning. It is the same word as *scot*, a contribution, in *scot-free*, free from payment, for which Shakespeare uses *shot-free* (*1 Henry IV.*, v. 3. 30). The literal meaning is that which is *shot* into the general fund, hence 'contribution'.

'shrew (ii. 3. 141), beshrew; a polite imprecation. From *shrew*, a scold; M.E. *shrewe*, wicked; O.E. *scrēawa*, a shrew-mouse, which was fabled to poison cattle to death by biting them.

silly (v. 3. 86), plain, simple; O.E. *sælig*, happy, blessed. Here we see the word in the course of its deterioration of meaning: 'timely, lucky, happy, blessed, innocent, simple, foolish'.

simular (v. 5. 200), counterfeit but specious.

slaver (i. 6. 104), exchange amorous kisses; Icel. *slafra*, to slaver. Cognate with *slabber*.

sluttery (i. 6. 43), the ways and dress of a slovenly woman. Of Scandinavian origin.

snuff (i. 6. 86), properly 'the part of a candle-wick charred by the flame, whether still burning or removed'. Here it evidently means 'the unsnuffed wick of a candle, darkening the flame', as in *Hamlet*, iv. 7. 116:

" There lives within the very flame of love
   A kind of wick or snuff that will abate it ".

Of Scandinavian origin.

stark (iv. 2. 209), stiff; used by Shakespeare only in speaking of a dead body. O.E. *stearc*, strong, stiff.

still (i. 1. 3, &c.), always, constantly.

straight - pight (v. 5. 164), straight-pitched, standing erect. *Pight* is the old form of *pitched*. Minerva was usually represented (after the colossal bronze statue at Athens) standing erect, the left foot advanced, wearing her ægis, and brandishing a spear.

strain (iv. 2. 24), inborn disposition, *or* race, stock (cf. *Pericles*, iv. 3. 24: " I do shame | To think of what a noble strain you are, | And of how coward a spirit "). " A strain of rareness " (iii. 4. 95) =a rare kind of conduct.

tanlings (iv. 4. 29), persons tanned or scorched by the sun: unique instance.

tent (iii. 4. 115), probe (as a wound). From *tent*, a roll of lint used to dilate a wound; derived through Fr. from Lat. *tentare*, to handle, test.

tirest (iii. 4. 94), preyest; tearest, as is done by birds of prey. Ultimately from O.E. *teran*, to tear.

whilst, the (iv. 2. 254), the while, an accus. of duration of time. *Whilst* is really the gen. case used adverbially, with epithetic *t*; hence *the whilst* is etymologically inaccurate.

witch (i. 6. 158), a male sorcerer. The application of the word to a man is in accordance with its etymology, for it can stand equally for O.E. *wicca*, a wizard, or *wicce*, a witch. *Wizard* is from the same root.

woe (v. 5. 2), woeful, sad ; cf. *Tempest*, v. 139: " I am woe for it ". This adjectival use is at least as old as Chaucer, who has (*Prologue to Canterbury Tales*, l. 351): " Wo was his cook but if his saucë were | Poynaunt and sharpe". Originally *woe* was an interjection, not uncommonly construed with the dat. of a noun, whence must have arisen its adjectival use.

yond (iii. 3. 10), yonder. The correct form of the adjective is *yon* (still common in provincial English), O.E. *geon* ; *yond* (O.E. *geond*, throughout) is properly a derivative preposition and adverb.

INDEX OF WORDS

For words not indexed here, see the Glossary.

demesnes, iii. 3. 70.
desert, i. 5. 73.
deserve, iii. 3. 54.
desire, i. 6. 52.
discovered, v. 5. 277.
disedged, iii. 4. 93.
distemper, iii. 4. 191.
doubt, i. 6. 94.
dull, ii. 2. 31.

embrace, iii. 4. 17.
encounter, i. 3. 32.
estates, v. 5. 22.
even, iii. 4. 181.
excellent, ii. 3. 15.
exhibition, i. 6. 118.
exorciser, iv. 2. 276.
extremity, iii. 4. 17.
eye-strings, i. 3. 17.

false, ii. 3. 68.
farther, i. 5. 65.
favour, i. 6. 41.
fear, i. 4. 85.
fear'd hopes, ii. 4. 6.
feated, i. 1. 49.
feather, i. 6. 178.
fellows, iii. 4. 90.
fit, iii. 4. 168.
fitment, v. 5. 409.
foot, v. 4. 116.
for, iii. 5. 70.
forbear, iv. 2. 278.
forfeiters, iii. 2. 36–39.
foundations, iii. 6. 7.
franchise, iii. 1. 55.
franklin, iii. 2. 76.
fraught, i. 1. 126.
freeness, v. 5. 421.
from, i. 4. 13; v. 5. 430.
full of view, iii. 4. 147.
fulness, iii. 6. 12.
furnaces, i. 6. 65.

gilded, v. 3. 34.
go even, i. 4. 39.
great morning, iv. 2. 61.
groom, iii. 6. 70.

habits, v. 1. 30.
haply, iv. 1. 17.
happy, iii. 4. 174.
hardness, iii. 6. 21.
heard of, ii. 4. 11.
holy, iii. 4. 177.
home, iii. 5. 92.
honesty, iii. 6. 70.
horse hairs, ii. 3. 29.

imperceiverant, iv. 1. 12.
imperious, iv. 2. 35.
importantly, iv. 4. 19.
in (=on), iii. 6. 50.
inclined, i. 6. 113.
ingenious, iv. 2. 186.
injurious, iii. 1. 46.
insultment, iii. 5. 137.
irregulous, iv. 2. 315.
it, iii. 3. 85.
it (*genitive*), iii. 4. 157.

jack, ii. 1. 1.
Jack-slave, ii. 1. 18.
jay, iii. 4. 48.
journal, iv. 2. 10.
jump, v. 4. 180.

lapse, iii. 6. 12.
leans, i. 5. 58.
leave, i. 3. 15.
lend, iii. 6. 24.
let blood, iv. 2. 168.

Mary-buds, ii. 3. 22.
may, iii. 2. 50.
mean, iii. 2. 49.
medicinable, iii. 2. 33.
mend you, ii. 4. 26.
mere, iv. 2. 92.
miracle, iv. 2. 29.
mortal, v. 3. 51.
mountaineer, iv. 2. 71.

nearer, iii. 5. 91.
nerves, iii. 3. 94.
nice, ii. 5. 8.
niceness, iii. 4. 155.
none, i. 6. 58.

GENERAL INDEX

ImTheStory.com

9 781290 767071